The Three Cloths of Christ by John C. Iannone

THE THREE CLOTHS OF CHRIST:
THE EMERGING TREASURES OF CHRISTIANITY

THE THREE CLOTHS OF CHRIST by John C. Iannone

THE THREE CLOTHS OF CHRIST by John C. Iannone

THE THREE CLOTHS OF CHRIST:
THE EMERGING TREASURES OF CHRISTIANITY

John C. Iannone

Published By:

NorthStar Production Studios, LLC

and Lulu Press

Kissimmee, Florida, USA

Copyright 2009 – Updated January 2010

ISBN 5800039217678

Registered: Writers Guild of America West

The Author welcomes your thoughts or ask questions at:

jciannone@gmail.com

or visit website:

www.shroudinfo.com

COVER PHOTO: 10th century image of King Abgar with Cloth circa. 40 A.D. Note Cloth is folded, doubled-in-four, called the "tetradiplon" in Greek. Known as the Mandylion, or little towel when folded. Courtesy of Archbishop Damianos, St. Catherine's Monastery, Mt. Sinai, Egypt.

THE THREE CLOTHS OF CHRIST   by   John C. Iannone

THE THREE CLOTHS OF CHRIST   by   John C. Iannone

TABLE OF CONTENTS

Introduction:---------------------------------------8

Chapter One: What is the Shroud of Turin? ----------------10

Chapter Two: Pollen, Mites and Flowers - A Unique Linen--28

Chapter Three: Ancient Coins Over The Eyes---------------39

Chapter Four: The Signature of Roman Crucifixion---------50

Chapter Five: The Blood on the Shroud--------------------68

Chapter Six: An Ancient Textile Consistent with Jewish
             Burial Practice-----------------------------75

Chapter Seven: How Were The Mysterious Images Formed?----89

Chapter Eight: Tracing The Historical Journey:
             The First Thousand Years--------------------104

Chapter Nine: The Journey Continues:
             The Second Thousand Years-------------------121

Chapter Ten: Art and The Shroud--------------------------143

Chapter Eleven: Resolving The Carbon-14 Controversy------155

Chapter Twelve: The Sudarium Christi: The Face
             Cloth of Jesus In The Tomb------------------168

Chapter Thirteen: The Veil Of Veronica-------------------177

Chapter Fourteen: The Image of Our Lady of Guadalupe-----207

AfterForward---215

Author Index---223

Subject Index--229

Photos---234

****

THE THREE CLOTHS OF CHRIST   by   John C. Iannone

THE THREE CLOTHS OF CHRIST   by   John C. Iannone

"There are more things in heaven and earth, Horatio, than are dreamed of in your philosophies."

                  Shakespeare's Hamlet, Act I, Scene 5

DEDICATION

Personal Dedication

This book is dedicated to my two wonderful sisters, Elaine and Kathryn, who are always there for me.

Professional Dedication

This book is also dedicated to two great Shroud scholars: Susan Benford and Dr. Ray Rogers whose recent passing has left a gap that will be hard to fill. Their tireless work has helped reverse the discrediting of the Holy Shroud established by the 1988 Carbon-14. With recent, updated information on the C-14 test, they have set Shroud studies on a new and exciting course. These scholars will be missed.

              * * * * * * * * * * * * *

THE THREE CLOTHS OF CHRIST by John C. Iannone

THE THREE CLOTHS OF CHRIST by John C. Iannone

INTRODUCTION

In 1998, at the invitation of Cardinal Giovanni Saldarini, then Custodian of the Holy Shroud, I was honored to be invited with fellow Sindonologists to have an extended viewing of the ancient linen. After having studied the Shroud intently for 20 years up to that point, it was an exciting journey representing a defining moment in my life.

Upon my return to the U.S., I felt compelled to lecture on this revered cloth. To date, I have studied the Shroud for 31 years and done over 160 presentations at Churches of all denominations – Catholic, Lutheran, Episcopal, Methodist, Presbyterian, Anglican, Baptist, Greek Orthodox, etc. and I have found the Holy Shroud to be a truly ecumenical subject of intense interest to many people, Christian and non-Christian.

Recently, I did a television program on Catholic TV in Massachusetts. The Producer asked me to discuss why I thought it was important that people understand the Holy Shroud. After some thought, I prepared my answer. I had believed in the Resurrection of our Lord before I ever heard of the Shroud. What occurred to me, however, was that if you come to understand and accept that the Shroud is the actual burial cloth of the historical Jesus of Nazareth – one that bears His images, His bloodstains and indications of His resurrection - then you must ask yourself the question:

> Why did Jesus leave His images on linen that have puzzled the greatest minds and given comfort to the ordinary person for two thousand years?

Was it an accident? Hardly. Was it a natural phenomenon? No. There are thousands of burial cloths from the period in Museums around the world. None have an image. Or, did He have a purpose for this miraculous event? The answer, as I hope you will find in this scientific and historical treatment in the following pages, is that, far from being accidental is was quite purposeful.

Embedded in this ancient linen is the compelling evidence of

THE THREE CLOTHS OF CHRIST by John C. Iannone

His Passion, Death and Resurrection. The Holy Shroud is a photograph, if you will, of the events wherein Jesus gave His life for us and rose again to give us hope. The ancient linen contains within its fabric a story – the greatest story ever told. Some writers call the Holy Shroud "The Fifth Gospel" – a witness which tells in images what the Gospels relay in words. I think of it as the **Visual Gospel**.

In my many presentations, I have been asked by people to talk about the sister cloths of the Holy Shroud, namely, the Sudarium Christi (Face Cloth in the Tomb mentioned in John's Gospel) and about the Veil of Veronica, an enduring Christian legend. Much has been learned about these sister cloths in recent times and I will discuss them all in this book. These are truly the "emerging treasures of Christianity." I have tried to write the science of the Shroud for ordinary people but have also included a comprehensive index of Authors and Subjects for those who wish to pursue further studies.

In April and May of 2010, Pope Benedict XVI has graciously decided to place the Holy Shroud on public exhibition for all the world to see and ponder. It may be the last time in the lifetime of many to have the opportunity to view the Holy Shroud. The Pope's decision to do this may well be as a result of recent findings by chemists and sindonologists that demonstrate that the Carbon-14 test of 1988 which seriously discredited the Shroud in the eyes of the world, has now been found to be compromised by a "spurious sample" in which a reweave, or repair, of Medieval cotton was mixed with ancient linen tested by the Carbon-14 Labs to compromise the testing, as we shall discuss.

It is my hope that readers will come to understand that the Holy Shroud is the most treasured artifact in Christian history. In its ancient fabric is a story – visually told – the greatest story of all times outlining what Jesus did for us.

Sincerely,

John C. Iannone

For additional information and photos, please go to my website www.shroudinfo.com.

THE THREE CLOTHS OF CHRIST by John C. Iannone

Chapter One

WHAT IS THE SHROUD OF TURIN?

"For those who believe, no proof is necessary. For those who do not believe, no proof will suffice."

Franz Werfel, The Song of Bernadette

Defining and Describing the Holy Shroud:

The Shroud, often called the "Holy Shroud," and "La Santa Sindone" in Italy, is most commonly referred to as the Shroud of Turin because it has been physically located in the Cathedral of St. John the Baptist in Turin, Italy since 1578. It could easily be call the Shroud of Jerusalem or simply The Holy Shroud since it originated in Jerusalem as we shall see.

Turin is approximately 400 miles northwest of Rome at the foot of the Italian-Swiss Alps. This precious cloth is considered by millions of Christians throughout the world to be the actual burial cloth of Jesus Christ. The ancient linen is a direct witness concealing within its fabric the compelling story of Jesus' Passion, Death and Resurrection. The Shroud is clearly the holiest relic in Christianity. The story containing the latest scientific and historical information on the Holy Shroud as well as that of its sister cloths - The *Sudarium Christi* (Face Cloth in the Tomb) and the legendary *Veronica Veil* - will be told in this book.

Physically, the Shroud is a remarkably well-preserved oblong piece of linen cloth 14'3" long (4.36 meters) and 3'7" wide (1.1 meters), weighing approximately 5 1/2 lbs (2.45 Kgs). The linen fibers are woven in a three-over-one herringbone twill with a Z-twist and consist of a fairly heavy yarn (34/100 of a millimeter thick) of Near Eastern or Mediterranean basin flax. Down the left front side

THE THREE CLOTHS OF CHRIST by John C. Iannone

(ventral side) of the Shroud is a border approximately 3 1/2 inches wide (8 centimeters from the edge) running the full length of the linen cloth. Once thought to be a side-strip sewn onto the main cloth, some have determined it to be a *selvedge*, that is, a piece of cloth woven into the main linen. It is done in such a manner as to require no hem. It should be noted that Shroud scholar Dr. Alan Whanger believes it to be a "bunching" of the cloth along its length to support its weight when held many times over the centuries along its length for viewing to the general populace.

The Selvedge:

Others speculate a different reason for adding the selvedge. Historian and renowned English sindonologist Ian Wilson speculates that the selvedge may have been added at a later date perhaps to center the image on the cloth for viewing. It is possible that when the body was laid onto the cloth it was not exactly centered from side to side making it appear off center. The selvedge would have "centered" the body. Wilson considers this the most logical explanation and points out that the selvedge was likely added at the same time as the fringe and gold covering (to be discussed later), the overall purpose being to transform the long cloth from a shroud to what seems to have been some sort of portrait which came to be known as the "Mandylion" or "little towel" in Greek. This is the Shroud doubled-in-four for manageability showing only the face.

Human Images on the Shroud:

On one side of the linen cloth are faint images of the front and back views of a man who appears to be laid out in an attitude of death consistent with Jewish burial customs of the Second Temple Period (the period of Jesus). In Jewish burials the hands were folded over the mid-section as opposed to the more Egyptian style of crossing the arms over the chest. The two views - or double image - show that the Man of the Shroud (as we shall call him at this point while building the case for authenticity) was laid out on His back on one end of the cloth with His head toward the center of the cloth. Then, after burial preparations were made, the cloth was folded over His head to cover or envelop the front of the body from head to foot.

THE THREE CLOTHS OF CHRIST by John C. Iannone

The color of the images is a faint *sepia* (straw color) contrasting with the off-white, ivory color of the original ancient cloth that the Apostles viewed. The images most resemble a scorch as one might discover on a linen handkerchief that has been lightly burned on the surface by an iron. When I had the opportunity for an extended viewing of the Shroud, I noticed that the closer one gets to the Shroud of Turin, the more the mysterious images disappear to the naked eye. The Shroud is best viewed from a distance of approximately six or more feet.

Bloodstains:

Along with the images are bloodstains that are reddish in color. Once thought by many to be "paint," these particles have now been clearly shown by blood chemists and hematologists to be true, human blood which we will discuss in detail later. The bloodstains are heaviest at the wrists and feet and at a wound on the right side of the chest corresponding precisely to the wounds inflicted on Jesus at the time of His crucifixion. In classical Roman style, Jesus was nailed through His wrists - the nail entering the high palm and exiting at the wrist. After He had hung on the cross for some time, a Roman soldier pierced His right side with a lance between the fifth and sixth ribs to ensure that He was, in fact, dead. This was done at the request of Pilate after the family requested the body.

Professor Gino Zanninotto, an Italian crucifixion expert, points out that the Romans used nails for crucifixion only in Palestine in the first and second centuries. The images also reflect bloodstains covering the top of the head and the face. In addition, many smaller bloodstains cover the front and back of the man, corresponding to the biblical description of the cap of thorns and the severe beating from a Roman whip (*flagrum*) inflicted on Jesus during His crucifixion. There are not signs of physical decomposition or bodily deterioration on the cloth. More will be said about the wounds and bloodstains on the Holy Shroud as seen by Pathologists and blood experts.

Scorches, Watermarks and Patches:

Other unique marks on the Shroud are long, longitudinal scorch marks of an incident that occurred on the night between the 3rd and 4th of December 1532 when a fire

THE THREE CLOTHS OF CHRIST   by   John C. Iannone

damaged the cloth as it lay in a silver casket reliquary set into the wall of the Sainte-Chapelle at Chambery (eastern France). The fire, set perhaps by an overturned candle, was so intense (estimated at 900-960 degrees Celsius or 1650-1750 degrees Fahrenheit) that the Shroud's silver casing had begun to melt. A drop of molten silver was found in recent times to have fallen on one edge of the Shroud's folds in this 1532 fire. The embedded silver droplet allowed scientists to estimate the heat of the fire because the melting point of silver is approximately 900 degrees Celsius.

Fortunately, due to the quick intervention of the Duke of Savoy's counselor Philip Lambert and two Franciscan priests, the casing was carried to safety. While there was damage to the Shroud itself, the images were barely touched (outer shoulders) by the intense fire. As a result of this fire, there are water stains from the dousing (creating several lozenge-shapes on the cloth) and scorch marks on the cloth along the fold lines. At this time, the cloth was folded in 48 sections. After the fire, the Shroud was rolled on a wooden roller with a Holland cloth backing. Later, the linen was changed by Princess Clotilde of Savoy in 1868 to the crimson silk-lined backing of the Shroud until 2002 when the backing was removed. After the silk backing was removed in 2002, the Shroud is now displayed flat.

In 1534, Cardinal Louis de Gorrevod sent the cloth to the nearby Convent of Poor Clares where a team of patient nuns painstakingly repaired the cloth. The nuns sewed on patches (seen on the Shroud until recently along the scorch marks). These patches were removed by a team of specialists in Turin in 2002 led by Mechthild Flury-Lemberg - a Swiss textile expert and one of the Custodians of the Cloth today and by Monsignor Ghiberti, also a Custodian.

Burn Holes:

Finally, visible on the cloth today are four sets of triple holes that appear to have been created prior to the fire of 1532. These same holes were seen in a rendering of the cloth done in 1192 in a drawing called the *Hungarian Pray Manuscript* and lend credence to the existence of the cloth well before the dating of carbon-14 scientists in 1988. We will discuss this later.

THE THREE CLOTHS OF CHRIST by John C. Iannone

The Shroud As A Photographic Negative:

One of the most fascinating aspects of the Shroud marking the beginning of the modern scientific study of the Cloth, was the accidental discovery in 1898 by a young amateur photographer (and lawyer) in Italy named Secondo Pia. Secondo was permitted to take two photographs of the Shroud during an exposition in Turin during a ceremony for the Royal Savoy family of Italy who had possession of the Shroud at that time. Photography was a relatively young science in the late 1800's. Secondo took his two photos in black-and-white on the evening of May 28, 1898. One photo he exposed for fourteen minutes and the other for twenty minutes on large glass photographic plates which he then took to his studio for development.

To Secondo's utter shock and amazement, as he describes in his *Journal*, as the images on the Shroud began to emerge, he noticed that they were developing as <u>*positives* instead of *negatives* on the negative plate</u>. This told him, to his disbelief, that the images as they appear to the human eye on the cloth were, therefore, negatives that, when photographed, produced <u>*positives on a negative plates*</u>. Secondo was awestruck. He realized that he was probably the first person in the world to look upon an actual "photograph" of Jesus. John Walsh, author of the book *The Shroud* writes:

>"The face with its closed eyes had acquired a reality that was nothing less than stupefying."

The black-and-white heightened the contrast. The question was raised: could an artist of the Medieval or Renaissance period have painted an image as a perfect photographic negative at a time when photographs were as yet unknown? Even if an artist could have done this, why would he forge a painting in the negative that could not have been understood or appreciated by the viewers of his day?

The photographs aroused interest by the scientific community as to the nature of the Shroud. The French Academy of Sciences in 1903 showed interest in the science of the Shroud and Professor Yves deLage of the French Academy called it a "bundle of imposing probabilities."

THE THREE CLOTHS OF CHRIST by John C. Iannone

The Enrie Photographs:

In 1931, Giuseppe Enrie, considered one of the finest professional Italian photographers of his day, was chosen by Cardinal Maurilio Fossati, the Archbishop of Turin, to take a series of photographs with special close-ups of the face and bloodstains. These photos revealed many details, including the possible presence of Roman coins over the eyes which was noted later (1978) from macro photographs taken by Fr. Francis Filas, S.J. at Loyola University and by Physicists John Jackson and Eric Jumper in the same year while viewing the Enrie Photos under a VP-8 Image Analyzer used by NASA. Additional photos were taken in 1969 and 1973 by Giovanni Battista Judica Cordiglia. This time they were taken in color and some of them under ultraviolet and infrared light during the investigation of a Commission - The Turin Commission - appointed by Cardinal Michele Pellegrino. Further photographs were taken in 1978 by Vernon Miller and Barrie Schwortz as part of the STURP team using slides and transparencies. Radiography, macrophotography, thermo graphic and quad-mosaic techniques were likewise use during these photo shoots. As Wilson points out:

> "Every technical advance in black-and-white photography has revealed the negative characteristics in greater clarity."

As of today, in spite of many theories, no one has been able to present a comprehensive and convincing theory as to how the mysterious images were created. However, some of the theories present a good degree of credibility as will be discussed. Wilson points out that the images have a curious "lack of physical outline." He states that:

> "Throughout the history of art, virtually until Turner and the Impressionists of the nineteenth century, artists relied to a greater or lesser degree on outlines to give shape to their work. The character of these and the manner of modeling any painting has always provided reliable dates from which the historian can make a confident judgment of dating and origin. However, in the case of the Shroud there is nothing on which to base any judgment, no other work with which to compare it."

THE THREE CLOTHS OF CHRIST   by   John C. Iannone

Ian Wilson, *The Mysterious Shroud*

The Man of the Shroud - A Description of Jesus?

The Man of the Shroud appears to have been a powerfully built man of approximately 30-45 years of age with long hair parted in the middle and falling to the shoulders. He has side locks, a mustache and a beard and he is naked. In refutation of a Medieval forgery theory, noted British genealogist Noel-Currer Briggs point out that:

> "The fourteenth century was not alone in disapproving men with long hair.(Medieval) Iconography depicted Jesus with fairly short hair."

Currer-Briggs even intimates that this very fact may have incited Medieval Inquisitors to attack the Knights Templar - the military/religious "warrior-monks" that were custodians of the Shroud after its disappearance from Constantinople in 1204 during the infamous Fourth Crusade. The Romans themselves - until the time of the Emperor Hadrian a century after the crucifixion tended to be clean-shaven while the Jews traced their long hair and beards back to the time of Moses. Aaron, Moses' brothers, for example, is specifically stated as having had a beard. In addition, Medieval artists never depicted Jesus as naked.

A Beard and A Braid:

On the back (posterior) image of the Shroud there appears to be a long strand of hair - a *braid* approximately 8-10 inches from the base of the head to a point midway between the shoulder blades that appears to be a *pigtail or ponytail*, common among Jewish males in Palestine during Jesus' time. The man's beard seems to have twin points *(forked)* characteristic of the Nazarene men of the day. There is also a *tuft of hair* falling over the brow - a feature noted in later art. Rev. Dr. Kenneth Stevenson of New York points out that the traditional hair style for an orthodox Jewish man 2000 years ago is much the same for him today: a ponytail and side locks appears to be what we see on the Shroud.

One of the world's most distinguished ethnologists, former Harvard Professor Dr. Carleton S. Coon, has associated the man with a very pure Semitic type found today among noble Arabs and Sephardic Jews. There are broad hints of Jewish

THE THREE CLOTHS OF CHRIST by John C. Iannone

ness in this hair styling. Wilson points out that the hair at the back of the head accords with what German biblical scholar H. Greeman has referred to as one of the most common fashions for Jewish men in antiquity. France scriptural authority Henri Daniel-Rops has supportively added the information that the Jews normally wore this pony tail "plaited and rolled up under their headgear" except on public holidays.

Height and Weight

By most estimates of Pathologists, the Man of the Shroud appears to have been 5'10 - 5'11" tall. Some maintain that this was very tall for an average man of that period. However, the idea that people of antiquity were significantly shorter than people today is simply a widespread popular fallacy. A University of California investigation of the skeletons of ten adult males from a recently discovered first-century Jewish burial ground in Jerusalem included one skeleton of even the upper height estimate of the Man of the Shroud. Approximately one of out 10 skeletons of the Essenes proved to be 6' or better. His weight is estimated to be between 170 - 180 lbs.

The Burial Attitude:

The body enveloped in the Shroud may have been set at a slight angle, the head bowed forward and possible supported by some pillow-type - likely stone - support. The arms are drawn very stiffly over the pelvis - left hand over right - and the right shoulder is seen to be lower than the left. The legs are decisively flexed at the knees and the left foot in partly over the right. Pathologists indicate that this was a body in a state of "*rigor mortis*" and reflects the position of the body when Jesus died on the Cross.

Rigor mortis set in quickly due to the long duration of His suffering. The head was bowed and the knees flexed. The shoulder may have been dislocated (according to the late Dr. Robert Bucklin - former Medical Examiner of Los Angeles) when His followers had to break the rigor and bring the arms into position from being extended on the Cross to being placed over the loins.

It appears then that the Man of the Shroud was of Jewish origin and that the bloodstains and wounds studied by

THE THREE CLOTHS OF CHRIST by John C. Iannone

forensic pathologists in their careful examination of the Shroud are remarkably coordinated with the testimony of the Gospels relative to the Roman crucifixion weapons and procedures employed in the death of the historical Jesus. His burial is consistent with Jewish burial practices of the day as outlined in the Mishna - the oral traditions of the Rabbi's written down in the First and Second centuries containing interpretations and scriptural ordinances regarding burial.

A Prayer Box?

More recent investigations of the Shroud by Dr. Alan Whanger, Professor Emeritus of Duke University in North Carolina, utilizing modern scientific instrumentation such as the PIOT (Polarized Image Overlay Technique) appear to reveal the presence of a *tephillin* - a Jewish phylactery or small prayer box that contains a portion of Scripture - attached to the forehead and the right arm. Shroud scholar Dr. Kenneth Stevenson discussed this possibility with Eleazor Erbach, an Orthodox Rabbi from Denver, Colorado. Rabbi Erbach not only confirmed its size and shape but also suggested that the broken blood flow on the right arm may have been caused by the corresponding arm phylactery.

Coins, Pollen, Limestone Dust and Dirt:

In addition to the possible phylactery, previous investigations of the Shroud point to the presence of Roman coins over the eyes (identified by some as *leptons* or *widow's mites* of the New Testament minted during the Governorship of Pontius Pilate). Also found were *pollen* from the ancient Near East; *calcium carbonate* (limestone dust) consistent with the cave-tombs; particles of dirt identified as *travertine aragonite* on the right heel, left knee cap and tip of the nose. This is dirt consistent with the soil around the cave tombs and is supportive with the legend of Jesus falling three times.

Floral Images and Mites:

The limestone dust is from the caves cut into the soft limestone of the hills outside the walls of Old Jerusalem. There are also skeletons of *mites* from the ancient Near East as well as *floral images* around the upper body area the Man of the Shroud having been *entombed with bunches and*

THE THREE CLOTHS OF CHRIST by John C. Iannone

bouquets of flowers. Such findings, to be discussed throughout this book, confirm the longevity, antiquity and provenance of the Shroud as coming from the Jerusalem area. As several authors point out, *if the Shroud was the work of a forger, its creation would be more "miraculous" than if it were the actual burial cloth of Jesus.*

The Shroud as a Well-Preserved Ancient Textile:

The fact the Shroud could have survived almost 2,000 years with little sign of deterioration should not be a surprise. There are many surviving Egyptian burial linens that are three times as old and have been preserved from 4000 - 6000 B.C. Jonathon D. Beard reported in *Popular Science* the finding of a 9,000 year-old piece of linen the size of a business card in an ancient village in southeast Turkey. What makes the Shroud unique, of course, it that there are *no other known cloths of antiquity bearing any images*, much less the full-length image of a man of Jewish heritage meeting all the criteria of someone subjected to Roman crucifixion. On some cloths there are signs of blood and decay, but no image. Robert Wilcox, examining clothes preserved in the Louvre in Paris pointed out that corpses wrapped in linen over extended periods of time will leave stains of the body's decomposition on the cloth. If and when the cloth rots, it will discolor.

Some consider the image to have been formed by some as yet unknown "natural phenomena." However, as Stevenson rightly points out:

> "If this type of body-on-cloth is the result of a natural process, why are there so many burial garments that have no image of the period buried in them?"

Sindonologist Robert Wilcox states that:

> "Even if (researchers) come up with some 'natural process,' the failure, so far, to find anything like the Shroud amongst the world's body cloths and artifacts leaves them with the further problem of why the process occurred only once in the history of the world, as far as is yet known."

The late Hematologist Dr. John Heller, a research scientist

THE THREE CLOTHS OF CHRIST   by   John C. Iannone

at the New England Institute of Medicine and author of the book *Report on the Shroud of Turin*, commented:

> "We do know, however, that there are thousand on thousands of pieces of funerary linens going back to millennia before Christ, and another huge number of linens of Coptic Christian burials. On none of these is there any image of any kind."

Shroud author Frank Tribbe points out that no other cloth of antiquity has been subjected to the "scientific investigation and ecclesiastical speculation" to which the Shroud has been subjected. The preservation of such cloths is generally due to the *exclusion of air (sealed) and to an arid climate*, both of which are factors in the Shroud's history. In its long history, the Shroud was locked away in various chests, reliquaries and containers rarely seeing the light of day. At one point in its history it was almost hermetically sealed in a stone wall in the City of Edessa (known as Urfa in modern Turkey) for nearly five hundred years (40 A.D. - 535 A.D.).

The Retting of Linen:

In addition, the first century Roman historian Pliny described the steps of processing yarn to include washing it in a "*struthium solution*" as a softener. Struthium is assumed to be "*soap weed*" and it was used to effectively preclude mildew, mold and decay. This "*retting process*" of linen in *saponaria or soap weed* could provide a clue to the Shroud's remarkable preservation, but scientifically no evidence of soap weed has been found on the Shroud.

Textile Tests on the Shroud: The Turin Commission:

In June 1969 Cardinal Pellegrino (then Archbishop of Turin) with approval of the Vatican and of King Umberto II of Savoy (owner of the cloth at that time) appointed a special commission of Italian scientists, among them the noted Egyptologist from the University of Turin and Superintendent of Egyptian Antiquities, Silvio Curto, to examine the Shroud. The Team, called the Turin Commission, was to conduct limited tests; advise the Cardinal about the storage and preservation of the Shroud and recommend a program of extensive scientific testing.

THE THREE CLOTHS OF CHRIST by John C. Iannone

The group was to perform non-destructive testing. They made examinations visually and with the microscope. In addition they utilized normal as well as with ultraviolet and infrared light. Having determined that the cloth was extraordinarily resistant to alterations from atmospheric changes, the Commission recommended more extensive examination and testing, including attempts to date the Shroud. They further suggested tests of select threads and small samples of the cloth as well as documentary video taping of the precious relic.

Later, in 1973, a French scholar, Professor Gilbert Raes of the Ghent Institute of Textile Technology in Belgium, was permitted to join the team to carefully examine two small linen samples: one 13 x 40 millimeters and the other 10 x 40 millimeters from the Shroud. Dr. Max Frei, a Swiss criminologist and botanist, also joined the team to study pollen samples on the Shroud. Dr. Raes reported that the Shroud was indeed woven of linen with a three-to-one herringbone twill with a Z-twist and that it is sewn with linen thread (all the warp, weft and sewing threads of the Shroud are of linen).

He noted that the yarn was indicative of a good-quality workmanship and the weave density an average of a little over thirty-five threads per centimeter, corresponding favorably with the thirty thread per centimeter average of the finest Egyptian mummy fabrics. The normal weave in Palestinian, Roman and Egyptian loom-technology was one-over-one. The three-to-one herringbone twill was a more expensive and more refined weave. It would have been a finer fabric of the period. We know from the Gospels that Joseph of Arimathea was a rich man and it was he who provided the Shroud used to bury Jesus (Mt. 27:57-61). In fact, the Gospel writers make it a point to say: "and Joseph was a wealthy man." so we would expect to find a finer fabric, which we do.

Cotton Fibers On The Shroud:

During the radiocarbon analysis done at Oxford in 1988 as well as in Carbon-14 labs in Zurich and Arizona, *cotton fibers were found on the Shroud*. According to Peter H. South, director of the Laboratory for Textile Analysis at Ambergate in Great Britain

THE THREE CLOTHS OF CHRIST by John C. Iannone

> "The cotton is a very fine dark yellow color, probably of Egyptian origin and very old. Unfortunately, how it found its way into the Shroud is impossible so say."

This finding of cotton on the Shroud from the Carbon-14 test compromised the Carbon-14 testing. The yellow color was due, as we shall discuss later, to the finding of a yellow Madder Root dye bound to some cotton threads used to make a Medieval repair of the cloth. These fibers, discovered in 2000 and tested in early 2002-4 compromised the Carbon-14 testing.

Dr. Raes, using polarized light for microscopic viewing, had also identified traces of cotton fibers (fibrils) that he classified as of the *Gossypium herbaceum* type, a cotton that existed in the Middle East of the first century. Professor Philip McNair of Birmingham University, England, supports these finds and points out that the occasional cotton fibrils in the Shroud were of the Gossypium herbaceum type that was cultivated in the Middle East during the first century, but was not known in Europe during the period when possible falsifying of the Shroud could have occurred.

The cotton traces indicated that the Shroud was woven on a loom that had been used previously to weave cotton cloth. Paul Maloney, a research archaeologist and sindonologist from Pennsylvania, notes that cotton was actually a part of the linen thread. Dr. Raes says that these finding support the contention that the Shroud linen was woven in the Middle East, since raw cotton was unknown in Europe until the ninth century when it was first planted in Spain by the Moors.

Cotton was first woven in Venice and Milan in the fourteenth century and cotton cloth was not seen in England until the fifteenth century. Cotton was grown in China and India in antiquity and was expertly woven in India several centuries before the Christian era. By the first century it was grown extensively in Mesopotamia and Egypt. Wilson notes that cotton is also known to have been introduced to the Middle East by the monarch Sennacherib during the seventh century B.C.

By the time of Christ it would certainly have been

THE THREE CLOTHS OF CHRIST by John C. Iannone

established in the environs of Palestine and, therefore, offers no difficulty to the authenticity of the Shroud. Dr. Raes concluded that this piece of linen could have been manufactured in the first century. He could not say with certainty that it was. The late John Tryer, a chartered textile technologist who worked in the field for twenty-five years as an associate of the Textile Institute of Manchester, England, discovered that while Middle East linens similar to the Shroud exist as far back as 3600 B.C. not much medieval linen has survived. He states that:

> "it would be reasonable to conclude that linen textiles with Z-twist yarns and woven 3-over-1 reversing twill similar to the Turin Shroud could have been produced in first-century Syria or Palestine."

The Mishna makes it very clear that cotton may be added to linen without fear of a transgression of the prohibition known as the "mixing of kinds" but that the slightest amount of wool mixed with linen would not have been tolerated. The Shroud, therefore would have been a perfectly proper burial linen for a Jew in the First century. *The Book of Leviticus* 19:19 states:

> "Neither shall a garment mingled of linen and wool come upon thee."

This was a prohibition against blending vegetable fiber (flax) with animal (wool) but not vegetable (linen) with vegetable (cotton). It is important to point out that we are dealing with two sources of cotton. One source was some cotton fibers that remained on and mixed with linen on the ancient loom used to create the Shroud. The other source that influenced the Carbon-14 test came from a Medieval cotton repair expertly rewoven into the Shroud.

We will return to this subject later and relay how these cotton fibers, thanks to the astute findings of American sindonologists, the late Sue Benford and her husband Joseph Marino in 2002, with the help of the late Dr. Ray Rogers - the STURP Team chemist, distorted and compromised the Carbon-14 testing of 1988. The cotton fibers were determined to have been a "repair" made on the Holy Shroud likely in the early Sixteenth century using cotton dyed with a madder-root dye (yellow) and bound to the cotton fibers with an aluminum mordant and gum-arabic binder.

THE THREE CLOTHS OF CHRIST   by   John C. Iannone

These cotton fibers were intricately rewoven into the linen by a process called "French invisible weaving" practiced at the time among reweavers who repaired the finest tapestries of Europe. The Turin scientists cut the fabrics presented to the Carbon-14 labs. The Labs did not note the mix of cotton and linen - thereby compromising the test results.

Linen and The Image:

In 1978 the STURP team with over 24 scientists conducted a thorough scientific investigation of the Shroud using the latest equipment. The group determined that the actual image was created by a phenomenon (as yet not clearly known) or a momentous event that caused a rapid cellulose degradation (aging) of the linen fibers, that is, an accelerated dehydration and oxidation of the very top linen fibrils of the cellulose fibers of the Shroud, thereby creating a sepia or straw-yellow colored image similar to that of a scorch - yet not created by heat.

Dr. Ray Roger, the Shroud chemist, just before his death, further noted that the discoloration was more like something that influenced the "surface debris" of the linen fibrils rather than the medullas of the linen. He indicated that starches on the surface - possibly from the retting process of the linen - left surface impurities. Whatever precipitated this rapid aging affected only the very top fibrils of the fibers of the linen. As noted previously, the images are a *surface phenomenon*. Most scientists compare it to a light scorch such as might be created if an iron touched a handkerchief for a short period. However, since the images do not fluoresce under ultra-violet light, it is not a scorch from heat.

What, then, caused this to happen? This is a central part of the mystery of the Shroud. No one has yet been able to provide a comprehensive explanation and we will discuss various theories later. Those who believe in the Resurrection of Jesus, myself included, believe that something startling occurred at the moment of the Resurrection - some phenomenon as yet not understood by science. This momentous event left its mark on the Shroud for us to ponder. It is *a photo of the Resurrection created - perhaps by light* - for all people of all eras to contemplate. Many call the Shroud the "silent witness" for this reason and claim that the Shroud is a modern witness

THE THREE CLOTHS OF CHRIST by John C. Iannone

to the Resurrection. I call it the "Visual Gospel."

Modern Display of the Shroud:

Today, as a result of the findings of scientists of the STURP Team and recommendations to Turin authorities, the Shroud is displayed on rare occasion in a new fashion.

1. The patches have been removed in 2002 and the area beneath them vacuumed to save the patches and particles for further study.

2 The cloth is laid out flat to avoid wrinkling and the "migration of particles" of blood from the folding and rolling done in the past.

3. The Cloth is kept behind a bullet-proof glass to protect it from random or planned acts of terrorism by an individual or group.

4. The casing is air-conditioned to approximately 68 degrees Fahrenheit to protect it from humidity.

5. It is also kept in an argon/nitrogen environment to protect it from environmental damage from pollutants. Turin is an industrial city where Fiat was manufactured.

6. It is rarely displayed to the public and this is done under soft-lighting.

Public Display of the Shroud in 2010:

The Linen was displayed in 1978, in 1998 and in 2000 to celebrate the anniversary of the founding of Christianity. In a surprise announcement, Pope Benedict XVI told the world that the Shroud - not expected to go on display again until 2025 - would now be displayed in Turin between April 5 to May 22, 2010.

Material Traces of Jesus' Life:

It should not come as a surprise that Jesus would leave "material traces" of His life on earth. On April 21, 1902, Yves Delage, Professor of Anatomy at the Paris Sorbonne and an agnostic, gave a lecture to his rationalist colleagues of the French Academy of Sciences. In this lecture he

THE THREE CLOTHS OF CHRIST by John C. Iannone

claimed that the body images on the Shroud were so physiologically flawless and meaningful that he found it impossible to believe they could be the work of an artist. As Yves Delage stated in a letter to Charles Ricket, Editor of the *Revue Scientifique* in response to his skeptical colleagues at the Academy of Sciences:

> "I willingly recognize that none of these given arguments offer the features of an irrefutable demonstration, but it must be recognized that their whole constitutes a bundle of imposing probabilities, some of which are very near being proven. A religious question has been needlessly injected into a problem which in itself is purely scientific, with the result that feelings have run high and reason has been led astray. If, instead of Christ there were a question of some person like a Sargon, an Achilles or one of the Pharaohs, no one would have thought of making any objection. In dealing with this question, I have been faithful to the true spirit of science, intent only on the truth, not concerned in the least whether or not it might impinge on the interests of any religious group. I recognize Christ as an historical personage and I see no reason why anyone should be scandalized that there still exist material traces of His earthly life."
>
> Quoted in Wilson: *The Mysterious Shroud*.

Contemporary Pathologist Dr. Frederick Zugibe, Medical Examiner in Rockland County and possessing a Ph. D in Anatomy, after over 50 years of study of the Shroud often states that "anatomy supports authenticity." Rev. Kim Dreisbach often talked of the "preponderance of evidence" in support of authenticity.

The Presence of Natron On The Shroud:

Dr. Garza-Valdez of the Microbiology Department of the University of Texas at San Antonio reported in June 1995 the presence of bacteria known as *natronococcus* (among other bacteria) on the Shroud. Microanalyst Dr. Giovanni Riggi also identified a substance chemically resembling natron. These bacteria thrive only in the presence of *sodium carbonate* (*natron*) used in preserving the mummies in

THE THREE CLOTHS OF CHRIST by John C. Iannone

ancient Egypt and for bleaching in ancient Turkey and Palestine. *The presence of such bacteria creates a presumption that the Shroud once had natron on it whose traces have disappeared over a long period of time.* This raises the question of who in the fourteenth century would have put natron from Turkey, Palestine or Egypt on the Shroud and why an individual would have done this.

****

THE THREE CLOTHS OF CHRIST by John C. Iannone

Chapter Two

POLLEN, MITES AND FLOWERS - ORIGINS OF THE SHROUD

"If the Shroud was a creation of the Middle Ages, then its forger must have ordered the mites (and pollen) to go with it."

Rev. Dr. Kenneth Stevenson

In our search for antiquity, the examination of the Shroud as a textile is only the beginning of the quest. More information has come to light in recent years that enables us to date the Shroud to ancient Palestine (contrary to the apparent finds of the Carbon-14 test which will be examined later). Among these tell-tale finds are the presence of pollen, mites and floral images on the Shroud.

Ancient Pollen On The Shroud?

The late Swiss botanist and criminologist Dr. Max Frei was permitted in 1973 and 1978 as part of the Turin Commission and the STURP Team to take sticky-tape samples of the surface debris of the linen (dirt, dust, mites and pollen grains) directly from the Shroud. Pollen grains are of special interest because they have an exceptionally hard outer shell, the *exine*, which can last literally millions of years. Dr. Frei was highly respected in Europe, having founded the scientific department of the Zurich Police. He wrote his doctoral thesis on the flora of Sicily and continued this study of the Shroud's pollen until his death in 1983.

The entire Frei Collection, formerly in the possession of the Association of Scientists and Scholars International for the Shroud of Turin (A.S.S.I.S.T.) was transferred to the United States in 1988 and placed under the guardianship of Dr. Alan Whanger, Professor Emeritus of Duke University in North Carolina where further studies have been done

THE THREE CLOTHS OF CHRIST by John C. Iannone

under the aegis of research archaeologist Paul C. Maloney.

Before his death in 1983, Dr. Frei had identified fifty-eight different types of pollen on the sticky tapes and further demonstrated that some of this grouping came from Jerusalem at the time of Jesus. Other pollen, he noted, came from Eastern Turkey and some from Europe, the final resting place of the Shroud. With regard to Turkey, Dr. Frei was certain that the Shroud had been in the area he describes as the Anatolian Steppe which he qualifies as a phytogeographical term for the region of the towns (modern) of Bitlis, Diyarbakier, Mardin, Urfa, Gaziantep and Malatya. *Urfa* is the modern Turkish name for the former Byzantine city of Edessa believed to have been home to the Shroud for 900 years from approximately 40 A.D. until 944 A.D. Edessa, sometimes called "The Blessed City" is roughly 400 miles north of Jerusalem and sat on the fringes of the Byzantine/Roman Empire.

At the time of his death, Frei was seeking to identify nineteen other pollens which would have brought the number to seventy-seven. Paul Maloney placed this work in the hands of Aharon Horowitz, an illustrious Israeli palynologist who noted that pollens found on the Shroud can be compared to pollens found in Palestine but not in North Africa. Professor Avinoam Danin of Hebrew University in Jerusalem, who was contacted by Dr. Whanger, is the chief expert in Israeli desert flora. Professor Danin agrees with Horowitz and adds that it is possible to demonstrate, on the basis of pollens present on the Shroud, an itinerary across the Negev to the highlands of Lebanon.

Some critics have proposed that pollen could have been airborne from the Middle East to Europe and made their way to the Shroud. However, Dr. Frei, responding to this claim stated:

> "Groups A, B, and C of plants on the Shroud from Palestine and Anatolia are so numerous, compared to species from Europe, that a casual contamination or a pollen-transport from the Near East by storms in different seasons cannot be responsible for their presence... the predominance of these pollen must be the result of the Shroud's stay in such countries. Migrating birds or contamination with desert plants by pilgrims can be excluded because they had no

THE THREE CLOTHS OF CHRIST by John C. Iannone

possibility of direct contact with the Shroud. It should also be noted that the prevailing winds in the region move from Europe to the Middle East, not the reverse."

> Kenneth Stevenson and Gary Habarmas: *The Shroud and the Controversy* (quoting Swiss criminologist Dr. Max Frei).

The Presence of Mites On The Shroud:

Dr. Frei concluded that many pollen matched species found "almost exclusively" in halophyte fossils from the Dead Sea. To Frei's mind, the weight of evidence mitigated against a Medieval fraud. Stevenson further points out that this was Dr. Frei's field of expertise and his work has been supported by Dr. Avinoam Danin of Hebrew University and by Turin microbiologist Dr. Giovanni Riggi Di Numana, who also found samples of mites, or:

> "....minute animal forms extremely similar in their aspects and dimension to those from Egyptian burial fabrics."

During Dr. Riggi's analysis of samples vacuumed from between the Shroud and its backing cloth in 1978, he isolated and identified a mite peculiar to ancient burial linens, specifically Egyptian mummy wrappings.

As Stevenson points out:

> "If the Shroud was a creation of the Middle Ages, then its forger must have ordered the mites (and pollen) to go with it."

As renowned archaeologist William Meacham further stated:

> "Pollen...is empirical data...ipso facto evidence of exposure to the air in those regions."

Some have voiced concern that the STURP team, in an independent investigation in 1978, found only one pollen on the Shroud. However, Dr. Max Frei utilized a hand application of a special sticky tape to the Shroud that ensured the transfer of pollen that the non-pressure method of STURP likely missed. Stevenson points out that the hand application of tape was much more likely to contact the pollen that almost certainly would have settled deeper into the fibers and crevices of the linen fabric. The purely surface roller method used by STURP barely disturbed the linen and did not penetrate to the level of the pollen.

Linking History and Science:

Historian Ian Wilson's study of ancient historical texts that links the Shroud with the Image of Edessa (a theory discussed further on) confirms Dr. Frei's scientific discovery of pollen from these areas. Wilson postulated that historical evidence supports scientific finds and that the Shroud was in Edessa in Eastern Turkey from shortly after Jesus' death until 944 A.D. and then in Constantinople until 1204 A.D. He quotes Dr. Frei as saying:

> "These plants are of great diagnostic value for our geographical studies, as identical plants are missing in all other countries where the Shroud has been exposed to the open air. Consequently a forgery, if produced somewhere in France during the Middle Ages, in a country lacking these typical halophytes, could not contain such characteristic pollen grains from the desert regions of Palestine."

Stevenson rightly states:

> "It is doubtful that a Medieval forger (*at a time when the microscope was unknown*) could have known, let alone produced, a cloth with just the right pollen spread from *Palestine, Turkey and France.*"

The pollen discovered by Dr. Frei represent these main groups:

1. Halophyte type desert plants which are "very typical" of the Palestine area around the Dead Sea and the Negev.

2. Steppic plants which are characteristic of the area of the Anatolian Steppe defined by Dr. Frei as including Urfa (ancient Edessa). This is the dry zone where no natural pollen can grow on account of inadequate summer rainfall.

3. A small group of plants that are characteristic of the environs of Istanbul. This city in modern Turkey was the

THE THREE CLOTHS OF CHRIST by John C. Iannone

Constantinople of the Byzantine Empire founded by the Emperor Constantine in 325. Before that, Constantinople was called Byzantium - a city with a long and great history.

4. Northern European plants that are consistent with the Shroud's known history in France and Italy. The Shroud was in Europe and specifically France from approximately 1205 and was moved to Turin in 1578.

Werner Bulst, S.J. in an article in *Shroud Spectrum International*, made the following observations:

> "Of the pollen from fifty-eight species of plants less than one-third grow in France or Italy. This astonishing, small number of European species can be explained by the history of the Shroud in Europe, for, normally kept in a closed reliquary, the Shroud was protected from pollen contamination. Only on special occasions was it exposed in the open...The spectrum of non-European species is highly astonishing. There is only one place where all these plants, with the exception of three grow in a very small radius: Jerusalem. This cannot be an accident. Pollen could have been carried to Europe on winds, but a transport of pollen from the Middle East is highly improbable."

Dr. Stevenson points out that:

> "Pollen analysis is acceptable evidence in a court of law and therefore certainly empirical data as to the Shroud's authenticity, antiquity, and non-European origin. The value of the presence of ancient pollen and mites on the Shroud should not be underestimated."

Rev. Kim Dreisbach advised that archaeologist and cave-tomb specialist James Strange of Florida, with assistance from Dr. Giovanni Riggi, found pollen on the outside of the Shroud differing from those on the inside (the imaged side). The outside pollen were *mineral coated*, reflecting the likelihood that the outside of the cloth came in contact with the limestone ledge of the grave.

A Cloth Ordered By a Medieval or Renaissance Forger?

But what of the argument advanced by some that a Medieval or Renaissance forger could have ordered or happened upon a

THE THREE CLOTHS OF CHRIST by John C. Iannone

burial cloth, even an ancient burial cloth, from the Near East already containing pollen and mites? Could not a Crusader have brought back a cloth from Palestine to Europe which then was utilized by a Medieval or Renaissance artist to create or fake the Shroud?

Kenneth Stevenson replies that:

> "After all, it is possible, though not very likely, that a forger could have been wise enough to order a cloth from Palestine, even that he might have ordered an 'old cloth' from Palestine. But to suppose he could have ordered a cloth woven in the Middle East and then specified that the cloth must be exposed to open air in the areas of both Western Turkey (Edessa) and Eastern Turkey (Istanbul) to endure the proper pollen spread boggles the imagination. Anyway, the existence of pollen would not be discovered for at least another six hundred years. Moreover, the historical path of the Shroud (from Jerusalem to Edessa to Constantinople to Europe) would not be reconstructed for nearly eight hundred years."

Flowers and Floral Images On The Shroud:

Very exciting recent information indicates that the Man of the Shroud was entombed with *bunches and bouquets of flowers* and that *floral materials were once placed on the Shroud of Turin* which left pollen grains the imprints of plants and flowers on the linen cloth. Such information provides substantial evidence regarding the origin - or provenance - of the precious cloth as coming from an area around Jerusalem.

In 1995, Israeli botanist and expert on the plant life of Israel, Dr. Avinoam Danin, a Professor at Hebrew University in Jerusalem, was asked by Dr. Alan Whanger, Professor Emeritus at Duke University in North Carolina, to confirm the presence of floral images which Alan and his wife Mary had noted on the 1931 Shroud photographs of Giuseppe Enrie. They were later joined by Dr. Uri Baruch of the Israel Antiquities Authority, a palynologist and expert on Israel's pollen. Danin studied the plant images and Baruch analyzed the pollen grains found by the late Swiss Criminologist and botanist Dr. Max Frei via the sticky tape collection of materials that Frei had taken from the Shroud

THE THREE CLOTHS OF CHRIST   by   John C. Iannone

in 1973 and 1978.

Image of a Chrysanthemum On The Shroud:

Twelve years earlier, in 1983, Oswald Schuermann, a German physics professor, advised Dr. Whanger that he could see flower like patterns around the face of the Man of the Shroud. In 1985, Whanger, utilizing 2nd generation Enrie photographs, spotted the faint outline of *petals of a flower* noted by Scheuermann and identified as *"the inflorescence of the crown chrysanthemum (Chrysanthemum coronarium)"* (Prof. Danin). Dr. Whanger, utilizing a magnifying lens, suddenly saw out of the corner of his eye the image of a large chrysanthemum-like flower on the *anatomic left side about fifteen centimeters lateral to and six centimeters above the midline top of the head*. Dr. Whanger utilized many life size second generation Enri photos of parts of the Shroud as well as the full length images from the Enrie negatives.

These were processed and enlarged by Gamma Photographic Laboratories of Chicago, Illinois. Some were processed with the specific request to maximize the detail in the off-body area. By standing some distance away from the photographs and looking at the off-body areas, definite patterns became apparent to Dr. Whanger. The Whangers continued to find many images of plants by examining the photographically enhanced excellent black and white photographs of Giuseppe Enri taken in 1931. The Whangers compared their findings with the authoritative botanical work of Michael Zohary and Naomi Feinbrun's *"Flora Palaestina"* to tentatively identify 28 types of plants. In 2009, I had the honor of meeting with Dr. Whanger and viewing not only the pollen collection of Dr. Max Frei but the enhanced images of Enrie's photos and the outline of floral images. It was a special meeting for which I am most grateful.

Whanger noted that all 28 plants grow in Israel. He reviewed drawings of the 1,900 plants depicted in Zohary's book and worked with flowers buds, stems, leaves and fruits that are reasonably clear. He then did side-by-side comparisons in a number of instances and used the Polarized Image Overlay Technique (PIOT). The Whangers approached Professor Danin who largely verified their conclusions.

THE THREE CLOTHS OF CHRIST by John C. Iannone

The Provenance or Origin of The Shroud:

Professor Danin, when speaking of the pollen grains and floral images, stated that they serve as "*geographic and calendar indicators*" demonstrating that the origin or provenance of the Shroud was definitely the Holy Land. Evidence further suggested that the flowers were picked in the Spring (calendar indicators) from an area in and around Jerusalem including an area between Jerusalem and Jericho. Danin noted that: "they could have been picked up fresh in the fields. A few of the species could be found in the markets of Jerusalem in the Spring of the year"... a period consistent with the time of the Passover and Crucifixion.

The floral images found by the Whangers with the help of Prof. Danin included hundreds of flowers - many in the vicinity of the head of the Man of the Shrouds well as:

> "many others including several bouquets extending down to the level of the waist." This including *some on the chest and abdomen* (Dr. Alan Whanger).

The Rock Rose - Cistus creticus:

In addition to the *Crown Chrysanthemum*, Danin confirmed the image of the *Rock Rose (Cistus creticus)* identifying images of a bouquet of Rock Rose lateral to the left cheek of the human figure on the Shroud. Dr. Frei had found grains of Rock Rose pollen as early as 1973. This finding was approved by Dr. Uri Baruch in 1998. As Professor Danin states:

> "The fact that the existence of this plant image on the shroud has been demonstrated by two independent botanical methods proves beyond a reasonable doubt that the plants of this species were placed on the Shroud at one time."

The Bean Caper Plant (Zygophyllum dumosum):

In 1997, Danin, while visiting the Whangers, noted a bouquet including "*bean caper plants*" (*Zygophyllum dumosum*) which the Whangers had noticed but had not fully identified and did not publish. In establishing the provenance of the Shroud, Danin indicates that Zygophyllum dumosum grows only in Israel, Jordan and Sinai, its appearance helps to

THE THREE CLOTHS OF CHRIST   by   John C. Iannone

definitely limit the Shroud's place of origin.

Thorn-Thistle Pollen (Gundelia tournefortii):

In a correspondence received by this author from Professor Danin, he advised:

> "At present I give a higher weight to Gundelia tournefortii because of the (presence) of plenty of pollen grains of the latter and its image on the Shroud. Both species, Zygophyllum dumosum (Bean Caper plant) and Gundelia tournefortii (thorn-thistle bush) are necessary for locating the origin of the Shroud."

Dr. Whanger notes that the Crown of Thorns was made mostly with the *Gundelia tournefortii tumbleweed.*

Drs. Whanger, Danin and Baruch point out that, while the presence of floral images and pollen grains on the Shroud defines the place of origin as the Holy Land, they do not, of themselves, identify the Man of the Shroud with the historical Jesus of Nazareth. This author concludes, after conversations with Professors Danin and Whanger in Turin, that such images and pollen grains coming from the Holy Land, most from an area in and around Jerusalem, strongly support, when combined with other bodies of evidence outlined in this book, the case for authenticity of the Shroud as the burial cloth of the historical Jesus of Nazareth.

Flower Images In Early Christian Art:

Dr. Whanger notes that there is ample evidence of the presence of flower images on the Shroud. Flowers congruent with the Shroud images were portrayed in numerous works of art. One of the earliest portraits of Christ in the third century in the Roman catacombs shows a patterning around the head very similar to the flower-banked facial image in the Mandylion frame. (The Mandylion is believed to be the Shroud folded and mounted in a frame with only the face showing). Another portrait of Christ from the early Fourth Century in a Roman catacomb has about 150 points of congruence with the Shroud's facial image and shows a number of flower images in the nimbus or halo.

THE THREE CLOTHS OF CHRIST by John C. Iannone

He notes that the *Pantocrator Icon* of St. Catherine's Monastery at Mount Sinai, probably produced around 550 A.D. at Edessa at the request of Byzantine Emperor Justinian I, is the most accurate of the many portraits he has studied which have been derived from the image on the Shroud and which has over 250 points of congruence with it. *In the halo of this icon are many dozens of images of flowers highly congruent with those on the Shroud of Turin.*

Even more striking are the very accurate copies of the images of the flowers on the Shroud on the *gold sollidus coins* of Justinian II struck in 692-695 A.D. Flowers are accurately portrayed on the gold coins of Constantine VII in 950 after the Shroud was brought with great ceremony to Constantinople. In the earlier years of the Shroud, floral images were quite vivid. It is not clear when or how the images of flowers became so indistinct or imperceptible or when this was lost on the Western Church. While visiting with Prof. Whanger, I had the good fortune of holding a ring of Justinian II which portrayed the facial images of the Holy Shroud.

Lack of Vanillin on the Shroud:

Further support for the antiquity of the cloth comes from a find by Shroud Chemist, the late Dr. Ray Rogers. Rogers noted that the substance vanillin is found in linen and disappears with aging. A medieval linen would have approximately one half of its vanillin and a cloth of the believed age of the Shroud would have lost its vanillin. He notes that the linens that wrapped the Dead Sea Parchment have a similar loss of all vanillin leading to the belief in the antiquity of the cloth.

Fragments Found At Masada:

The Fortress of Masada on the shores of the Dead Sea was the winter palace of King Herod as well as the location where the Zealots took their final stand against the conquering Romans in 72 A.D. Mechthild Flury-Lemberg, a Swiss textile expert and custodian of the Holy Shroud, noted recently that fragments of fabric found at Masada had a form of stitching similar to that found of the side of the Holy Shroud. The stitching, she notes, has never been found on any Medieval or Renaissance fabrics and helps date the cloth to the period of Herod.

THE THREE CLOTHS OF CHRIST by John C. Iannone

Although the Carbon-14 tests of 1988 dated the cloth from the period 1260-1390, new findings to be discussed later, have refuted the date and demonstrated that the test was compromised by a mixture of medieval cotton and ancient linen.

****

THE THREE CLOTHS OF CHRIST   by   John C. Iannone

THE THREE CLOTHS OF CHRIST by John C. Iannone

Chapter Three

ANCIENT COINS OVER THE EYES

"The result...revealed objects resting on the eyes, objects which resembled small disks or 'buttons'"

Drs. John Jackson and Eric Jumper

One of the most significant discoveries favoring the first century dating of the Shroud comes from the identification of images of ancient Roman coins - believed to be *leptons* - minted during the reign of Pontius Pilate – found over the eyes of the Man of the Shroud.

The VP-8 Image Analyzer:

The story, as related by Ian Wilson, begins on February 19, 1976 at the Sandia Scientific Laboratories in Albuquerque, New Mexico. Research physicists Drs. John Jackson and Eric Jumper were, at the time, Captains in the U.S. Air Force and Instructors in Albuquerque (later associated with the U.S. Air Force Academy in Colorado). Ever since he was a teenager, Dr. Jackson had been interested in the Shroud as a hobby and wanted to gain a better understanding of how the image might have been formed. On that day, Jackson and Jumper visited the Sandia Lab and were introduced by William Mottern, an industrial radiographer, to a recently developed instrument known as the Interpretation Systems VP-8 Image Analyzer, a spin-off of the NASA Space Program research. They were joined shortly thereafter by Dr. Kenneth Stevenson and Dr. Giles Carter.

Discovering a Three Dimensional Image:

This instrument was utilized to interpret light and dark as functions of distance in space. Essentially, the VP-8 Image Analyzer translated light and shade, as on a black-and-white photograph, into relief, viewable in dimension on a television monitor. As an example, two photographs taken at

THE THREE CLOTHS OF CHRIST by John C. Iannone

varying angles on a lunar surface could be fed into the VP-8 Image Analyzer and seen in their original relief on a TV screen, providing a three dimensional view. Such relief would not normally be expected from a single photograph of a person, which would contain insufficient relief information. Recently, I had the privilege of sitting with Optical Specialist Kevin Moran in his laboratory in North Carolina and viewing the image of the Shroud photograph through the VP-8 Image Analyzer. The results were startling and I could well understand the excitement of the STURP scientists when they first viewed the three dimensionality of the image.

The group decided to place one of the high quality 1931 Enrie photos of the Shroud into the Analyzer, not expecting to see anything meaningful. However, as Wilson relates:

> "It was...with some astonishment that, after the Shroud negative had been placed in the Analyzer, the two scientists found themselves looking at a convincing, properly three-dimensional image which could be consistently rotated without distortion, the only anomalies being creases and the 1532 fire marks."

It appeared that the Shroud was encoded with *relief information* of the body it once enveloped reflecting light and dark as functions of cloth-to-body distance. Subsequent experiments revealed that no paintings produced the same effect under the Analyzer. The three-dimensional information of the Shroud image discovered in 1976 was now added to the photographic negativity of the Shroud image (with actual positive blood) discovered by Secondo Pia in 1898 and enhanced by the photographs of Giuseppe Enrie in 1931 to deepen the mystery surrounding the formation of the images on the Shroud. Further progress was obtained by Giovanni Tamburelli, professor at the University of Turin, above all with respect to the three-dimensional aspects of the facial features of the Man of the Shroud.

Discovery of Coin Images:

The story of the coins begins two years later in July 1978 with an article in *The Numismatist* magazine. Drs. Jackson, Jumper and Stevenson made another startling discovery. The investigators stated in their article in *The Numismatist* that:

THE THREE CLOTHS OF CHRIST   by   John C. Iannone

> "The result of this process (VP-8 Image Analyzer)...revealed objects resting on the eyes, objects which resembled small disks or 'buttons'...In summary...the objects are circular, about the same size and flat."

They noted that the object on the anatomical right eye (the eye as seen on the negative image) was more noticeable. The thickness of the objects was approximately 1 to 5 millimeters and the average diameter was approximately 14 millimeters. The researchers theorized that these objects could be *coins*. They mentioned this to Ian Wilson to determine what coins he, as an historian, thought might be likely candidates. Wilson noted that several coins from the time of Pontius Pilate were possible on the score of their size -about the size of a United States dime. He favored a *lepton*, the traditional *Widow's Mite* of the Bible. The authors state:

> "The result of his (Ian Wilson's) study produced the possibility of a Roman bronze lepton of Pontius minted between 29 - 31 A.D. One of Wilson's observations was that it lacked the image of Caesar and was, therefore, likely to be in the possession of Orthodox Jews. Rather amazingly, the size and shape of the lepton are perfect."

The researchers further noted the observation of what appeared to be a "backward question mark" on the object on the left eye that seemed to correspond to the striking *Augur's Wand (lituus*, or astrologer's staff) on a lepton. Italian numismatic expert Mario Moroni also identified these as leptons.

The Filas Report

In 1979, the late Rev. Francis Filas, a Jesuit priest and professor of theology at Loyola University in Chicago, photographed an enlargement of the face of the Shroud that he had been using on television programs. The enlargement was made from a second generation sepia print based on the original 1931 photographic plates of Guiseppe Enrie. Fr Filas stated:

> "To my surprise, I happened to notice a sort of design directly over the right eye."

THE THREE CLOTHS OF CHRIST by John C. Iannone

He brought the print to Michael Marx, a Greek classical numismatist in Chicago. As Marx scanned the photograph with his magnifier, he called Filas' attention to what appears to be *four curving capital letters:* **U C A I**. They obtained Frederick W. Madden's *A History of Jewish Coinage and of Money in the Old and New Testament* and consulted the catalog of all Pontius Pilate coins in the British Museum. The projected objects on the eyes matched in size and shape to a coin of Pontius Pilate. Letter-like shapes that Filas (and later Dr. Robert M. Haralick of the Spatial Data Analysis Laboratory at Virginia's Polytechnic Institute and State University) read as **UCAI** occur in the correct position on the projected object on the lepton of Pilate.

Using high magnification photography of the right eye on a large print of the Giuseppe Enrie negative revealed four letters: **U C A I**. The VP-8 Image Analyzer showed raised letters. Fr. Filas identified these as belonging to the lepton (or Widow's Mite) of Pontius Pilate where the words **TIBERIOU CAISAROS** were found. The **U C A I** was arranged in a coin-like curve surrounding a shape resembling a shepherd's staff. The tiny lepton of Pilate (a coin consisting of 96.5 percent copper and 3.5 percent tin) bares an astrologer's staff (*lituus*) accompanied by the inscription **TIBERIOU KAISAROS**.

However, how does one explain the use of **U C A I** versus **U K A I**? Fr. Filas surmised that the Shroud's **U C A I** might be the central letters with a **C** substituted for the Greek **K**, a contention received with considerable skepticism until there came to light two actual examples (now six) of Pilate leptons with precisely this misspelling. Filas noted that the **U C A I** was angled from the 9:30 to the 11:30 o'clock around the curve of the astrologer's staff. The lituus was a constant motif in coins minted by Pilate between 29-32 A.D. but never minted again by any official in Palestine nor anywhere else in the Roman world as an independent symbol.

In addition, a clipped area of the coin from the 1:30 to 3:30 O'clock was evident. William Yarbrough, a numismatist in Atlanta, Georgia, provided Fr. Filas with an actual Pilate coin. Later, a confrere of Michael Marx, John Aiello, contributed another Pilate coin that exhibited a more elegant style. Michael Avi-Yonah's modern *Prolegomenon*

THE THREE CLOTHS OF CHRIST by John C. Iannone

to the re-issuance of Madden's *History of Jewish Coinage and of Money in the Old and New Testament*, made the point that Pilate minted his coins in the Roman years of Tiberius, 16-18 (corresponding to 30-32 A.D.).

Fr. Filas concluded that there existed a combination of size, position, angular rotation, relative mutual proportion, accuracy of duplication (with the exception of a **C** on the Shroud where a **K** existed on the Pontius Pilate coins that were examined) and parity (i.e. turned in the proper direction) that proved beyond reasonable doubt that these were real coins and not just "weave anomalies" of the linen of the Shroud. He goes on to say that the mathematical probability suggests that to have four letters so appear in the correct positioning around the lituus would be in the range of one chance in eight million.

The Julia Lepton Over the Left Eye

The image of the coin area over the left eye is less distinct, but, as Dr. Alan Whanger stated:

> "We are able to determine that another Filas coin, a 'Julia' lepton struck only in 29 A.D. by Pontius Pilate (and named after Julia, the mother of Tiberius Caesar) matches this rather well, having 73 points of congruence in an area smaller than a finger print."

The Julia lepton was also identified (independently) by Dr. Baima Ballone (forensic medicine) and Dr. Nello Balossino (computer sciences) both of the University of Turin.

Coins Over The Eyes: An Ancient Jewish Burial Custom?

Recent archaeological digs have unearthed skeletons around Jericho that date back to the time of Christ with coins placed on the head. In En Boquq in the desert of Judah, a skeleton dating to the second century was found with coins in each of the eye sockets - evidence that Jews, on occasion, placed coins over the eyes of the deceased in the time of Jesus. Some critics, however, state that it was not necessary to place coins over Jesus' eyes. Professor James Cameron, a pathologist, points out that such closing of the eyelids would have been quite unnecessary in the case of an individual who had died upright, the weight of the super orbital muscles performing this function automatically.

THE THREE CLOTHS OF CHRIST by John C. Iannone

However, this opinion is not shared by U.S. pathologist Dr. Robert Bucklin, formerly of the Los Angeles Medical Examiner's Office.

Additionally, Cameron's statement assumes that the purpose of the coins was to keep the eyes closed. There were, however, other reasons for such a practice in antiquity. The Greeks, for example, placed coins over the eyes as a tribute by the deceased to the mythical Charon, who had to ferry the dead across the mythical River Styx. Early Christian graves revealed that coins were sometimes placed in the hand, pocket or mouth of early Christians who were buried. The Gates of Heaven had replaced the River Styx.

It is quite possible that this Christian custom found its roots from the tradition that coins were placed over the eyes of Jesus and that the practice, even among the Jews, had a purpose other that the physical one of keeping the eyes closed. The purpose may not be clear, but placing coins over the eyes was a custom of antiquity. Objects were, in fact, found over the eyes of the Man of the Shroud and such placement of coins has been noted by archaeologists (such as Zvi Greenhut of the Israel Antiquities Authority) on occasion in Jewish burials and is consistent with the customs of antiquity.

The Haralick Report

It became apparent that computer enhancement might be an important avenue to allow identification. Fr. Filas subsequently submitted the coin and Shroud image for comparative analysis at the Virginia Polytechnic Institute and State University's Spatial Data Analysis Laboratory. Dr. Robert Haralick, then at the Institute, offered cautious support to Filas' hypothesis while stressing the fundamental problem that science has no way of determining whether what appears as a coin inscription is anything but a random quirk of the Shroud's weave. In the abstract introducing his report, Dr. Haralick advises:

> "A number of digital enhancements were performed on imagery digitalized from the 1931 Enrie photographs of the Shroud and a 1978 STURP photograph taken by Vernon Miller. The enhancements provide supporting evidence that the raised area of the Shroud image contains remnants of patterns similar to those of a known

THE THREE CLOTHS OF CHRIST by John C. Iannone

Pontius Pilate coin dating from 29 A.D."

After extensive study, Dr. Haralick concludes:

> "Thus, in the enlargement of the right eye image we find supporting evidence for a bright, oval area: a shepherd's staff pattern as the main feature in the bright area; and bright segment patterns just to the side and top of the staff pattern which in varying degrees match the letters **OUCAIC**."

Haralick goes on to caution the reader that:

> "The evidence cannot be said to be conclusive evidence that an image of the Pontius Pilate coin appears in the right eye of the Enrie Shroud Images. However, the evidence is definitely supporting evidence because there is some degree of match between what one would expect to find if the Shroud did indeed contain a faint image of the Pilate coin and what we can in fact observe in the original and in digitally produced images."

Several years ago I had the opportunity of a telephone interview with Dr. Haralick. I asked him frankly if this could be a coin over the eye of Jesus. His answer was cautious and he said:

> "While I cannot say definitively that these were coins over the eyes of Jesus, I can say that what I find is consistent with anything I would expect to find if they were coins over the eyes of Jesus."

The Problem of the U C A I vs. U K A I:

The problem still remained that the letters on the Shroud coin read **U C A I**, whereas the Pontius Pilate coin in Fr. Filas' possession read **U K A I**. Logic said that if a coin maker were to make an error, the substitution of a **C** for a **K** in a Roman province was the most logical error to make. The pronunciation of "Caesar" in Latin and "Kaisaros" in Greek would have been identical for the hard K sound. In addition, repeated admonitions in modern coin manuals and from numismatists indicate that the coins of Pontius Pilate are, as a class, of *wretched technical quality, poorly pressed, off-center and showing misspellings.*

THE THREE CLOTHS OF CHRIST by John C. Iannone

An Actual Maverick Coin Found:

In 1981 Fr. Filas took the photograph of the Pilate coin he had received from William Yarbrough to Gamma Laboratories in Chicago and asked them to enlarge the coin to about twenty-five times life size in black-and-white. When Fr. Filas mounted the photo and stepped back to look at it, he noticed a definite **C** where the **K** of Kaisaros should have been located. He could not believe his eyes or believe that *he had in his possession a coin with a maverick misspelling that had never been know to exist before this*. The coin provided concrete proof that the misspelling had to exist in the past not only on the Shroud but also on an earlier example as well.

In 1982 a second misspelled coin was found. A coin dealer advised Fr. Filas that he had just sold a batch of Pilate leptons to the Rare Coin Department of the Marshall Field Department Store in Chicago. On November 12, 1981 Peter Meissner, Manager of Field's coin sales, showed Fr. Filas his Pilate coins. The third coin viewed under the magnifier seemed to read **"CAISAROS"** confirming the misspelling of **C** for **K**.

The Polarized Image Overlay Technique (PIOT):

Dr. Alan Whanger utilized his PIOT to examine the areas over the eyes of the Man of the Shroud and published his results in April 1982. As he describes the technique:

> "Subsequently, in 1981 we developed a method for exacting image comparison which we called the polarized image overlay technique in which the two images for comparison are projected one on top of the other on the same screen through polarizing filters at right angles to each other. By observing these images through a third polarizing filter which is rotated, one can shift from one image to the other and compare the two images in great detail."

In an article in 1985, Dr. Whanger tells us that, using the polarized image overlay technique with a photograph of Filas' coin and a computer enhanced photograph of the area over the right eye, produced by Log E/Interpretation Systems of Overland Park, Kansas, from the 1931 Enrie photograph:

THE THREE CLOTHS OF CHRIST by John C. Iannone

"We found that there is a nearly perfect match between these two images. Using the same technique of image overlay, we were able to identify the rest of the eroded letters **RIOU CAICAROC** with a reasonable degree of certainty and found congruencies between the coin and the Shroud image on several of these letters."

Whanger goes on to say that:

"Our conclusion is that indeed there is an identifiable coin image over the right eye of the Shroud of Turin and it is so similar to a known coin that the two coins must have been struck from the same die."

Whanger also states that the use of the polarized image overlay technique:

"...enabled us to confirm that indeed there is an image of a coin over the right eye and that the coin from which the image was formed was a die mate of a rare Pontius Pilate *lepton*, the only known one of its striking in existence."
      (Note: to date six examples have now been found).

The Coronal Discharge

In 1982 Dr. Whanger observed that the congruencies between the image on the Shroud and the actual coins (i.e. the die mate) were on the *elevated points and irregularities* on the coin's surface, following a pattern that one would expect from a *coronal-type high energy discharge*. Oswald Scheuermann, with Whanger's collaboration, picked up and pursued this line of investigation Scheuerann had developed remarkable skill and experience in producing coronal type images both photographically and on linen. Dr. Whanger states:

"His (Scheuermann's) methods are similar to electrophotography or Kirlian photography. He had produced coronal images of, and off of, a wide variety of materials which have enabled us to have much better ideas of what various images might look like and this has made it much easier to identify and understand images and patterns seen on the Shroud, even though the exact mechanism of formation of the Shroud image

THE THREE CLOTHS OF CHRIST   by   John C. Iannone

remains a mystery."

Dr. Whanger advised me recently that the mechanism that formed the coin images and likely the floral images were of the nature of a coronal-discharge differing from the mechanism that created the Shroud images, as we will discuss later.

He further notes that coronal-type images tend to come off of pointed and irregular surfaces as well as margins. Where the object is in touch with the surface (Shroud, linen, photographic plate), the image tends to be dense. Where the object is partially in contact with the surface, the outline is dense and partial, with a light central area. The presence of such coronal discharges and the ability to duplicate them on linen seems to provide further proof (or certainly lend credence to the claim), that there were in fact real coins over the eyes on the Shroud and not just quirks or anomalies of the linen weave of the Shroud. It should be noted that Optical Specialist Kevin Moran of Charlotte, North Carolina, questions this conclusion of coronal discharges and more research is recommended.

Conclusion

The preponderance of evidence strongly supports that there were, in fact, ancient Roman coins (*leptons*) over the eyes of the Man of the Shroud and that such a practice did exist in Jewish burials. Such evidence further obviates a Medieval forgery. Dr. Kenneth Stevenson of the STURP team sums it up this way:

> "There is definitely something in both locations, not merely anomalies in the weave patterns of the cloth as some Shroud opponents and even team members have suggested. All of the three-dimensional image that I (Stevenson) have examined, give evidence of something round and solid on the eyes. The fact remains that something is there, and the most logical explanation still suggests that they are coins."
>
> Stevenson & Habermas: *The Shroud and the Controversy*.

****

THE THREE CLOTHS OF CHRIST by John C. Iannone

Chapter Four

THE SIGNATURE OF ROMAN CRUCIFIXION: MATCHING WORDS, WEAPONS AND WOUNDS

"So many there be that stand gazing in horror; was ever a human form so mishandled, human beauty ever so defaced?"

Isaiah 52:14

Identifying the Man of the Shroud:

In building the case for authenticity, we have been careful up until now to identify the images on the Shroud as belonging to the Man of the Shroud without identifying him. We will now attempt to identify this Man with the historical Jesus of Nazareth. It is logical to ask *who* precisely is the individual whose mysterious images appear so vividly on the Shroud? Could the image be of some other Jewish man of the period who might have been crucified?

There is a "signature" built into the evidence that says that this was not just any man crucified during this period. It is the historical Jesus. We know this from the historical pedigree which we will trace shortly when we review the 2000 year journey of the Linen. However, Pathologists who have studied the Shroud images and the Shroud itself tell us that there is a match between the words of the New Testament, the wounds depicted on the Shroud and the weapons and methods utilized to crucify victims that point to only one person whose images appears on the cloth - the historical Jesus of Nazareth.

I have often called the study of the pathology of the Shroud the greatest CSI, or Crime Scene Investigation, of all time.

THE THREE CLOTHS OF CHRIST by John C. Iannone

Matching Words, Weapons and Wounds:

In studying the Shroud, the New Testament accounts of the passion, death and resurrection provided by the four Evangelists correlate precisely with Roman crucifixion practices and weapons as known from scripture, history and archaeology. Further, contemporary forensic pathologists and surgeons have viewed the wounds apparent on the images of the Shroud and have demonstrated how this information correlates exactly with the statements from the New Testament. This unique match of the words of the Gospels, the Roman weapons and the wounds inflicted provide a "signature" or "fingerprint" that identifies the Man of the Shroud with the historical Jesus of Nazareth.

It is, as just mentioned, the greatest Crime Scene Investigation - CSI - and Cold Case investigation in history.

Ian Wilson advises:

> "It is important...that we consider carefully to what extent the crucifixion visible on the Shroud is compatible with that recorded of Jesus Christ; also to what extent the entire picture furnished by the Shroud and its image is compatible with what is known of everyday life in the New Testament."

Dr. Kenneth Stevenson points out that:

> "..an artist or forger could attempt a duplication. But, if there are many similarities, including some an artist or forger would likely miss or be unable to reproduce, and if there are no differences, then the probability that Jesus was the man enveloped in the Shroud increases dramatically."

As Donald Lynn of STURP noted in 1979:

> "Indeed, if this were the work of a forger, this accomplishment itself would be more miraculous than the contention that the Shroud is the actual burial cloth of Jesus."

THE THREE CLOTHS OF CHRIST by John C. Iannone

Roman Crucifixion

Crucifixion was a particularly ignoble form of capital punishment. The Romans reserved it for non-Roman citizens of the Empire, particularly captives of war, civil rebels, criminals and slaves in the Provinces. Both men and women were crucified. It was a common form of punishment throughout the Empire for almost four hundred years. It was not, however, uniquely Roman. In fact, crucifixion was practiced long before the Romans by the Scythians, Persians, Phoenicians and Carthaginians. Thousands of Jews and Gentiles went to their deaths in this manner.

Alexander the Great crucified over two thousand inhabitants in the city of Tyre. During the siege and capture of Jerusalem by the Romans in 70 A.D, almost five hundred Jews a day were crucified for several days. The Jewish Historian Josephus relates that many hundreds were crucified until the Romans "ran out of wood." Crucifixion was ultimately banned by the Emperor Constantine in the year 313 A.D. It was designed to create fear of what would happen if citizens did not bow to the will of Rome or was involved in insurrection.

The Roman historian Tacitus wrote extensively in his *Annals* (15:44) about the different techniques of crucifixion. Various types of crosses were used, including the conventional cross (T-shaped) believed by most scholars to have been used in the crucifixion of Jesus. However, the Romans also used Y-shaped and X-shaped crosses and a Tau cross in the form of a T with no extension above the crossbeam. Sometimes the victims were nailed to the crossbeam and sometimes they were tied with leather thongs. On occasion, a small seat (*sedile*) was provided for the buttocks. The feet might be perched on a small shelf or nailed to the cross separately with two nails or together with one nail. St. Peter requested to be crucified upside down so as not to imitate the manner of Jesus' crucifixion.

The Inscription: I.N.R.I :

Often, in crucifixes found in Churches we find an inscription over the head of Jesus: I.N.R.I. These letters reflect the Latin title that Pontius Pilate had written over the head of Jesus on the Cross (John 19:19). Latin was the official language of the Roman Empire.

THE THREE CLOTHS OF CHRIST by John C. Iannone

The words were "Iesvs Nazarenvs Rex Ivdaeorvm." Latin uses "I" instead of the English "J", and "V" instead of "U" (i.e., Jesus Nazarenus Rex Judaeorum). The English translation is "Jesus of Nazareth, the King of the Jews." The Early Church adopted the first letters of each word of this inscription "INRI" as a symbol. Throughout the centuries INRI has appeared in many paintings of the crucifixion.

Pilate's title was actually written in three languages: Hebrew, Greek and Latin and the words were designed to state to the crowds the reason for the crucifixion of any person. In this case, Jesus was condemned for treason for calling Himself a King.

> "And Pilate wrote a title, and put it on the cross. And the writing was, JESUS OF NAZARETH, THE KING OF THE JEWS. This title then read many of the Jews: for the place where Jesus was crucified was nigh to the city: and it was written in Hebrew, and Greek, and Latin. Then said the chief priests of the Jews to Pilate, "Write not, 'The King of the Jews;' but that he said, 'I am King of the Jews'." Pilate answered, "What I have written I have written."
> -John 19:19-22

For this reason, most scholars believe that the cross utilized for Jesus was a T-cross with wood extending above the head allowing for the inscription to be nailed over the head. Normally, the Romans left the uprights (*stipes*) in position at the place of crucifixion and made the prisoner carry a cross-beam (*patibulum*) which was then hoisted and attached to the upright.

Some of the very weapons and methods utilized to crucify Jesus, as outlined in the New Testament texts and as reinforced by the finds of archaeology, and the combination of such unique weapons and methods when compared with the wounds appearing on the Shroud provide a "signature" of the crucifixion of Jesus.

The Biblical / Historical Accounts:

We begin with a careful examination of what each of the Gospel writers has to say about what actually happened to

THE THREE CLOTHS OF CHRIST by John C. Iannone

Jesus. The author notes that the information may at times be graphic, but such information reflects the harsh reality of Jesus' sacrifice and is critical to making the case for identification of the Man of the Shroud with Jesus. Many pathologists and surgeons have studied the Shroud, most notably Dr. Robert Bucklin; Dr. Pierre Barbet; Dr. Frederick Zugibe, Dr. Anthony Save; Dr. Joseph Gambeschia; Dr. Herman Moedder; Dr. David Willis and Dr. Yves Delage...and many more.

1. Jesus is Arrested In the Garden of Gethsemane:

The Passion narratives establish that Jesus was arrested by "men with swords and clubs" (Mt. 26:47) and taken off to Caiaphas the High Priest (see also Mk. 14:43; Lk 22:47-53 and Jn. 18:1-11). The fact that the arresting mob bore swords and clubs would indicate that they were not very gentle with Jesus and physically abused Him during the arrest. We must remember that Jesus had "sweat blood" in anticipation of His passion. Doctors call this *haematidrosis*. This weakened Him.

2. Jesus is Struck with Fists:

In the presence of the chief priests and scribes of the Sanhedrin, Jesus was struck:

> "Then they spat in His face and struck Him with their fists; others said as they hit Him, 'Prophesy to us, Messiah! Who was it who struck you?" (Mt. 26:67-68).

> "Then some began to spit on Him and covering His face, they struck Him with their fists, saying: 'Prophesy!' And the Temple attendants took Him away, beating Him as they went." Mk 14: 65; Lk 22:63-65.

> "When He said these things one of the attendants who was standing by gave Jesus a slap in the face..." (Jn. 18:22)

We note several references to Jesus being hit with fists and having blows rained on Him. The late Dr. Robert Bucklin, former Medical Examiner of Los Angeles County and forensic pathologist, carefully studied the full-length photos of the Shroud and analyzed the wounds and weapons that may have cause them. In his classic video *The Silent*

THE THREE CLOTHS OF CHRIST by John C. Iannone

Witness as well as in various medical journals, Dr. Bucklin outlines his findings. He notes that there are several facial and head injuries. Among these, he noted that Jesus was violently struck on the right cheek. There is swelling a partial closing of the right eye and a contusion below the right eye.

The nose of Jesus appears elongated and Bucklin indicates that there appears to be a separation of the nasal cartilage and possible fracture incurred by a blow or a fall. Also, the tip of the nose has an abrasion as if the victim has fallen or been struck. We noted earlier that particles of dirt (travertine aragonite) were found on the tip of the nose reflecting a fall with arms restricted. There is a rivulet of blood and saliva on the right side of the mouth

3. Jesus is Bound and Taken to Pilate:

Matthew 27:2 notes:

> "After they had Him bound, they led Him away" (see also Mk 15:1 and Lk 23:1).

Luke adds that Jesus was then sent to Herod. He goes on:

> "After Herod and his soldiers had treated Him with contempt and mocked Him, he had Him dressed in fine apparel and sent Him back to Pilate." (Lk. 23:11).

The fine apparel was to mock Him as a King. Jesus was not allowed to be put to death under Jewish law. He was sent by the Sanhedrin to Pilate to induce the Romans to utilize capital punishment against Jesus as a "rebel" because He claimed He was the "King of the Jews" (Jn 18:34) - thereby appearing to usurp the authority of a Roman Emperor.

The Sanhedrin has originally accused Him of saying He would raise the temple in three days - an act of *blasphemy* that would not be recognized in a Roman court. So they changed the charges from blasphemy to *treason* before Pilate.

4. Jesus is Questioned by Pilate and Scourged with Roman Whips: The Flagrum.

Pilate, after an appeal to the crowd for the release of

THE THREE CLOTHS OF CHRIST by John C. Iannone

Jesus, ultimately yielded to the crowd and ordered Jesus scourged and readied for crucifixion:

> "He (Pilate) had Jesus scourged and then handed Him over to be crucified (Mt. 27:26; Mk. 15:15; Jn 19:1)

He was turned over to the Romans soldiers, traditionally four men led by a fifth (a Centurion called the *Exactor mortis*) - a team specially trained in crucifixion procedures and techniques. The Romans utilized a whip that consisted of three leather thongs attached to a wood or leather handle, each thong having two dumbbell-shaped pieces of bone or lead on the end. *The Dictionary of Greek and Roman Antiquity* identifies this as the Roman *flagrum* frequently mentioned in the accounts of the Christian Martyrs. It was dreaded for its *plumbatae* - pellets of lead or bone attached to the end of the leather thongs.

Examples of the *flagrum* are illustrated occasionally on Roman coins. During the excavation of Herculaneum, the sister city of Pompeii destroyed by the volcano Vesuvius in 79 A.D., an actual specimen was discovered. Each whip mark (estimated between 60-120 lashes) would leave six welts or contusions in the flesh. Such marks, each about 3.7 cm long, frequently caused *contusions* or *hematomas*, that is, welling of blood under the flesh tissue without necessarily breaking the skin.

Jesus was apparently *whipped by two men of slightly different sizes*, one on each side, accounting for the different angles of the whip marks on His front and back. Dr. Bucklin indicates that the Shroud whip marks are spread from the tops of the shoulders to the lower reaches of the calves in a fanned-out pattern. From horizontal across the loins, they fan upward over the upper back, criss-cross over the shoulders and fan downward on the thighs and calves.

Bucklin point out that there are double puncture type wounds going lateral to downward, apparently inflicted by an implement with sharp edges with a flicking motion. Such a whipping left many marks on the front and back of Jesus. Jewish practices limited the scourging of a victim to 39 lashes. Roman scourging, however, was unlimited, but is was incumbent on the solders whipping the victim not to kill Him. In such a case, the scourger could be made to

THE THREE CLOTHS OF CHRIST by John C. Iannone

substitute for the victim. The lashers, therefore, became artists at keeping the victim alive.

5. Jesus was Crowned (Capped) with Thorns:

The Governor's soldiers stripped Jesus and crowned Him with thorns:

> "Then they stripped Him and put a scarlet robe on Him, and after having twisted some thorns into a crown they put this on His head." (Mt. 27: 27-29; also Mk 15:27 and Jn 19: 1-2).

Bucklin tells us that Jesus' forehead and scalp were pierced with many sharp objects with blood visible in the hair on top of Jesus' head, on the sides of His face and on His forehead. Blood is also visible on the hair at the back of His head. The blood flow on the back of the neck shows seven of twelve trickles directed to the left; three to the right and two perpendicular. The hair on the left is soaked with blood. This is consistent with the manner in which Jesus' head was tilted on the Cross - the blood following gravity.

The "Epsilon Mark" or a reverse 3 looking like the Greek epsilon is seen on the forehead. Pathologists attribute this to a blood trickle following the furrowed brow.

The Uniqueness of the Crown of Thorns:

Such wounds are consistent with a capping of thorns. We noted earlier that Professor Avinoam Danin of Hebrew University in Jerusalem identified pollen from "*Gundelia tournefortii*" - the thorn-thistle bush. Capping with thorns was a unique event in crucifixion history, and no other victim, to our knowledge, was ever recorded as having been capped with thorns.

The Roman historians Tacitus, Suetonius and Pliny-the-Younger and the Jewish historians Josephus and Philo of Alexandria talk of many crucifixions in their writings, but none mentions anyone being crowned with thorns. *Herein is one part of the "signature" of Jesus' crucifixion and not just that of any other Jewish man being crucified.*

Artists, medieval and otherwise, have traditionally

THE THREE CLOTHS OF CHRIST by John C. Iannone

depicted a circlet or crown of thorns and not a cap but the evidence on the Shroud indicates it was a cap pressed on the top of Jesus' head. The New Testament used the word "*stephanos*" for the cap of thorns - a word used at the time to refer to the laurel wreath crown of the Emperor.

6. Jesus Carries A Cross:

The Romans made Jesus carry a cross and then forced Simon the Cyrene to carry it for Him because of His weakened state. Dr. Frederick Zugibe, a pathologist and Chief Medical Examiner of Rockland County, New York, (also a Doctor of Anatomy and student of the Shroud for over 50 years) points out that Jesus must have been suffering great fatigue at this point from His agony in the garden where He sweat blood (*haematidrosis*); from the night-long trial that included beating, flogging, abuse, hunger and exposure to the chilly night air. The team of Roman soldiers could not let Him die before the appointed time. They solicited the help of Simon the Cyrene. We read in the New Testament that:

> "As they were going out, they came across a man from Cyrene, Simon by name, and enlisted him to carry His Cross." (Mt. 27:32; Mk. 15:21 and Lk 23:26).

The Gospel of John states:

> "So they took Jesus in charge. And carrying the cross Himself, He went out to what was called 'the Place of the Skull' in Hebrew Golgotha, where they crucified Him and with Him two others..." (Jn. 19: 17-18).

Normally, the Romans would leave the upright piece of the cross *(stipes)* in place at Golgotha and have the victim carry a heavy crossbeam (*patibulum*) weighing from 50-100 pounds across both shoulders. If there was more than one victim (such as the two thieves crucified with Jesus) the Romans would tie a rope connecting the ankles of the victims to the ends of the *patibulum*, preventing the victims from running away or swinging the beam to hit a soldier. Any effort to do this would literally pull the victim's own legs from under him causing him to fall to the ground.

THE THREE CLOTHS OF CHRIST by John C. Iannone

Chafing Marks On Shoulders:

The evidence on the Shroud, as Bucklin points out, shows that the man has large rub marks or "chafing marks" on both sides of the upper back area in the scapular region. These rub marks were formed after the scourging because the scourge marks are overridden by the chafing marks in these areas. While they could have been formed from the rubbing motion of the back of the Cross, they are more consistent with the carrying of the patibulum (or cross beam) across the shoulders.

Pathologist Dr. Cameron points out that:

> "...in the shoulder regions these injuries appear to have been succeeded by some major source of abrasion, evident from the appearance of rubbing high on the left shoulder blade and lower down on the right."

Dr. Cameron interprets this as the carrying of some heavy weight on the back, inevitably recalling the crossbeam. From experiments with volunteers, Cameron observed that a right-handed person with a heavy beam tied to his outstretched arms tends naturally to carry this beam high on his left shoulder and lower down on his right. When he falls, he will most likely fall on his left knee.

7. Jesus Falls:

The observations of Dr. Cameron and others is consistent with the wound on the Shroud showing serious damage to the left knee. There are *microscopic dirt particles* embedded in the Shroud linen on the left knee - as pointed out earlier. Traces of a local soil - *Travertine Aragonite* - are embedded in the left knee. We note that, while the Gospels do not mention Jesus falling, Christian tradition has Jesus falling three times and the Stations of the Cross in many Churches recalls this tradition. Pathologist Dr. Robert Bucklin points out that the left leg of Jesus is tied to the lower part of the cross beam being carried on His shoulders. His left knee cap is damaged in a fall. Dirt on the left knee, left eyebrow and left cheek and damage to His right eyebrow and center of the forehead indicate a series of falls, traditionally considered to be three. There is dirt on the tip of the nose.

THE THREE CLOTHS OF CHRIST by John C. Iannone

8. Jesus is Nailed to the Cross:

We know from archaeological discoveries of Roman work-sites and the discovery of the bones of a crucifixion victim, Jehohanan, that the Romans used seven inch iron roofing spikes. Roman nails were made of iron with a gradually tapering square shaft from the head to the points. About 30 years ago, seven tons of home-made nails (almost a million nails) were unearthed in Scotland by Professor I.A. Richmond, Professor of Archaeology of the Roman Empire at Oxford, at the site of a Roman fortress at Inchtuthill built in 83 A.D. Although the Passion narratives do not specifically state that nails were used, we know they were used from a later Resurrection account in which Jesus invites the Apostle Thomas to place his hand in the place where the nails pierced Jesus' hands. We recall the words of the Prophet Isaiah:

> "They have pierced my hands and my feet; they have numbered all my bones." (Psalm 21: 16-17).

In the Gospel of John, Jesus makes a post-Resurrection appearance to the Apostles in Thomas' absence. Later, the Apostles relate the appearance to Thomas who tells them:

> "Unless I see the marks that the nails made in His hands and put my finger into the holes they made, and put my hand into His side, I won't believe. (Jn 20:25).

Eight days later, Jesus appeared again and permitted Thomas to put his fingers into the wounds of the hand and side (Jn 20:26). In Luke, Jesus told the Apostles to "look at my hands and my feet," asking them to witness the nail wounds (Lk 24:39). Earlier in John, before the Apostles tell Thomas that they have seen the Lord, Jesus appeared to the Apostles and "showed then His hands and His side." (Jn 20:20).

A: Nails Through The Wrists Versus the Palms:

The wound on the Shroud appear to be through the wrists and the feet. The nails through the wrists are contrary to the depiction of Christian art throughout the centuries which shows the nails through the palms. Throughout the history of the church, the punctures in Jesus' hands have been

THE THREE CLOTHS OF CHRIST   by   John C. Iannone

pictured in the palms. Art Historian Philip McNair claims that in his entire experience with hundreds of examples of medieval art, the nail wounds are always located in the palms of Jesus. The reality of the Crucifixion contradicts art in this area.

Dr. Pierre Barbet, a French surgeon and Shroud scholar who wrote a classic work on the crucifixion entitled *A Doctor At Calvary* (1953) demonstrated that nails through the center of the palms would not hold a man on the cross. Such nails would easily tear through the flesh. According to Barbet's extensive studies on this issue, Jesus would have been nailed through the wrists. He indicates an area called the Space of Destot - and he notes a point in the wrists where eight bones meet.

This raises an interesting question. The Gospel writers (in our contemporary translations) talk of the "hand." However, in Biblical Greek, hand is "*chier*" and in Aramaic "yad" and there is only one word used in Greek and Aramaic for hand, wrist and forearm, and this is "chier." So, the biblical word could be translated as wrist.

B: The Missing (Hidden) Thumbs:

It is also interesting to note that one does not see the thumbs on the Shroud, the left hand (anatomically) being over the right. It is confusing in that when one sees the Shroud with the naked eye (viewing the photographic reversal) the right hand appears to be over the left. In actuality, the left is over the right. Dr. Barbet had noticed that the thumbs were missing. He noted that when a nail is driven through the wrists, the Median nerve of the hand (where the crease in your palm closest to the thumb meets the wrist) is damaged or severed, this forces the thumb to close into the palm.

Looking at the Shroud photos, the thumb of the upper hand (left over right) cannot be seen - a unique physiological phenomenon. Dr. Robert Bucklin once advised that, in his investigation of 30,000 autopsies in the Medical Examiner's office in Los Angeles, whenever he came upon a victim that sustained damage to the Median nerve - perhaps from fending off a knife attack - the thumbs were drawn into the palm.

Pathologists, while they may not agree on all the details,

THE THREE CLOTHS OF CHRIST by John C. Iannone

do agree that nails entered high in the palm or low wrist and exited in the wrists and not in the center of the palm as depicted in art. Further, the thumb image is missing - a detail not likely known in the relatively primitive pathology of the Middle ages and contrary to any medieval artist's or forger's then contemporary artistic information

Dr. Zugibe notes that the left wrist is punctured and has two divergent streams bifurcating around the small ulna bone (bump on the wrist). Bucklin notes that there are also two divergent streams of blood on the forearm relating to the two angles of blood flow from the changing position of the arms on the cross as Jesus lifted Himself up to breathe and then dropped back down again. He also notes that there is a 35 degree angle formed from the rivulets of blood flowing from the hand, again showing the positions of the body on the cross.

There is injury to the feet as seen on the dorsal image. The right foot is planted more firmly on the cloth and is saturated with blood showing evidence of an exit wound in the sole. The left foot is slightly elevated over the right - likely from the left foot being placed over the right. One nail was used to secure both feet entering the second metatarsal space of the foot. This is a position of the legs from rigor mortis when the body was taken down and the knees are also slightly flexed reflecting the position on the Cross.

C: **Evidence of Dirt:**

We noted earlier that evidence of dirt (soil) appears on the Shroud. During the 1978 investigation of the Shroud, Dr. Eric Jumper and Optical Engineer Dr. Sam Pellicori rigged up a microscope and aligned it with the blood soaked heel of the Shroud. Careful examination under full magnification determined that there was in fact *dirt on the right heel*. It was a dramatic moment for the STURP team. They noted that is was, however, logical. No one was crucified wearing shoes or sandals, so it is safe to assume that dirt would be present.

Dr. Joseph Kohlbeck of the Hercules Labs in Colorado identified it as *travertine argonite*, and Dr. Levi Setti of the Enrico Fermi Institute outside Chicago, Illinois, confirmed the find. Dirt was also noted on the left knee

THE THREE CLOTHS OF CHRIST by John C. Iannone

and tip of the nose supporting the legend that Jesus fell three times.

D: The Crucifixion of Jehohanan:

Frank Tribbe, author of *Portrait of Jesus?* recounts that in 1968, during construction excavation in Jerusalem, workers discovered an ancient Jewish cemetery in northern Jerusalem called Givat'at ha'Mivtar. Archaeologists found a group of burials dated precisely to the Roman massacre that occurred during the Jewish revolt of 70 A.D. The skeletons were preserved in stone burial chests called *ossuaries* which contained only the bones of the deceased after the flesh had decayed. One of these boxes contained the bones of Jehohanan Ben Ha'galgol (identified by the name written in Aramaic on his ossuary). He had been crucified.

A seven inch spike was still sideways through his heel bones, through a block of acacia wood, and had splinters of olive wood from the upright of the cross (stipes) still adhering to its tip. Nails had also been driven through his lower forearm where the radius bones were noticeably worn from the grating on the nail as Jehohanan pulled himself up so he could breathe. The tibia and fibula bones of his calves were crushed from the Roman practice of crucifragium - the procedure of breaking the leg bones to hasten death.

This did not happen in the case of Jesus whose leg bones were not broken. Instead, the Centurion lanced Him in the side to ensure He was dead. Archaeologist Vasilius Tzaferis and Hebrew University pathologist Nicu Hass examined Jehohanan's bones and reported on them in the *Israel Exploration Journal* in 1970.

Up until the time of the discovery of Jehohanan's grave, no actual victims of crucifixion had been found. Ian Wilson surmises that the reason for this was almost certainly because the telltale evidence, the presence of nails, was never found. The Romans believed that nails used in a crucifixion were highly efficacious in curing epilepsy, fever, swellings and stings. Hence, these rarely remained with the body of a crucifixion victim. They were likely taken and kept as amulets by soldiers or interested bystanders. Given the legends of the nails of Jesus being a relic of the Crucifixion, it is entirely possible that the Apostles and followers kept the nails of their crucified

THE THREE CLOTHS OF CHRIST by John C. Iannone

Lord.

9. The Sign Placed Over The Cross:

When they reached Golgotha, they gave Jesus wine mixed with fall (a bitter herb) and crucified Him. They then place a titulus (or sign) over His head saying:

> "This is Jesus, the King of the Jews." (Mt. 27:37; Mk 15:26).

John says:

> "Now Pilate wrote out a notice and had it fixed to the cross. It read: 'Jesus of Nazareth, King of the Jews.'" (Jn. 19:19)

It was written in Aramaic, Greek and Latin. Usually, the titulus was placed above the head, although in the case of Jehohanan it was placed at the feet.

10. Jesus is Mocked and Dies:

Jesus was mocked by passers-by and died at the ninth hour (3:00 P.M.) (Mt. 27: 39-56; Mk. 15: 29-39; Lk 23: 44-46; and Jn 19:29-30). The ninth hour would be 3:00 P.M. or in mid-afternoon. The Jewish day began at 6:00 in the morning.

11. The Crucifragium and Lancing of the Side:

John adds two unique aspects of the Crucifixion not covered by other Evangelists, and these indeed contribute strongly to the "signature" of Jesus. John notes:

> "It was Preparation Day and to prevent the bodies remaining on the Cross during the Sabbath - since the Sabbath was a day of special solemnity - the Jews asked Pilate to have the legs broken and the bodies taken away. Consequently, the soldiers came and broke the legs of the first man who had been crucified with Him and then of the other. When they came to Jesus they found He was already dead, and so instead of breaking His legs, one of the soldiers pierced His side with a lance; and immediately there came out blood and water." (Jn 19: 31-34).

THE THREE CLOTHS OF CHRIST   by   John C. Iannone

This particular day was quite important since it was the beginning of a double religious holiday: the Passover and the Sabbath. Sundown would occur shortly and the bodies could not remain on the crosses under Jewish law. The Romans employed a practice called crucifragium, mentioned earlier, which consisted of breaking the legs of the victim to prevent him from raising himself up to breathe, and thereby hastening death. The Jews were anxious to end the crucifixion before the onset of the Sabbath at sundown. The Sabbath generally began when the high priest could spot three stars.

Pathologists have confirmed that the legs of the Man of the Shroud were not broken, reinforcing the New Testament texts about Jesus. John here quotes Psalm 34:20 and Exodus 12:46 to show that Jesus' legs were not broken as foretold in the Scriptures saying:

> "This is the evidence of one who saw it - trustworthy evidence, and he knows he speaks the truth - and he gives it so that you may believe as well. 'Not one bone of His will be broken.' " (Jn. 19:35-36.).

In addition, the soldiers saw that Jesus was already dead and pierced His side with a *lancea* (A Roman lance) between the fifth and sixth ribs on the anatomical right side of His body. Origen (3rd century) notes the thrust was administered in military custom *sub alas* (below the armpits). The wound, as identified by Pathologists on the Shroud was 1 3/4" high and 7/16" wide (4.4 by 1.5 centimeters). From excavated examples, the lance blade corresponds exactly to the elliptical wound on the side of the victim visible on the Shroud. The lance appears to have been standard issue for the soldiers (*militia*) of the garrison at Antonia and other fortresses guarding Jerusalem. Archaeologist William Meacham notes it does not match the typical points of the *hasta* (spear) or *hasta veliarie* (short spear) or *pilum* (javelin) used by the infantry. In the New Testament we read:

> "They will look on the one whom they have pierced."
> (Jn. 19: 35-37).

THE THREE CLOTHS OF CHRIST by John C. Iannone

A: Blood and Water:

John tells us that after Jesus was pierced with the lance:

> "Immediately there came out blood and water." (Jn. 19:34).

This was a unique event not understood by the Evangelists, but explained in modern medical pathology. Dr. Bucklin pointed out that in the hours He hung there, the plasma (serum) and blood corpuscles would have separated in the pericardial sack (surrounding the heart), and in the lungs (pleural edema) with the plasma rising to the top. Piercing of this sack caused the blood first and then the serum to ooze out, giving the appearance to medically untrained soldiers or followers at the foot of the Cross that it was blood mixed with water. This blood and serum flowed from the lance wound on Jesus' right side and when He was laid down on the Shroud and carried to the tomb horizontally, the blood and serum flowed downward off the side and pooling around the back across the kidneys.

Pathologists state this is very evident on the Shroud and again links the lancing, blood flow and carrying of the body of Jesus with the images of the crucifixion wounds.

12. The Burial Attitude - Signs of Rigor Mortis:

It is worth noting that pathologists and anthropologists have studied the body's reconstructed burial attitude, which they indicate is a body in a state of rigor mortis. Under conditions of high stress and prolonged suffering, rigor mortis would have set in quickly while Jesus was still on the Cross. As Ian Wilson pointed out:

> "It (the body) had, for instance, to have been set at a slight angle, the head raised by some pillow type support; the arms drawn very stiffly over the pelvis; the right shoulder set lower than the left; the legs decisively flexed at the knees and the left foot is partly over the right. If the Shroud is a forgery, the care with which even the post-crucifixion lie of the body had been thought out is quite remarkable."

Bucklin noted that the right shoulder set lower than the

THE THREE CLOTHS OF CHRIST by John C. Iannone

left could be a result of a dislocation when the rigor of the arms was broken to move the hands onto position over the loins.

Conclusion:

When taken in totally, the perfect match of the words, weapons and wounds provide a signature that there is only one person in history matching this combination of wounds. This is a man who was:

1. Severely **scourged** with a Roman whip - a flagrum.

2. Carried a **heavy beam** which left its markings on His shoulders.

3. Was **nailed** in the wrists and feet.

4. Was crowned with a **cap of thorns** to mock His Kingship - an event unique in ancient literature.

5. Was **lanced** in the side instead of the common practice of crucifragium.

6. Severely **beaten and punched** with swellings on His face.

All this was on a cloth always **historically associated with Jesus** throughout history.

We can now safely say that this was not the image of just any man crucified in this period, but it is clearly the image of the historical Jesus of Nazareth. Forensic pathology and science is reinforced by the fact that this cloth was also traced historically to only one man - its historical pedigree pointing to Jesus of Nazareth.

****

Chapter Five

THE BLOOD ON THE SHROUD

"It is certain that there is blood on the Shroud as it is that there is blood in your veins."

         Hematologist Dr. John Heller

When the STURP team went to Turin, one of the major questions they sought to answer was whether the substance on the Shroud was real, human blood or some form of paint, ink, dye, powder or other substance, even mammalian blood. Their studies were to prove that they were dealing with real human blood. This finding made the Shroud "unfakable" by any Medieval artist.

The late Dr. Alan Adler, a research chemist from Western Connecticut University who worked with Dr. John Heller at the New England Institute, after extensive examination of the blood declared:

> "It is certain that there is blood on the Shroud as it is that there is blood in your veins. The marks on the Shroud of exuded blood, belong to a man who was tortured and crucified. It cannot be from the 14th century, but is much older and far more consistent with what we know of the crucifixion of Christ."

The STURP team noted that, whereas the image fibers are a surface phenomenon, limited to the top fibrils of the fibers of the Shroud, the blood in places saturates the cloth and penetrates through.

a. Blood Type is Real, Human and Type AB:

The blood present on the Shroud has been studied in Europe by Dr. Pier Luigi Baima Ballone, professor of forensic

THE THREE CLOTHS OF CHRIST by John C. Iannone

medicine (Turin University); Jose Delfin Blanco, Spanish specialist in legal medicine and by hematologist Carlo Goldoni in addition to Drs. Adler and Heller, chemists in the United States. They confirm that the blood on the Shroud is human blood, indicating that "in light of its characteristics it would seem to appear as belonging to blood type AB." Dr. Garza Valdez of the University of Texas once pointed out that in the world population there are four basic blood types: A, B, O and AB and the rarest blood type on Earth - type AB - is found in about 3-5% of the world population. The majority of cases, he notes, are in the Middle East. In fact, AB blood is considered a "bio-type" of the Middle East.

b. Evidence of Trauma and Stress:

In the early stages of the blood studies, one Pathologist mentioned that the blood on the Shroud appeared "redder" than he would expect ancient blood to look - generally more black. However, when Adler and Heller investigated particles they noted a high content of the bile pigment "*bilirubin*" released in the body when the hemoglobin begins to break down. This would account, they noted, for the redder coloring of the blood since the pigment *bilirubin* (literally bile that is red) is released into the blood providing its red coloring. They point out that this *occurs in a person suffering from high stress or trauma* - certainly characteristic of Jesus in His passion.

"Not when, but how":

Blood specialists of ancient blood noted that it is *not when a person (historically) dies but how (the manner in which) they died* that determines the coloring of their blood. There are, in fact, samples in existence of blood that is much older than 2,000 years that is still red from the presence of bilirubin.

c. Veins and Arteries:

Physicians Giuseppe Caselli (1939), Pierre Barbet (1950), Sabastian Rodante (1982) as well as Dr. Zugibe and Dr. Bucklin (1980's and 90's) carefully examined the blood flows on the forehead with special reference to the location of the veins and arteries of the scalp. Shroud author Frank Tribbe notes:

THE THREE CLOTHS OF CHRIST by John C. Iannone

> "They were able to conclude with absolute certainty that each discernible rivulet of blood shows distinctive characteristics of either venous flow or arterial flow in every case correct for the location of the thorn puncture from which the rivulet starts."

Arterial blood flow is always to be distinguished by the spurts of blood that emerge from a wound due to heart pulses; conversely, thicker venous blood flow is slow and steady and coagulates more quickly.

d. Ancient DNA:

Dr. Dan Scavone of the University of Southern Indiana reports in an article of October 13, 1995 that in September 1994, Dr. Victor Tryon, Director of DNA Technologies of the University of Texas Health and Science Center in San Antonio, Texas:

> "…isolated three genes from Shroud blood remnants. He has obtained a segment of the Betaglobin gene from Chromosome 11 and the Ameligenin gene from both the X and Y chromosomes. Together with blood analysis, the DNA research also identified that the occipital blood (back of the head of the Shroud) is that of an adult human male."

Dr. Tryon noted in a CBS special *The Mysterious Man of the Shroud* (Executive Producer Terry A. Landau, April 1997) that the blood was *human, male and contained degraded DNA consistent with the supposition of ancient blood*. Further, Dr. Dan Scavone (University of Indiana) noted that embedded in a blood-glob from the occipital region of the head is a microscopic textile fragment (five-microns in diameter) appearing to be woven of camel hair. This possible, but questionable identification, could be important for authenticating the Shroud.

I had the honor of speaking with Dr. Tryon over the telephone in the mid-1990s and asked if this could be identified as the blood of Jesus. He answered by saying:

> "While I cannot say as a scientist that this is the blood of Jesus, I can say that it is consistent with anything I would expect to find if it were the blood of Jesus."

THE THREE CLOTHS OF CHRIST   by   John C. Iannone

It should be noted that there was some controversy as to how the fibers were obtained, and Dr. Tryon assumed these were properly turned over. However, the fibers were obtained by Dr. Giovanni Riggi Di Numana from fibers and blood specks of the Shroud and provided to Dr. Tryon by Riggi in 1994. Italian writers Ida Molinari and Alberto Chiara in *Famiglia Christiana* (Volume 4, 1996) report that the removal of he fibers was not authorized (a removal unknown to Dr. Tryon) and some dispute remained with the then Papal Custodian, Cardinal Giovanni Saldarini. However, in the opinion of this author, even if the samples were not obtained with proper approval, this would not invalidate the scientific findings of Dr. Victor Tryon.

We are now looking at the:

1.   Blood of a male (Ameligenin X and Y chromosomes);

2. ...who likely died in ancient times (highly degraded DNA consistent with the supposition of ancient blood);

3. ...likely in the Middle East (Bio-Type AB);

4. ...under conditions of great trauma and stress (high levels of bile pigment bilirubin coloring the blood).

This certainly fits the *profile of the historic Jesus*.

e. Blood of a Deceased Man:

Unfortunately, there are theories today such as that of Rabbi Hugh Schoenfeld in the "Passover Plot," and that of Holger Kersten and Elmar Gruber in *The Jesus Conspiracy*, specious and misleading at best, that Jesus never really died. Somehow, they maintain, He survived the crucifixion and was in a coma in the tomb. Therefore, they state, this was a plot, a conspiracy and Jesus never really died. Obviously, if He never died, then He never rose from the dead. And as St. Paul once said:

   "If Jesus didn't rise, our faith is in vain."

Such theories attempt to undermine our faith.

THE THREE CLOTHS OF CHRIST by John C. Iannone

However, as blood specialists and pathologists clearly point out: this is the body of a deceased man in *a state of rigor mortis*. In addition, the blood and serum flow after He was lanced clearly point to a *post-mortem blood condition* - the plasma of the blood (serum) having separated from the red blood cells. In addition, blood chemists and hematologists have noticed the presence, under ultraviolet light, of *serum albumin retraction rings or haloes* around wounds such as those on the back where scourging occurred. This is virtually unfakable.

Serum albumin is a blood protein. Drs. Adler and Heller noted that whereas the bodily images have a mist-like quality with no sharp lines, the bloodstains are richer and darker in color and have more precise lines. They also have a "halo effect" typically suggestive of the separation of blood and serum, which happens after the heart has stopped. This reinforces that the blood is not only human but that it represents a post-mortem event - a deceased man.

f. Blood Clots:

Dr. Gilbert Lavoie of Boston, former President of the World Health Organization (WHO) conducted a study of the blood clotting on the Shroud. He noted that blood contains fibrinogen - a protein that circulates in the plasma and turns to fibrin when exposed to an open wound, helping in the clotting factor by forming a web-like blockage of blood flows - assuming it is not a major wound or severed artery. A clot begins to form and a moist jelly like substance eventually hardens to a scab and heals.....that is, if we live. However, something different happens if we die in the process of forming a clot. This unique event was captured on the Holy Shroud and is evidence of the post-mortem situation.

Dr. Lavoie noted, that from a few hours after death, blood clots that are forming, rather than hardening, *re-liquefy* (a process called fibrinolysis) and are absorbed by the linen. They are characterized by a serum-albumin haloes or retraction rings and are further evidence of a post-mortem event and also indicate the virtual impossibility of a medieval artist being able to know this and to duplicate it.

THE THREE CLOTHS OF CHRIST by John C. Iannone

Summary: A Profile of the Blood Of Jesus

Blood was on cloth before image. When particles are lifted or dissolved, there is no image under them. The blood was on the Shroud before whatever mechanism formed the image. As Dr. Heller, supported by renowned artist (and Particle Physicist) Isabel Piczek who has painted over 400 murals on Church walls, stated:

"Surely, this was a weird way to paint a picture."

If a forger had painted or created a picture and added human blood to make it realistic, he would likely have added the blood afterward and over part of this painting, not the reverse. In addition, a Medieval artist would never have known about the chemistry of human blood and the presence of post-mortem serum haloes.

Profile:

1. Blood saturates and penetrates the cloth.

2. It is real human blood with **heme porphryins** - no indications of paint or any substance appearing like blood.

3. Blood is **Type AB** - a Bio-Type of the Middle East.

4. Blood has high levels of **bilirubin** making it redder than normal ancient blood. Indicates person died in trauma under conditions of great stress.

5. Blood contains a **highly degraded DNA** consistent with supposition of ancient blood.

6. Blood has **Ameligenin X & Y chromosomes** - a male human blood.

7. There is a separation of blood plasma and serum. Indications under ultraviolet light of **serum albumin halos** and rings around wounds reflect a post-mortem blood flow.

8. Blood shows **venial and arterial** blood flow.

9. Gospels indicate that when Jesus was lanced in the side there flowed out "blood and water." This is the separation

THE THREE CLOTHS OF CHRIST by John C. Iannone

of plasma/serum and the red blood cells. Again, indications of a **post-mortem situation.**

10. Blood clots indicate re-liquification of clots after death and transferred to cloth with **serum albumin halos seen under ultraviolet light.**

****

THE THREE CLOTHS OF CHRIST   by   John C. Iannone

THE THREE CLOTHS OF CHRIST by John C. Iannone

Chapter Six

AN ANCIENT TEXTILE CONSISTENT WITH JEWISH BURIAL PRACTICES

"The Shroud represents a bundle of imposing probabilities."

Professor Yves Delage

We turn now to the Jewish burial practices of the Second Temple Period (from approximately 100 B.C. to 100 A.D.) encompassing the period of Jesus' earthly life to compare what the Gospels tell us of the death and burial of Jesus with known burial practices of the period.

The Gospel of John (19:40) tell us that Jesus was entombed

"following Jewish burial custom."

The late sindonologist Fr. Edward A. Wuenschel, C.Ss.R., author of *The Holy Shroud*, reminded us that the Shroud:

"is surely an archaeological object of the most profound significance bearing directly upon the principal phases of the Passion and upon the manner of Christ's burial."

Much can be learned from sources which include:

a. The accounts of the Gospels;

b. The information from Jewish historians Josephus and Philo of Alexandria.

c. The Mishna (rabbinic literature written down by the Rabbis in the first and second centuries from the oral

THE THREE CLOTHS OF CHRIST   by   John C. Iannone

traditions);

d.   *The Tractate Mourning* - a Talmudic document;

e.   The Medieval Jewish *Code of Law*;

f.   The findings of archaeology;

h.   Early Roman law;

i.   The *Moed Katan* - from the Babylonian Talmud

Corroborating and Non-Contradictory Evidence

With the extensive excavations in 1967 of the Jewish necropolis (cemetery) at Jericho and the discovery of many tombs around Jerusalem such as the large necropolis on the Mount of Olives near the church built on the site where the Gospels say Jesus wept over the city (*Dominus Flevit*) and the cemetery of the Essenes at the desert community of Qumran on the northwest shore of the Dead Sea, much information has been collected clarifying early Jewish burial practices. This enables us, along with other documentation, to put together a composite picture of Jewish burial practices. Examining the Shroud and the procedures used to bury Jesus in light of this new information provides still further corroborating evidence of the Shroud's antiquity and authenticity.

Ancient Jewish Beliefs Regarding Death, Burial and Resurrection:

Let us first provide some background on the evolution of ancient Jewish theological thought, especially during the Second Temple Period regarding the death, burial and idea of resurrection.

Primary Burial

When an individual died, the family was required to bury him or her as quickly as possible because of the climactic conditions favoring the rapid onset of decay. Primary burial involved burial in either a wooden coffin in the ground or envelopment in a shroud in a cave tomb cut into the soft limestone rocks. In the area of Jerusalem, most people were buried in the cave tombs carved out of the soft

THE THREE CLOTHS OF CHRIST by John C. Iannone

limestone outside and near the walls of the city. Cemeteries were required to be outside the city walls. Coffins made of wood were more rare, probably caused by a desire to avoid anything that would prolong the process of decomposition of the body as well as because of the scarcity of wood in the region.

The body was usually enveloped in a shroud (a large linen sheet called a *sindon* in the New Testament) and laid on a stone shelf in the cave tomb where preparation of the body commenced. A mourning period for the family of from seven to thirty days ensued (depending upon the rapidness of decay in the cave tomb). The body would be allowed to decay until only the bones remained, usually a period of one year. The Jews of this period believed that sins of individuals are in the flesh, and expiation of sin was achieved through decay of that flesh. When only the bones remained, the body was then considered pure and the bones ready for placement in ossuaries (small stone jars used for collecting and preserving bones).

The burial or entombment of Jesus was consistent with the primary burial procedures of the Jews. The New Testament relates that Joseph of Arimathea (a distinguished member of the Sanhedrin - the Jewish religious ruling body) entombed Jesus in a cave tomb cut from the rock nearby the crucifixion site on Golgotha (Calvary) and enveloped Him in a Shroud.

> "Joseph took the body, wrapped it in a clean linen shroud and placed it in his new tomb which he had hewn in the rock. Then, he rolled a large stone across the entrance of the tomb and went away."
>
> (Mt. 27: 59-60)

Rt. Rev. John A.T. Robinson noted:

> "The corpse of Jesus enfolded in a simple linen cloth passing lengthwise over the head and covering the whole body back and front is not, I submit, what any forger with medical or modern presuppositions would have thought of; but it makes complete sense of the texts and conforms with the other ancient evidence."

It was not customary in the ancient or medieval world for

THE THREE CLOTHS OF CHRIST   by   John C. Iannone

an artist to paint on linen. In addition, painting Jesus naked was unheard of. The Shroud represents a true Jewish burial in a linen shroud.

Secondary Burial:

After a period of about one year, the family was responsible for carefully collecting the bones of the deceased and placing them in an *ossuary* - usually a limestone box - and normally inscribed with a name. The purpose of this was to keep the bones together in preparation for the physical resurrection. The Hassidim (the righteous of early Maccabean times) and the Pharisees - strong in the time of Jesus - believed in a physical resurrection. The Sadducees denied such a resurrection. During the time of Jesus, belief in a physical resurrection was strong among the Jews.

The Afterlife and Resurrection in Ancient Jewish Thought

Much of the information on Jewish religious thought about death and burial is contained in the *Tractate Mourning* (*Samahot* - literally "Rejoicings."). With the help of the library staff at Jewish Theological Seminary in New York City, I was introduced to this document in the mid-1990s and learned from this writing and from the staff the burial customs of the period. This third century Talmudic Tractate contains regulations dating back to the time of Jesus relating to death, burial and mourning. In this Tractate, the ideas of the fate of the dead are clear. It involved a descent into a nether world (Sheol) called at times "dust" (Ps. 22:30 or Is. 26:19 or described as a "pit" (Is. 14:15 and Prov. 28:17). It is conceived as a dark place (Job 10:21-22) where one descends, never to return. There, one is counted among the "shadows," the "weak ones" never to rise again (Is. 26:14). The dead are described as being cut of from the living and even from God (Ps. 88:10-12 and 115:17).

L.Y. Rahmani of the Israel Department of Antiquities and Museums in Jerusalem tells us that:

> "The concept of the nether world as conceived in Jewish thought...called for some provision of the fundamental necessities for those going down into a place of darkness, and some sort of existence is

THE THREE CLOTHS OF CHRIST by John C. Iannone

implied."

This idea of a vague, shadowy existence gave way gradually to a more defined concept of an afterlife and belief in a physical resurrection. The biblical reference for such a resurrection is first encountered in Daniel 12:2 written as late as the second century B.C. after the start of Antiochus IV Epiphanes' persecution. He notes that from the Maccabean times forward, we encounter this end-times thinking (with Daniel 12:2 and 2 Maccabees 7:14) We read of seven brethren and their mother enduring every torture commanded by the wicked king, proudly declaring their belief that:

> "the King of the Universe will raise us up to an everlasting renewal of life, because we have died for His laws."

By the time of Jesus, belief in a physical resurrection, especially among the Pharisees, was well established in Jerusalem. Rahmani tells us that:

> "belief in a personal and physical resurrection eventually evolved into a fundamental principle of Jewish faith."

It is against the background that we look at the Resurrection of Jesus. The followers of Jesus would have been very careful to bury Jesus according Jewish law and customs. They did not understand at the time of burial that Jesus was going to rise from the dead on Sunday morning.

The Cave Tombs

Hundreds of cave tombs have been unearthed in recent archaeological digs in Palestine relating to the Herodian and Roman periods. The Jewish law required that people be buried outside the town limits. We have learned much about these cave tombs, especially from the work of the late noted archaeologist Dr. Eugenia Nitowski, formerly a Carmelite nun (Sr. Damien of the Cross) who was among the foremost authorities on the Jewish (Jerusalem) cave tombs and from other recently published articles in archaeological journals.

In a descriptive article in the *Biblical Archaeology*

THE THREE CLOTHS OF CHRIST by John C. Iannone

Review, Rachel Hachlili also described excavated tombs similar to the one in which Jesus was laid. Hachlili describes these tombs as hewn from rock (a soft, chalky limestone identified as *calcium carbonate*) cut into the hillsides forming a man-made cave or chamber. The floor was square, about eight feet on a side. Usually, a pit about five feet square, was dug into the floor of the room as a place for mourners to stand. This created ledges or benches along the sides of the tomb where the deceased would be laid down temporarily. Here they would be placed on a large linen sheet or shroud (sindon) and the face cloth (*sudarium*) which covered the face to this point was removed and folded to one side.

The height of the caves from the benches to the ceiling was only three to four feet and the pit in the center increased this height to about six feet, allowing a person to stand upright inside the tomb. In addition, burial recesses, or loculi (kokim in Hebrew) were hewn into the walls above the benches on three sides of the tomb chamber. These loculi were semicircular in shape and longer than the height of a man of approximately six feet, or long enough in fact to place in it a body, coffin or ossuary.

The entry was narrow and closed of by a circular blocking stone that was rolled into place and sealed with mortar and small stones. In the Resurrection narrative, the stone sealing Jesus' tomb was moved away (Jn 201). There were perhaps a few steps leading from the high entry way to the center pit. Usually each *loculus* or burial recess within the chamber was also sealed off by blocking stones, bricks or small stones held together by mortar or mud.

Dr. Eugenia Nitowski noticed a white, chalky substance (*calcium carbonate*) on her clothing while in the tombs. Chemical analysis from samples sent back to the United States revealed this to be limestone dust, also found on the Shroud, which picked up traces of the soft limestone when Jesus was laid on the ledge of the tomb on the sindon or burial linen. We noted earlier that pollen was discovered on the backside of the Shroud where it came in contact with the stone ledge and became embedded in the linen fibers. It was, in fact, calcified pollen from the limestone.

THE THREE CLOTHS OF CHRIST by John C. Iannone

The Primary Burial - The Linen Cloth

After the death of Jesus, the New Testament tells us that Joseph of Arimathea went to Pilate to ask for the body before the commencement of the Sabbath which began at sunset with the sighting of the first three stars. Time was pressing because the bodies of the dead were not to be handled during the Sabbath. The ancient historian Josephus in his *Jewish Wars* tells us that:

> "The Jews are so careful about funeral rites that even those who are crucified because they were found guilty are taken down and buried before sunset."

This included even suicides and the bodies of enemies. Pilate was astonished that Jesus had expired so quickly, Roman crucifixion being designed to make victims suffer for a longer period. Jesus, however, had been suffering for many hours with the agony in the Garden where He sweat blood and from the severe scourging, capping with thorns, nails in hands and feet and beating by the guards, including hunger and exposure to the chilly night air. He was greatly weakened.

Pilate gave permission for His removal from the Cross. We note here that there was placed around His head while on the Cross and after He died a customary **sudarium** or face cloth which remained on His head until He was laid in the tomb. At which time the *Sudarium Christi* was removed and folded to one side, as three of the Gospel writers note.

> "Joseph took the body and *wrapped* it in a clean linen *shroud* and placed it in his new tomb which he had hewn into the rock." Matt. 27:59

> "Pilate was amazed that He was already dead...and after learning it from the Centurion he bestowed the corpse on Joseph. So Joseph bought a linen *shroud* and took Jesus down, *wrapped* Him in the linen *shroud* and placed Him in a tomb that had been hewn out of rock." Mk. 15:46

> "He (Joseph) came to Pilate and asked for Jesus' body, and after taking it down, he *wrapped* it in a linen shroud and placed it in a tomb hewn out of rock in which no one had yet been laid." Lk 23:53.

THE THREE CLOTHS OF CHRIST by John C. Iannone

The New Testament word for "shroud" in Greek is *sindon*. The Gospels utilize this word when referring to the main cloth in which Jesus was entombed. Sindon is defined in the Greek lexicons as a "large linen sheet" which we know the Shroud to be. In this case it is 14'3 inches by 3' 7 inches. The Gospel writers go on to utilized the Greek term *entulissa*, which is defined as *"folded over the body"* generally translated as "wrapped" in the sense of being "*enveloped*."

The picture portrayed here is that of a large linen sheet stretched out on the ledge of the cave tomb. Jesus was placed at one end on His back with His head toward the center of the cloth. The Sudarium was removed from around His head and folded to one side. After the body was prepared with burial spices and strewn with flowers and coins over the eyes, the sheet was drawn over the front of His body. He was not wrapped mummy style.

The Burial Strips: Othonia

Another term is introduced by the New testament writers, namely *othonia,* defined as "binding cloths or strips of linen." We read in John 19:40:

> "They took Jesus' body and bound it in linen cloths (*othoniois*) with the spices, as is the custom among the Jews in preparing for burial."

Luke 24:12 also used the term:

> "But Peter got up and ran to the tomb and when he stooped down he saw only the linen cloths (othonia)."

The late Shroud author Werner Bulst, S.J. pointed out that *othonia* as used in John 19:40 refers to a narrow cloth, a strip, such as is used for bandaging a wound. This is equivalent to bindings (*keriai*) with which Lazarus was bound (Jn.11:44). Likewise the verb *deo* found in John 11:44 and 19:40 always meant to bind in the strict sense and never "to wrap up, in or envelop" indicating that these were bandage strips differing from the larger cloth.

These binding strips were likely used to bind the hands and feet to permit easy carrying of the body, especially through the narrow entrance to the cave-tombs and to secure the position of the body (with hands folded across the

THE THREE CLOTHS OF CHRIST by John C. Iannone

loins). Rigor mortis likely began on the Cross and the rigor of the arms broken to bring them over the loins and keep them in position by binding them together.

Bulst points out that on the body image of the Shroud there is a gap above the wrists where blood flow seems interrupted:

> "Strangely, a little above the wrists, there is a gap of about a hand's breadth with no trace of blood that trickled and caked along the forearm muscle of the Crucified. The blood transfers on the forearms are otherwise unusually clear and sharply outlined. The missing imprint above the wrists on either forearm would be readily explained if a linen strip had been bound about them here and knotted to keep the arms in the position as they are seen on the Cloth. Without some such bond, this position of the arms would be impossible."

Bulst goes on to relate that the feet appear to have been similarly bound above the ankles.

> "The imprints of these extremities (on the Shroud) are noticeably dim both on the frontal and dorsal view."

This would imply that something (linen strips or othonia) interfered with the image-formation process.

The Chin Band:

New Testament writers speak of a chin band. There was a practice of placing a chin-band around the chin and tying it over the top of the head to keep the mouth closed and slow down the process of decomposition. Rahmani, referring to the *Tractate Mourning (Semahot)* says that:

> "When death had taken place, the eyes of the deceased were closed, as were all orifices. The mouth was bound up so as not to stay agape."

Analysis of the Shroud shows that there does appear to be a chin band round the face of Jesus and a break in the flow of blood down the arms supporting that the wrists were bound with linen strips. With regard to the chin band, Wuenschel referred to Paul Vignon in stating:

THE THREE CLOTHS OF CHRIST by John C. Iannone

"The presence of the chin-band offers a very reasonable explanation of the blank space which interrupts the imprint at the top of the head of the Shroud of Turin."

Robinson further indicates that:

"The vertical dark strips on either side of the face between the cheeks and locks, otherwise so odd, could similarly be caused by the band holding back the intervening hair."

This also provides a logical explanation of why one does not notice the ears of Jesus on the Shroud Image. Likewise, since orifices (such as ears) had to be covered - a chin band would accomplish this objective.

The *Jewish Encyclopedia*, Vol. 3, pp. 434-436, 1925 edition states:

"The mouth was shut and kept in position by a band."

The Resurrection of Lazarus:

Further support of the chin-band and binding of hands and feet can be found in the story of the resurrection of Lazarus which appears only in John, Chapter 11. The Gospel of John relates that:

"After saying this, (Jesus) called out in a loud voice, 'Lazarus!' Come out!"

Lazarus came out with his hands and feet bound with thongs (*keriais*, or grave cloths) and a cloth (*sudario*) around his face (*peridedeto*). Jesus said to them,

"Unbind him and let him go!"

Peridedeto is translated as "bound about/to bind around about" as with a chin band and strips around the wrists and ankles. *Keriai* were a kind of binder of twisted rushes, somewhat like a thong with which bedsteads were strung, and which were used to hold the hands and feet in place for burial in lieu of linen strips.

THE THREE CLOTHS OF CHRIST   by   John C. Iannone

We will talk more about the third term - *the Sudarium* - when we discuss the Face Cloth in the Tomb (*Sudarium Christi*) in a later Chapter.

The Attitude of the Body:

The body of Jesus was laid on the Shroud with the head toward the center of the cloth. The arms were placed, left hand over right, over the area of the loins. In support of this burial attitude, Reverend Sox deemed that the Shroud was authentic because the arms appear placed "modestly across the loins rather than at the side of the body."

Ian Wilson goes on to say that:

> "in Judea, a number of skeletons excavated in the Essene cemetery at Qumran on the shores of the Dead Sea (ca. 200 B.C. to 70 A.D) were *laid out flat, facing upward, elbows bent slightly and hand across the pelvis, exactly the attitude visible on the Shroud.*"

The Essenes were a pious group in this period who differentiated themselves from the Pharisees and Sadducees and lived a highly disciplined life apart in the Desert of Qumran, just off the Dead Sea, in anticipation of the coming Messiah. They lived a quiet, contemplative, Monk-like existence away from the worldliness of the hustle and bustle of Jerusalem and the Temple area. The Egyptian burial custom, in contrast, placed the arms criss-crossed over the chest.

Aloe and Myrrh:

We know that burial spices (aloe and myrrh) were placed inside the Shroud along with flowers. John 19: 39-41 states:

> "Then Nicodemus came, too - the one who had first come to Jesus at night - bringing a mixture of myrrh
> and aloes, weighing about a hundred pounds. So they took the body of Jesus and bound it in linen cloths with the spices, as is the custom among the Jews in preparing for burial."

Dr. Biaima Ballone, Professor of Legal Medicine at the

THE THREE CLOTHS OF CHRIST   by   John C. Iannone

University of Turin, identified traces of aloe and myrrh on the Shroud, principally in the bloodstained areas. Weunschel clarifies that these two spices were in the form of a dry powder. In the ancient world, aloe and myrrh were common articles of commerce. Myrrh is a gum resin exuding from the trees of the genus commiphora or balsamodendren myrrh and quickly becomes dry and solid as its volatile oil evaporates. Aloe is an herb obtained by evaporating the juice of the leaves of several spices of aloe, a genus of the liliacaeae. The aloe and myrrh is distinguished from the perfumed oil or unguent comprised of spices mixed with oil (Lk 23: 56) which the women prepared for the morning after the Sabbath.

Weunschel (quoting Paul Vignon) states:

> "The fact that the spices were in powdered form has a special significance with regard to the Shroud of Turin. Certain features of the imprints show that there was powder on the linen sheet at the time when it enveloped the body."

The purpose of the spices was generally to delay the process of decomposition to permit a mourning period and to serve as a perfume to combat the odor of decay until the women could return the morning after the Sabbath to properly cleanse and prepare the body. It must be remembered that none of the Apostles or disciples anticipated the Resurrection of Jesus, even though He had prepared them for this momentous event.

No Evidence of Corruption or Decay

There is no evidence on the Shroud of decomposition or corruption because Jesus was only in the tomb approximately thirty to thirty-six hours prior to His Resurrection. The New Testament proclaims that Jesus' body did not experience corruption. In Acts 2: 22-32 we read that Peter addressed the crowd, and quoting King David concerning the Messiah, tells the crowd that God could not:

> "allow His Holy One to suffer death's decay."
> (Ps. 16: 8-11).

As Dr. Kenneth Stevenson noted, many of the ancient burial cloths in existence today, while not having any type of image, do contain marks of decomposition of bodies. The

THE THREE CLOTHS OF CHRIST   by   John C. Iannone

Shroud, however, exhibits no signs of bodily decomposition or corruption.

The Shroud As An Ancient Textile:

We know that the Shroud is, in fact, an ancient textile consistent with the period of Jesus from the following:

First: The measurements of the Shroud are 14' 3' by 3' 7'. These seem like odd measurements. However, the unit of measurement at the time of Jesus was the *cubit* and the cubit in Palestine was 21.6 inches by modern standards. If you translate the Shroud into cubits, it precisely *2 cubits x 8 cubits*, consistent with the looms of the period.

Second: The Shroud is a finely woven 3-over-1 herringbone weave - a very fine fabric of the period. Normal shrouds were one-over-one weave. We know, however, that the Shroud of Jesus was bought by Joseph of Arimathea. The Gospel writers make it a point to say that "Joseph was a wealthy man." So, we would expect a finer fabric.

Third: One of the contemporary Custodians of the Holy Shroud in Turin is Mechthild Flury-Lemberg, a Swiss textile expert. Flury-Lemberg reports findings recently at the Fortress of Masada - Herod's winter palace high on a plateau overlooking the Dead Sea - of fragments of linen with a unique stitching on them which is also found on the side of the Shroud. She notes that this stitching has not been found in Medieval or Renaissance tapestries or cloths.

Fourth: The main Shroud Chemist for the STURP Team, the late Dr. Ray Rogers, pointed out that the Shroud contains no *vanillin*. Vanillin is a substance, an organic compound, found in linen and its presence deteriorates over time. The absence of vanillin in the linen of the Shroud indicates to him the linen's antiquity. It is similar in this respect to the linen which bound the Dead Sea Scrolls which were written on papyrus, wrapped in linen and placed in sealed clay jars.

New findings related to the Carbon-14 tests of 1988 which refute the evidence will be presented later regarding the Shroud as an ancient textile.

THE THREE CLOTHS OF CHRIST by John C. Iannone

Fingerprints On The Heel?

An intriguing statement made by Monsignor Giulio Ricci, former President of the Roman Center for the Study of the Passion of Christ and the Holy Shroud in his 1978 book entitled *The Way of the Cross in the Light of the Holy Shroud* (pp.63-64) warrants repeating here. He noted the presence of *fingerprints* on the left heel made from one of the bearers of the body of Jesus. Ricci states:

> "These prints (on the heel) were caused by the blood that would have flowed out of the hole in the feet, which had just been freed from the nails, due to the edema occurring either before death through circulatory insufficiency or after death through hypostasis (Dr. Giordano). The blood ran down and concentrated in the area of the heels, where it left some unusual marks which allow perfect reconstruction of the hand to be made, with the fingers bent and tensed, showing the effort needed to carry the weight. The little finger and the ring and middle fingers of the left hand (of the individual bearing Jesus' body), in contact with the heel, were surrounded by the blood running from the hole in the left foot. The same thing happened with the right hand on the right heel, though the imprint is less clear."

Ricci believed that this was evidence that the bearers of the body might have carried the body to the tomb feet first. It is also possible that Jesus' body was placed on a litter, and carried the relatively short distance to the tomb.

In summary, it is now evident that the Shroud is, in fact, an ancient linen textile. Further, the words of the New Testament describing what happened to Jesus, in all aspects of the passion and death, are supported by documents relating the ancient Jewish burial customs of the Second Temple period.

****

THE THREE CLOTHS OF CHRIST by John C. Iannone

Chapter Seven

How Were The Mysterious Images Formed?

"I am forced to conclude that the image was formed by a burst of radiant energy - light if you like."

Dr. Ray Rogers, Physical Chemist of the STURP Team

The most intriguing aspect of the study of the Shroud is the question of what mechanism actually formed the mysterious images on the linen. Despite exhaustive investigation by scientists from all disciples, no one has yet provided a comprehensive or conclusive proof of the process of image formation. However some of the answers will make one ponder.

Characteristics of The Image On The Shroud:

Let us first revisit some facts about the images. The images are of the frontal and dorsal side of Jesus crucified and laid out in an attitude of death according to Jewish burial custom. The full, life-size images appear to be a *sepia or straw-yellow* in color as one might expect from a light scorch on linen and oxidation over two thousand years. When STURP scientists first focused their microscopes on the linen, they were intrigued by the fact that *the image is limited to the very top fibrils of the fibers of the linen*. There is no evidence of any substance that created the image. There is no paint, no dye, ink, powder or caulk - in essence no substance creating the image.

A Surface Phenomenon:

STURP referred to it as a *"surface phenomenon."* There is *no penetration of any substance or saturation and no cohesion of fibers* such as one might expect from a paint with binders. In addition there are *no brush strokes or*

THE THREE CLOTHS OF CHRIST by John C. Iannone

directionality of strokes such as would be characteristic of an artist, nor any outline formed by an artist - the "horizon event" in art as related by world-famed artist Isabel Piczek. Further, there is an inverse relationship between the cloth-to-body distance and the intensity of the 3-dimensional image. The farther the cloth was from the body it covered, the less intense the image. No artist could create such a perfect 3-D relationship between cloth-body distance and intensity of images.

Where there is blood, there is no image, leading to the conclusion that *the blood was on the Shroud first before whatever mechanism forming the image took place*. The blood interfered with the image formation process on those particular spots. When one approaches the cloth, as this author did, the closer one gets to the image, the harder it is to see, being best viewed from a distance of six to ten feet - a distance that is not realistic for an artist to have painted the Shroud. This also refutes the theory that an artist painted the image and then added real human (ancient) blood for effect.

In a 1981 meeting at New London, Connecticut, scientists reported:

> "No pigments, paints, dyes or stains have been found on the fibrils. X-Ray fluorescence and microchemistry on the fibrils preclude the possibility of paint being used as a method for creating the image. Ultraviolet and infrared evaluation confirm these studies.

The late Dr. John Heller, then Professor of Medical Physics at Yale and Director of the New England Institute of Medicine, noted that:

> "At the end of months of work, we had pretty well eliminated all paints, pigments, dyes and stains. Where did this leave us? There were images of a man that produced 3-D read-outs in a VP-8 Analyzer and the images were not the result of any colorant that had been added."

To answer whether the image may have been caused by heat such as a light scorch-from-heat, scientists applied X-Ray Fluorescence. *The image did not fluoresce* indicating that it was *not created by heat*.

THE THREE CLOTHS OF CHRIST by John C. Iannone

The Rise and Fall of the Iron-Oxide Theory:

The late Dr. Walter McCrone, a noted Microanalyst with his own research laboratory (Walter C. McCrone Associates, Inc.) in Chicago, Illinois noted the presence of some particles of iron oxide on the Shroud from samples given to him. He was not one of the STURP scientists who personally examine the Shroud. He deduced from the flecks that this was some sort of paint. McCrone had an international reputation from his discovery of the Vineland Map forgery. In 1957, an American book dealer found a map apparently dating from the fifteenth century and copied from an earlier Viking map, showing parts of North America. Speculation arose that the Vikings beat Columbus to North America by some 500 years.

Walter McCrone received the map for Yale University and studied it, only to discover in 1974 that the ink contained anatase (titanium dioxide) which had only been invented in the 1920's. He declared the map a forgery. However, as is pointed out by Picknett and Clive, McCrone's findings have been called into question. In 1987 physicists at the University of California examined the map using a method of particle induced X-ray emissions and found only minute amounts of titanium - more than 1,000 times less than that claimed by McCrone, which, as they point out, one would expect to find in medieval ink. Perhaps the Vineland Map is genuine after all. More importantly, McCrone's judgment regarding the Shroud was further called into question.

McCrone, as mentioned, had not been with the team that examined the Shroud first hand. He claimed that the pigment Venetian red, made by grinding iron oxide into a powder, was solely responsible for the Shroud image. However, the STURP scientists who examined the cloth directly reported that, while there was iron oxide evenly distributed throughout the cloth, and not limited to the image areas, these particles have *nothing to do with the formation of the images.* Scientists point out that in the production of linen, the flax plant is retted, that is, soaked in water in a pond, vat or other receptacle, sometimes for several says to separate the stalks and fibers. This soaking in water allows the linen to absorb iron from the water which is evenly distributed throughout. The fact that the iron is evenly distributed and is in a pure state (versus iron oxide used in Medieval paints which has manganese and other

THE THREE CLOTHS OF CHRIST by John C. Iannone

substances) demonstrates that the iron oxide is not involved in the formation of the image.

Medieval Sanctification of Paintings:

It is known that often, in the long history of the Shroud, artists would be allowed to paint copies of the Shroud to bring back to their hometowns churches. These artists were allowed to lay their paintings over the Shroud to somehow sanctify such paintings. They did not understand the microscopic transfer of particles. The microscope was not invented for another two centuries. This process left an occasional microscopic trace of paint or pigment on the cloth from the artist' painting. In addition, chemists noted that some flecks could have been from blood. With the folding and rolling up of the Shroud over the years, some flecks of iron oxide from blood could easily have fallen on other parts of the Shroud.

What Caused the Image - Some Theories:

The Shroud is a linen cloth and linen is composed of cellulose fibers that, in turn, are composed of carbon, oxygen and hydrogen. Scientists who have studied the Shroud directly utilizing many tests concluded that the image was formed by some process the caused an accelerated dehydration, oxidation and degradation (rapid aging) of the Shroud's topmost cellulose fibrils from an energy source causing a scorch like effect but not a scorch from heat.

More recent studies by Dr. Ray Rogers in 2002-2005 indicated to him that it wasn't the medullas of the linen that were affected, but rather a discoloration of the *surface impurities* on the linen fibrils - impurities such as starch from the retting process. However, a question remains: what process caused this scorch-like effect?

A Natural Process?

Could some natural process have created the image? We will review some theories along this line. However, contradicting this theory is the fact that, if the image was created by some process of nature, why is there no record of any other image among the many burial cloths remaining from antiquity? There are, for example, many Egyptian funerary cloths in museums and other locations

THE THREE CLOTHS OF CHRIST by John C. Iannone

throughout the world. At most, a very limited few have some marks on them, primarily from decomposition of tissue of the deceased or perhaps bloodstained. None, however, has anything like an image - and certainly nothing approaching the clarity of the full-body images on the Shroud. In addition, there is no sign of decomposition on the Shroud. The New Testament tells us that Jesus was not in the tomb very long (perhaps 30 to 36 hours) and in Acts 2:22-32 we read that Jesus' body did not experience corruption but was resurrected instead. Could some other natural process provide a clue?

The Vaporgraph Theory:

In 1902, biologist Paul Vignon, who devoted much of his life at the Sorbonne and the Institut Catholique de Paris to the scientific study of the Shroud, hypothesized that a natural process, namely, the presence of sweat, ammonia, blood and the burial spices (aloe and myrrh) combined with the heat of the body to create a chemical gas that diffused upward toward the cloth and accounted for the image. Dying in great agony does produce febrile (fever) sweat containing urea, which ferments into carbonate of ammonia giving off an ammonia vapor. In the time frame of the grave, such a vapor could cause a light brown stain on linen.

Vignon's work was taken up by Michel Adge, a professor of chemistry and Giovanni Imbalzano, professor of mathematics and physics as well as by John D. German of the USAF Weapons Laboratory. John A. De Salvo of Northwestern College of Chiropractics in his Revised Vaporgraphic-Direct Contact Hypotheses placed a great deal of importance on the presence of lactic acid in perspiration as a factor in the production of the image. Robert Wilcox summarized the objections to the theory saying:

> "As far as chemical being able to make such an image, lab tests have shown that chemicals diffuse and run through linen fibers, and thus produce a blurry, and certainly non 3-D Image."

This may rule out Archaeologist Dr. Eugenia Nitowski's "post-mortem fever" theory of image formation. The *image on the Shroud does not show signs of diffusion or of penetration*. Vaporgraphs do not account for a three-

THE THREE CLOTHS OF CHRIST by John C. Iannone

dimensional image. In addition, the Shroud image is a surface phenomenon. Vapors do not travel upward in a straight or parallel line, but diffuse and create an unclear image. Finally, vaporgraphic theories cannot account for the transfer of images of hair, or coins, or flowers. STURP physicist Dr. Eric Jumper noted that the process was an "image forming process" that acted through space, not by contact. Further, there is a relationship between "intensity versus distance," that is, the closer the body to the cloth, the more intense the image.

Finally, Jumper notes that the images were not "pressure sensitive," that is, the image on the back of the body has the same shadowing characteristics and lack of saturation as the front even though the body was lying with full weight on the cloth. In addition, *vapors would ascend and not descend* to form the back images.

Note: It is possible that the presence of aloe and myrrh "sensitized" the cloth to receive the image which was created by something other than by vapors.

The Volkringer Effect:

Dr. Jean Volckringer, formerly Chief of Apothecary at St. Joseph's Hospital in Paris and member of the French Academy of Sciences, discovered that certain leaves, which had been left between the pages of a book for over a hundred years, formed a highly detailed negative image on the paper several pages away. This theory was advanced to explain potentially the image on the Shroud. He noted that the heavy paper covering these plants is not uncommonly imprinted with a striking image of the specimen involved.

Some of the parallels of these to the Shroud are remarkable, being sepia in color and featuring considerable observable detail of roots, veins, stems and leaves. The imprints also have inverse relief characteristics becoming fainter the greater the distance of any part of the plant from the paper, and reproducing without direct contact over the distance. They also have a three-dimensionality when viewed under a VP8 Image Analyzer.

Volckringer noted the important fact that the plant images are formed from an undoubted dehydration, degradation and oxidation of the cellulose of the rag paper in which the

THE THREE CLOTHS OF CHRIST   by   John C. Iannone

plant specimen has been pressed. Somehow, the plants projected or radiated their image to the paper.

The puzzle is that, as discussed previously, if the image formation process on the Shroud was from a natural source such as the Volkringer effect, then why do such images not appear on many hundreds of Egyptian and other burial cloths in possession of our museums throughout the world? In addition, the Volckringer effect takes time, perhaps decades. Jesus was, however, in the tomb for perhaps twenty-four to thirty-six hours. It is not likely that this process took place in such a short time. However, there does seem to be some relationship of the process creating the Volckringer effect and the process that created the Shroud Image but it does not explain the presence of the images.

The Kerlian Aura:

In the late 1940's, Ralph Graeber, a nuclear engineer, spoke of Kirlian photography as a type of radiation possibly involved in the formation of images on the Shroud. In 1939 Semyon Kirlian, then a Soviet electrician, was observing a demonstration of a high-frequency machine being used in electrotherapy. He noticed a tiny flash of light between the electrodes attached to the patient and the patient's skin. Kirlian attempted to photograph this process by holding a piece of film between the two and placed his hand on the film. As Wilcox points out:

> "Although Kirlian got a severe burn for his efforts, he also got a brilliant photograph of his hand, with a luminescence, or halo, or aura, along the contours of the fingers."

He then photographed all sorts of objects, inanimate and alive, ranging from leaves, coins and fingers as well as the entire human body. The results were always the same: a glowing luminescence that seemed to radiate from the subject in a myriad of hues - red, blue, green, yellow and white. Soviet scientists called it "*bio-radiation*" or an "*energy body*" that somehow was inside and emanated from all things. *Kirlian photography demonstrated that the human body emits radiation and Ralph Graeber first related such radiation as having a possible relation to the images on the Shroud.*

THE THREE CLOTHS OF CHRIST by John C. Iannone

Kerlian Auras and Halos:

Jesus' aura or halo, Graeber speculated, was strong enough to leave marks on the cloth when no other bodies that had been put in shrouds ever had. Kirilan photography demonstrated that both mental and physical stress increased the loss of life-energy from the body. Since Jesus suffered from both extreme mental anguish and physical torture, the intensity level of radiation from His body would have been very great in the tomb. Additionally Graeber points out that as Jesus was the Son of God, His aura was no doubt strong than that of any person.

The crucial differences between the two types of radiation (Volckringer and Kirlian) are in the variables of intensity, exposure duration, and possibly development time. The Volckringer images were produced by a *low intensity exposure over a long period of time*. The Shroud images appear to have been produced by *a high intensity exposure over a short period of time, even an instantaneous intense milliburst of radiant energy.*

Healers and Cures:

American researchers Thelma Moss and Kendall Johnson of the University of California in Los Angeles confirmed much about the Kirlian process (called "radiation field photography") and added some new and fascinating data. They studied the aura of a person claiming to be a healer. Energy flowing out of the healer's body into the body of a patient is often the explanation healers give of the phenomenon that apparently takes place. The results of the Moss-Johnson tests were reported in the October 16, 1972 issue of *Time* Magazine. They noted that *after a cure, the healer's aura was significantly diminished and the patient's aura was correspondingly increased.*

Jesus was a master healer and curer and the intensity of His aura must have been great. The Gospels tell us that Jesus was a man with a power - a power He is specifically recorded to have felt drawn from Him as in the case of the woman with the hemorrhage who touched the hem of His robe. In Mark 5:30 we read:

> "Jesus Himself, realizing at once that power had gone out from Him, turned around in the crowd and said,

THE THREE CLOTHS OF CHRIST by John C. Iannone

'Who touched my cloak?'" (Mk.5:30).

Volckringer-Kirlian Radiation:

Robert Wilcox discussed with Graeber the type of radiation possibly involved in the Volckringer-Kirlian emanations. Graeber suspected it was in the ultraviolet region of electro-magnetic radiation. Ultraviolet radiation was close to visible light which is why some sensitive individuals were able to perceive human auras. Ultraviolet rays could burn, given enough intensity, and therefore could have caused the scorched look that the Shroud images appear to have. Graeber, however, did not care for the term "scorched" because *he believed that the mysterious radiation tracing on the Shroud was somewhat analogous to heat but without heat's harshness, perhaps more like* **light** *on a photographic place.*

The Hiroshima-Nagasaki Atomic Bomb Blasts:

Dr. Ray Rogers, working as a physical chemist of the Los Alamos Laboratory's Design Engineering Division and a STURP member, said (about the Shroud images):

"I am forced to conclude that the image was formed by a burst of radiant energy, **light** if you like."

The emphasis is again on **radiant energy from light coming from within the body** versus **heat.** Professor Alan Adler, a chemist of Western Connecticut State College, concluded that *the Shroud images could have been created only by high-level energy* which he could not name. The physical body that lay on the Shroud of Turin must have *radiated as a very high intensity for a very short period of time, perhaps milliseconds.* This radiant light, which Frank Tribbe termed a "*flash photolysis*," has had historical parallels where permanent images were formed by the light and power in the atomic bomb blast at Hiroshima. Dr. Everett James, a radiologist formerly of Vanderbilt University and Dr. Alan Whanger of Duke University called it an *auto radiograph* emanating from within the body.

In 1976 STURP scientists in the Los Alamos Laboratory (operated by the University of California for the U.S. Department of Energy) issued a public statement suggesting that one scientific hypothesis:

THE THREE CLOTHS OF CHRIST by John C. Iannone

"draws an analogy between the mysterious images on the Shroud and the fact that images were formed on stones by the fireball radiation from the atomic bomb at Hiroshima."

In 1946, just after the blast, John R. Hersey published an article in the *New Yorker Magazine* on the Hiroshima images and elaborated on them in his book Hiroshima. U.S. Army and Air Force photographs as well as Japanese photographs provide a variety of views of this phenomenon. Hersey said that:

"The bomb had, in some places, left prints of the shadows that had been caused by its light."

Scientists noted that the blast discolored some concrete to a light reddish tint and scaled off granite surfaces. The light produced by the Hiroshima-Nagasaki blasts was so brilliant that it caused shadows of upright objects. The radiant energy of the blast was so powerful that it permanently "etched" those shadows onto both flat, horizontal surfaces such as concrete roadways and vertical surfaces and on the side of a gas storage tank.

There was even the shadow of a man in a cart posed in the act of whipping his horse. Obviously, the man, cart and horse - just seconds from the epicenter - were incinerated in the blast, leaving only the shadow. Scientists at a conference in Albuquerque, New Mexico, sitting just two hours drive from the site of the first atomic bomb blast at Alamogordo in 1945 considered that *some kind of thermonuclear flash created the images.*

An Energy Source from Within Jesus' Body:

There are parallels with the Shroud that indicate that, rather than a substance, some kind of energy force or source seems to have been responsible for the images. The Shroud images were seemingly *created from within rather than from without* by a process of necessity far more controlled than the blast from an atomic bomb. The information of the 1973 Turin Commission report indicated that the image affected only the topmost surface of the fibrils (confirmed by the 1978 STURP Team) and whatever created the images had neither seeped into nor penetrated

THE THREE CLOTHS OF CHRIST   by   John C. Iannone

the fibers. The image fibers were insoluble and resistant to acids. This energy source was powerful enough to project the image onto the linen from a distance of up to four centimeters (according to physicists John Jackson and Eric Jumper), yet gentle enough not to cause distortion in the areas where there would have been direct contact on the dorsal image where the cloth received the full weight of the body.

The image was created with a *marked upward-downward direction - a vertical collimated radiation* - without any diffusion and leaving no imprint of the sides of the body or top of the head. Additionally, the image did not discriminate between registering the body surface as well as hair, blood, flowers and inanimate objects - the coins over the eyes and a phylactery, or small prayer box attached to the forehead. Physicist Dr. Eric Jumper argued that any diffusion process would have involved penetration of the fibers and any remotely lingering laser beam would have caused complete destruction. Whatever created the images must have been some extremely high intensity, short duration burst (milliseconds) acting evenly upward and downward.

The Phenomenon of the Resurrection of Jesus:

Physicists began to suspect that the image itself pointed toward a unique event, an event involving a milliburst of radiant energy emanating as light from within the body of Jesus, one involving **light** which left the scorch-like (but not a scorch from heat) images on the Shroud. This is a challenging theory that hints that *a momentous, unprecedented event occurred at the moment of Jesus' Resurrection. Here science and faith meet.* It was as if Jesus was leaving for all mankind to ponder a photography of His moment of great triumph - a photography that was registered on linen and that contained in the linen a compelling story of all aspects of His passion, death and resurrection.

Scientists point to a brilliant flashing light upon His return to life that delicately scorched or seared His image on the Shroud. Often, in doing many lectures on the Holy Shroud, I am asked by Pastors of all faiths why I think it is so important to understand the Shroud and whether this may make people think this is somehow an article of faith

THE THREE CLOTHS OF CHRIST by John C. Iannone

or that belief in Jesus is contingent on belief in the Holy Shroud. I clarify that our belief in the Resurrection stands on the Gospels and on our faith. However, if we accept the authenticity of the Holy Shroud as the burial cloth of the historical Jesus, one that contains His images, bloodstains and evidence of His resurrection, we must ask ourselves the key question: *Why did Jesus do this? Why did He leave His mysterious images on linen? He must have had a reason and it is one we should take seriously.*

Was it an accident or a natural phenomenon? The evidence does not support that it was an accident or natural phenomenon. Jesus did this with a purpose: the cloth tells a compelling story and allows us to study and understand what He did for us presented for all levels of faith from the simple believing Christian to the most educated of scientists. It deepens and enhances our faith.

We should not be surprised that the phenomenon of the Resurrection was somehow involved with light or radiant energy. It is interesting to note that Jesus is referred to in the New Testament as the "Light of the World."

The Transfiguration:

In a passage in the New Testament related by Matthew, Mark and Luke, called the Transfiguration, Jesus takes three Apostles (Peter, James and John) up on a mountain and there is "transfigured" before them. He reveals to them, before His crucifixion, *a glimpse of his glorified body*. The New Testament writers talk of this unique event as follows:

> "HIS FACE SHONE LIKE THE SUN AND HIS CLOTHES BECAME WHITE AS THE LIGHT." Matt. 17
>
> "HIS CLOTHES BECAME DAZZLING WHITE, WHITER THAN ANYONE IN THE WORLD COULD BLEACH THEM." Mark 9.
>
> "THE APPEARANCE OF HIS FACE CHANGED AND HIS CLOTHES BECAME AS BRIGHT AS A FLASH OF LIGHTENING." Luke 9.

Attention is focused on the terms "white as the light"; "dazzling white"; "bright as a flash of lightening." The Angels at the Tomb are described in similar fashion.

THE THREE CLOTHS OF CHRIST by John C. Iannone

The Near-Death Experience and The Light:

Several years ago, after extensive research and interviews, I published a book entitled: "*Glimpses of the Afterlife: The Near Death Experience in Science, Faith and History.*" After interviewing many people and studying the work of noted doctors such as Drs. Raymond Moody, Elizabeth Kubler-Ross, Melvin Morse, Kenneth Ring and Michael Sabom who had hundreds of dialogues with patients encountering a near death experience, I was drawn by what Dr. Raymond Moody stated. I had heard this same thing told to me by people who had encountered the Near Death Experience. Dr. Moody explained:

> "Perhaps the most common element in NDE's is an encounter with very bright light of unearthly brilliance which does not hurt eyes. They are enveloped by a loving, warm Being."

Again, there is an encounter with a "very bright light of unearthly brilliance."

Physicists who have studied the Holy Shroud images are perplexed by the mechanism that created them, saying that there is some form of radiant energy emanating from within the body but not knowing exactly what it was. They theorize that a form of "particle radiation" occurred at the moment of the Resurrection...a physiological consequence of a spiritual event.

Former Harvard Physicist Dr. Thomas Phillips, talking to his colleagues who found this difficult to grasp once stated:

> "We never had a Resurrection to study before, so how do we know what would have happened when God raised his Son to life?"

Woman Healed By Jesus:

In Mark 5: 20 we learn of the story of the woman who approached Jesus who was walking in a crowd. She had suffered from a hemorrhage for 12 years and wanted only to touch the hem of Jesus' garment. She did so. Jesus stopped and asked who had touched Him. The Apostles were puzzled because He was being jostled by a crowd. However, He knew

THE THREE CLOTHS OF CHRIST by John C. Iannone

someone had touched Him and that "power went out of Him" The New Testament Greek uses the term "*dunamin*" - meaning power or energy. As we shall see later, early Christian writings such as the Acts of Pilate (380) and later "The Avenging of the Saviour" identified this woman as the Veronica who wiped Jesus' face on the Via Dolorosa on which He left his mysterious facial imprint.

Radiant Energy from Within:

It is fascinating to note that scientists believe that the power or milliburst of energy emanated *from within the body and not from outside the body*. Jesus' own body emanated the radiant energy which restored Him to life. Research done by Dr. Giles Carter, a Chemist of East Michigan University in the early 1980's and by Dr. Alan Whanger of Duke University in the 1990's, trained in radiology, both theorized some form of *x-radiation emanated* from within the body, burning, as it were, the image delicately in a flash of light onto the Cloth. Shroud photographer Barrie Schwortz pointed out that there are "no shadows" on the Shroud as might be expected if the source of light was external to the body. This theory supports the fact that light emanated from within.

Images of Bones and Teeth?

A light bulb, for example, lit from within has no shadows on itself. The energy flowed from within and *both scientists have noted the image of bones of the hand - metatarsals and phalanges - appearing on digitalized photos*. Dr. Whanger even points out the presence of approximately 20 teeth, again suggesting a collimated x-radiation acting vertically emanating from within the body. Recently, I sat with Dr. Whanger in his laboratory at home and viewed the presence of bones of the hands and teeth utilizing his PIOT, or Polarized Image Overlay Technique. I was astonished by the results shown via the polarized filters at right angles to each other with a third filter moving at different angles.

Enter Nuclear Medicine:

Dr. August Accetta in Huntington Beach, California once performed an experiment in nuclear medicine in his study of the Holy Shroud. Using a nuclear dye, methylene diphosphate, he injected himself in the presence of physicist Dr. John Jackson. They waited six hours and took photos with a Gamma camera. Dr. Accetta noticed that he could see phalanges and metatarsals of the hand, lending support to an x-radiation from within the body.

Further work continues attempting to determine the type of energy of the electromagnetic spectrum that may have been involved in the formation of the image. As some physicist state, such a discovery would revolutionize physics as we know it.

****

THE THREE CLOTHS OF CHRIST   by   John C. Iannone

THE THREE CLOTHS OF CHRIST by John C. Iannone

Chapter Eight

TRACING THE HISTORICAL JOURNEY: THE FIRST THOUSAND YEARS

"If instead of Christ, there were a question of some person like...an Achilles or one of the Pharaohs, no one would have thought of making any objection."

>> Professor Yves Delage - French Academy of Science

As science delved into the mysteries of the Shroud, historians began searching ancient and modern manuscripts hoping to shed light on the presence of the Shroud in literary or liturgical texts over the past 2,000 years. Historians have located a number of texts that have enabled us to recreate a plausible history of the Shroud that compliments scientific findings. While some of the historical information is circumstantial, the sum total of information provides a strong link between the modern Shroud of Turin and the ancient Shroud from the Tomb of Jesus. This evidence taken in its totality represents the "preponderance of evidence" noted by the late Shroud scholar the Rev. Kim Driesbach of Atlanta.

The Silence of the New Testament:

The most logical place to start is in the New Testament itself. It appears puzzling that the Gospels writers, while speaking in some detail of the grave cloths, do not mention the images on the Shroud. One would think that the Apostles would go about Jerusalem showing everyone the images they had found on the burial cloth. Perhaps they did...in secret. However, there were good reasons for the follower of Jesus to keep the existence of the Shroud quiet and to talk almost "in code." Most likely, Peter, as the leader, took control of the Shroud and guarded it carefully. Of necessity, the Apostles could not openly display the grave cloths of their Risen Lord.

THE THREE CLOTHS OF CHRIST by John C. Iannone

First, as a record of Jesus' passion, it was something very precious to the early Church. Out of fear that it might be mishandled or even destroyed, it would not have been exposed to the eyes of the enemies of the early Church or to the curious.

Second, Jewish religious regulations strictly forbade the handling of burial cloths, especially a bloody one of victims of violent death. Many Jews would not have understood or accepted the preservation of this bloody burial cloth by Jesus' followers.

Third, the Jews throughout the Old ad New Testament period considered graven images (drawings, paintings, statues depicting God) as blasphemous. This is especially true in that the Shroud contained images of a naked man. If the Apostles had used, in a public manner, the images of a naked Jesus depicted on a bloody burial cloth this act would have been considered as blasphemous and would have further jeopardized the very lives of the early disciples.

Fourth, Jesus was, after all, considered a criminal and crucified by the Romans. Any public display of His images with a claim that He had risen would certainly have created conflict with the Romans - especially a claim that He was the Son of God.

Peter and the Apostles, therefore, could not effectively utilize the Shroud openly as a proselytizing tool to convert their fellow Jews in or around Jerusalem. We surmise from later evidence that the Apostles made the decision to have the Shroud brought to a safe haven away from the dangers the early Church faced in Palestine, especially around Jerusalem. This would account for the silence of the New Testament.

Apocryphal Texts:

There were good reasons for the silence of the New Testament concerning the Shroud (apart from the Crucifixion accounts of the burial cloths which were written between 65 A.D. in the Gospel of Mark and approx. 100 A.D. {Gospel of John} after the Shroud left Jerusalem. Some Apocryphal texts (texts not recognized in the official Canon of literature which formed the New Testament) however, do make reference to the funeral cloths of Jesus:

St. Jerome, for example, quotes a passage from the *Gospel*

THE THREE CLOTHS OF CHRIST by John C. Iannone

of the Hebrews (second century) and cites what is probably the most ancient non-biblical reference we have to the Shroud:

> "Now the Lord, after having given the Shroud to the servant of the priest, appeared to James."

Other texts read:

> "After having given the Shroud to Simon Peter..."

and this interpretation would seem to agree with what St. Paul says:

> "He appeared to Cephas (Peter) then to the Twelve. Finally, He appears to James."

"*The Mysteries of the Acts of the Savior*" also of the second century, reports that the Lord Himself, appearing to Joseph of Arimathea, showed him the Shroud (*Sindon*) and the Face Cloth (*Sudario*).

Texts from the Egyptian Church (third and fourth centuries) mention that bodies are wrapped in a shroud with aromatic spices, "as Joseph of Arimathea and Nicodemus had done with the body of the Lord, as the Shroud shows."

Pope Sylvester I, addressing the famed Council of Nicea in 324 A.D. called by Constantine the Great, decreed that a (white)linen cloth was henceforth to be used on all altars during the Mass in memory of the shroud in which Jesus was buried. This custom prevails to the current day.

While the persecutions raged around them during the first three centuries, the Christian community jealously guarded the relics of the martyrs. It is logical to assume that the greatest veneration and care would have been reserved for the burial cloth of Jesus. Where, then, could the nascent Church safely send the Shroud?

The Journey to Edessa in Turkey:

J.B. Segal wrote a classic book entitled *Edessa: The Blessed City*. He describes this great metropolis and its colorful history as a jewel in the Byzantine Empire. Byzantium, later called Constantinople (now Istanbul), was the capital of the ancient Byzantine Empire covering most of what is now modern Turkey. Ancient Edessa (modern Urfa)

THE THREE CLOTHS OF CHRIST   by   John C. Iannone

was a city about 400 miles north of Jerusalem. At that time, Edessa was within the Roman Province of Osrhoene and on the outskirts of the Roman Empire. As such, it was close to the borders of the Parthian (Persian) Empire to the East - basically modern Iraq and Iran. Edessa was a cosmopolitan city that became the seat of an early Christian community similar to the one in Antioch between Edessa and Jerusalem. Many early Jews-turned-Christian fled from the persecution in Palestine and settled in other cities such as Antioch and Edessa, especially after the Romans laid siege to Jerusalem in 70 A.D.

What rationale may have prompted Peter and the Apostles to send the Shroud for safe-keeping to Edessa? Interestingly, science confirms the presence of the Shroud in Edessa. Swiss criminologist Dr. Max Frei found pollen on the Shroud from both the area around Jerusalem and from the area of Edessa, Constantinople and Europe. This find supports historians in saying that Edessa was the home of the Shroud for many Centuries (900 years). What, therefore, is the historical rationale for believing that the Shroud moved to Edessa?

Ancient Edessa (modern Urfa in Turkey) was located in Syria of New Testament times. There was considerable interaction between the Syrians and the inhabitants of Palestine. Matthew 4:24-25 tells us that:

> "News of Him (Jesus) went out through all Syria and they brought Him all who were sick with various diseases and were suffering torment - the demon-possessed, epileptics, paralytics - and He healed them."

Josephus, the early Jewish historian, talks of close contact between Jerusalem and the Jewish inhabitants of northern Mesopotamia. Mesopotamia (literally the delta between two rivers, the Tigris and the Euphrates) was near Edessa. We know from early sources that there were trade routes between Edessa, Antioch, Jerusalem and Egypt. Ananias, the courier for King Abgar in Edessa, visited the Praetor of Egypt on King Abgar's behalf. These caravan routes linked these great cities and travelers would have heard the stories of Jesus and inquired on their journeys.

Therefore, Edessa was a likely place to send the Shroud for safe haven. The strength of the evidence from early

THE THREE CLOTHS OF CHRIST by John C. Iannone

literary sources indicates that Edessa did become the home of the Shroud for many centuries (from approximately 40 A.D. - 944 A.D.).

The Legend of King Abgar:

The fact that Edessa was a logical and credible place to bring the Shroud does not necessarily mean that it was brought there. However, support for Edessa comes from the persistent legends surrounding King Abgar that appear in the early Christian literature. King Abgar V Ouchama (the Dark) was King of Edessa from about 13-50 A.D. during Jesus' life on earth. King Abgar had heard about the activities of Jesus curing the sick and he himself was suffering from leprosy. The legend, related by early Historian Eusebius in 325 A.D. relates that Abgar sent a letter to Jesus and sent Ananias, his emissary, to deliver the letter to Jesus to encourage Him to come to Edessa.

Thaddaeus (Addai) Brings the Shroud To Edessa:

The legend, which has several variations, maintains that Jesus sent word back to King Abgar that, after His death, He would have someone come to Edessa to cure Abgar. After Jesus' passion, death and resurrection, Thaddaeus (called Addai in Syrian), a disciple, was sent by Thomas the Apostle to cure the King of leprosy and to establish the Church in Edessa. But what did he bring with him?

Eusebius The Historian:

The legends first appear in the writings of an early and famed historian of the Church, Eusebius of Caesarea. In his *Ecclesiastical History* written about 320-325 A.D. Eusebius uses a Syrian text from the Edessa archives and speaks of the letter Abgar sent to Jesus. Eusebius tells us that Abgar was wasting away with an incurable disease and he heard about Jesus and His miracles. He then sent a letter carrier, *Ananias*, to Jesus asking for delivery from his disease. Eusebius mentions that the Apostle Thomas sent the Disciple Thaddeus to Edessa who healed Abgar of his leprosy and founded the Church in Edessa.

The Pilgrim Egeria:

Egeria, a pilgrim to Edessa traveling from Gaul in 381-384 mentions in her *Diaries* that the Bishop of the city, in showing her the places of interest in Edessa, took her to

THE THREE CLOTHS OF CHRIST by John C. Iannone

the gate which Ananias entered bearing the letter of Jesus. No mention is made, however, of any image of the Lord. Possibly the Shroud was hidden away because of the persecutions of the first three centuries. Memory of it may have faded to the general populace and been carefully guarded by the Bishop and his people.

The Core of the Abgar Legend:

Eusebius does not mention any portrait, but several authors suggest that Eusebius may have deliberately suppressed any such mention in his text since he was opposed to images as idolatrous. An image, however, is mentioned by later authors and became known as The Image of Edessa. We have, in Eusebius, the beginnings of the Abgar Legend, a persistent legend of the early Church lasting for over a millennium that Abgar knew and communicated with Jesus; that the Apostle Thomas, after Jesus' death, send Thaddaeus to Abgar to cure him and initiate the Church in Edessa; and that a "portrait" of Jesus was brought to Edessa that came, over time, to be considered as divinely wrought - an "acheiropoietos" - image not made by human hands.

Edessa - The Likely Place:

Given the persecutions of the early Church in Jerusalem and the likelihood that the Shroud needed to find safe haven outside Palestine; given the link between Jerusalem and Syria and the early Christian community in Edessa; given the persistence of the Abgar Legend suggesting that a "portrait" did exist in Edessa for centuries; given the scientific findings of Dr. Max Frei that pollen on the Shroud came from the area around Edessa (the Anatolian Steppe); and given the Shroud historian Ian Wilson's correlation between the Image of Edessa rediscovered (or) revealed in Edessa in 524-544 and the artistic revolution that followed this rediscovery, the case is compelling that the Shroud did indeed move to Edessa and was one and the same as the Image of Edessa and the Mandylion (little towel - the Shroud folded) - of later Byzantine literature.

The Doctrine of Addai:

Somewhere in the latter part of the fourth century (350 to 400 A.D.) another Syrian text emerges called the *Doctrine of Addai*. Addai is the Syrian name for the disciple Thaddaeus. Here, the Abgar Legend reappears, but no mention

THE THREE CLOTHS OF CHRIST by John C. Iannone

is made of a "portrait" that Ananias "painted" of Jesus along with mention of a letter which Abgar had written to Jesus. In this document, Jesus gives a verbal response to Abgar. The document relates that:

> "Ananias...took and painted the portrait of Jesus with choice pigments."

It is the first mention of the "portrait" in Edessa and reiterates that Thomas sent Thaddaeus to Edessa to cure Abgar.

Acts of the Holy Apostle Thaddaeus:

In the early sixth century, a document called the *Acts of the Holy Apostle Thaddaeus* again recalls the Legend of Abgar. This document is quite important since it repeats the Abgar Legend and expands on it by introducing another major clue in the early literature: namely The *Tetradiplon*. The text reads:

> "And Ananias, having gone and given the letter, was carefully looking at Christ, but was unable to fix Him in his mind. And He (Jesus) knew as knowing the heart and asked to wash Himself, and a towel (Greek: tetradiplon) was given to Him and when He had washed Himself, He wiped His face with it. And His image having been imprinted upon the linen, He gave it to Ananias, saying "Give this, and take back this message to Him that sent thee (Abgar): 'Peace be to thee and to thy city.' "

The basic rudiments of the Legend are repeated. However, a new element is added: a *mysterious image on linen* is introduced, an image of Jesus called the *tetradiplon.* The image is elevated from a "painting" to a "mysterious image on linen cloth" imprinted by Jesus when wiping His face with a towel (tetradiplon). It appears that in the earliest legends, the Shroud may have been considered initially as a "painting" by those who could not understand the images. It came to be recognized as an image of Jesus "not made-by-human-hands (*acheiropoietos*) and began to be elevated to a "mysterious image" and later to a divinely wrought image. Attention is called now to this new word *tetradiplon*.

The Tetradiplon:

The word "towel" used in the text intrigues Shroud

THE THREE CLOTHS OF CHRIST   by   John C. Iannone

historians because the literal translation of the Greek word used (*tetradiplon*) means *doubled-in-four*. *Tetradiplon* is an unusual Greek work lending credibility to the contention that this was a full-length linen cloth folded to show only the face (otherwise called the *Image of Edessa* and also *The Mandylion* or "Little Towel") in a horizontal, or landscape form (width greater than height) rather than the normal vertical or portrait form (height greater than width) utilized by artists when painting a face. Such a horizontal versus vertical image-on-cloth lends credence to the image on the burial cloth.

An artist would likely have worked on a vertical plane and not likely on linen cloth in painting on the face. The term *Mandylion* (little towel) was, it appears, used later on as a reference to this smaller, folded cloth-image showing only the face on the Shroud. According to Professor Lampe of Cambridge University and editor of the *Lexicon of Patristic Greek*, the word tetradiplon is found only twice in Greek Byzantine literature - both times in reference to this linen cloth. The second example is from the tenth century liturgical homily called *Monthly Lection (*part of the *Festival of Sources)* written in the year 945 A.D. In this text we read that after Jesus had washed:

> "...After Jesus had washed there was given to Him a piece of cloth folded four times (*rhakos tetradiplon*) and after washing, He imprinted on it His undefiled and divine face."

Ian Wilson describes the process to mean doubled, then redoubled and doubled again, i.e. doubling three times that has the effect of "doubling-in-four," producing EIGHT SECTIONS. As he point out, when folded in this manner the result is unmistakable:

> "The face along appears, disembodied on a landscape aspect background in a manner of the most striking similarity to the early artist's copies of the Image of Edessa."

This also helps explain why some authors refer only to the face of Jesus on cloth and others to His full body image. Most saw only the face of the folded Shroud (Image of Edessa or Mandylion) and were not ordinarily permitted to see the cloth stretched out. This would make sense in that a 14' cloth would be far more manageable if folded.

THE THREE CLOTHS OF CHRIST by John C. Iannone

The Raking-Light Test of Physicist Dr. John Jackson:

An important link between the Shroud and the tetradiplon comes from the scientific tests performed in 1978 in Turin by the S.T.U.R.P. Team. One of these tests performed by Dr. John Jackson, a physicist then stationed at the Air Force Academy in Colorado and now founder along with his wife Rebecca of the Turin Shroud Center of Colorado, was called the "raking-light test" and utilized high magnification. To his surprise, the raking-light test and the use of high magnification verified fold marks on the Shroud corresponding exactly to what would have appeared if the Shroud was "doubled-in-four" when it was hidden away in the walls of Edessa. This enhances the credibility that the Image of Edessa, the Mandylion, and the Shroud of Turin are one and the same cloth.

The Image, Lost (or Hidden Away) and Found:

The Image of Edessa, which Ian Wilson came to identify as the Shroud, had been sealed up for protection in the walls of the ancient city of Edessa to save it from persecution launched by the grandson of King Abgar. We learn this from the later Byzantine authors. The Shroud remained sealed for several centuries until somewhere between 525-544 when it was rediscovered. Perhaps it was a carefully guarded secret of the Bishops and was brought out at a critical time. The rediscovery or unveiling of the cloth happened allegedly during an attack on Edessa by the Persian King Chosroes. Steven Runciman of Cambridge relates that during the attack in 544 A.D., the Persians built a fortification to scale the walls of Edessa. The Edessans, in turn, dug a tunnel to attempt to set fire to the wooded fortification of the Persians from below the ground. While tunneling under the wall, they found the Image of Edessa.

Wilson quotes Procopius of Caesarea, the historian of the period who, in his work *On The Persian Wars*, tells us:

> "In 540 King Chosroes I of Persia had declared war on the (Roman) Empire; and in 544 he advanced in full force into Mesopotamia and laid siege to Edessa. The walls of Edessa were tall and strong, but the Persians built a huge tower to overtop them; whence from their great number they could swamp the garrison. But before the tower was completed, the defenders burrowed underneath it, made a chamber and filled it with

THE THREE CLOTHS OF CHRIST by John C. Iannone

> highly flammable material and set it ablaze..."

Wilson, however, believes the rediscovery may have been a bit earlier possibly around 525. He links the rediscovery with the famous flood of Edessa. In 525 the river flooded and severely damaged the walls of Edessa. During the repair of the walls, Wilson believes that the Icon (Image of Edessa) was rediscovered during repairs. He tells us:

> "The Bishop Eulalius went prayerfully to the spot, made a thorough search and found the sacred image intact."

While historians disagree on the exact date of the rediscovery, they do agree that a rediscovery took place between 525-544. Wilson notes that the Emperor Justinian I dispatched engineers to Edessa in 525 to divert the river to prevent future floods. The Emperor also commissioned the construction of a beautiful shrine for the Icon, the Cathedral of Hagia Sophia in Edessa, which became home of the Image of Edessa until 944. The Hagia Sophia of Edessa is not the same at the famed Hagia Sophia of Istanbul. It should be noted that in the 700's and 800's the Moslem invasion took control of Edessa and the Hagia Sophia was converted to a Mosque. The Moslems had control of the Holy Shroud until approximately 944 A.D when a Christian army was sent to Edessa to rescue the cloth and the Moslems surrendered it for silver. The possession of the Shroud by the early Jewish-turned-Christian community, followed by the Moslems and then Christians again over the centuries gives the Shroud an ecumenical dimension.

The Bubonic Plague - The Shroud as a Palladium:

In recent research, I have speculated that the cause of bringing the image out from hiding may have been due to the fact that the Empire was devastated with the Bubonic Plague which came out of Africa. In 535 A.D. there was a severe plague that caused many to scramble for food. It is likely that the Persians was seeking food and supplies and attacked Edessa. The Image was likely kept under close watch of the Bishops and not well known to the populace. It is possible that the Image was brought out of hiding as a "palladium" - a protection and consolation for the people. Pallus Athaena was a Greek goddess whose statue would be brought out during times of plague, famine or war to protect Greek cities.

THE THREE CLOTHS OF CHRIST by John C. Iannone

The Changing Image of Jesus In Art

Wilson describes at length the impact of this rediscovery or unveiling on the art of the period. Prior to the rediscover, the common images of Jesus in the Roman Empire (with a few rare exceptions that do not resemble the Shroud), were of a young, beardless, Apollo-like man with short hair and no moustache pictured usually in profile. Jesus was most often depicted as a Shepherd, Teacher or Healer. The themes were mostly of the risen, glorified Christ.

After the rediscovery of the Image of Edessa, he notes, Christian art takes a radical turn. Jesus' images in art appear remarkably similar to that of the Shroud of Turin, with Jesus as a bearded man with long hair, moustache, pictured frontally. He notes particularly the front of the Image as a full facial Image. The rediscovery or unveiling and its impact on Eastern and Western art is discussed in a later chapter. Wilson is credited with making the important link between the Image of Edessa, the Mandylion and the Shroud of Turin as being one and the same.

The Ecclesiastical History of Evagrius:

In 590 A.D., Evagrius Scholasticus became Bishop of Edessa. He wrote an Ecclesiastical History wherein he recalls the Legend of Abgar and states that Edessa was protected by an Icon, a divinely wrought portrait:

> "They bring the divinely wrought image which hands did not form, but which Christ our Lord sent to Abgar on his desiring to see Him."

The Image, now recognized as a "divinely wrought image," was kept in the Cathedral of Hagia Sophia in Edessa and remained there until the year 944 A.D. During the Moslem invasion, the Hagia Sophia became a mosque.

Over the next few centuries prior to the movement of the Image to Constantinople, we find a number of other isolated tests that provide further clues to the Shroud's existence and presence in Edessa.

Braulio, Bishop of Saragossa (Spain):

In 635-651, Braulio in his *Epistle 42* says:

THE THREE CLOTHS OF CHRIST by John C. Iannone

> "It is possible that many things happened then which have not been written down, just as we read of the linen cloths and the Shroud in which the body of Christ was wrapped, that they were found, yet we do not hear that they were preserved; still I do not suppose that the Apostles neglected to save these."

During the 8th and 9th centuries, the Image of Edessa was often cited as an authoritative example in defense of the use of sacred images in church against the Iconoclasts by such notables as Andrew of Crete, St. John Damascene, Pope Gregory II, Patriarchs Germanus I (both of whom are involved with the Veil of Veronica as we will discuss later) and Nicephorus, John of Jerusalem, James of Antioch and Basil of Jerusalem.

The *Himation* of St. John Damascene:

In 730, St. John Damascene, a Syrian Christian, in his work *On Holy Images* says:

> "A tradition has come down to us that Abgar, King of Edessa, was drawn vehemently to divine love by hearing of our Lord and that he sent envoys to ask for His likeness. If this were refused, they were ordered to have a likeness painted. Then He, who is All-knowing and All-powerful, is said to have taken a strip of cloth and left His likeness upon the cloth which it retains to this day."

We call attention to the strip of cloth (*himation* in Greek). The Greek scholar Henry George Liddell in his *Greek-English Lexicon* defines a himation as:

> "a piece of dress; in usage always as an outer garment, formed by an oblong piece of cloth."

Further on he relates it to a "Roman toga" and grave cloths. His definition suggests a large piece of linen (sindon) like the Shroud.

Pope Stephen III:

In 769, in his *Good Friday Sermon*, Pope Stephen III says:

> "He stretched His whole body on a cloth, white as snow, on which the glorious image of the Lord's face and the length of His whole body was so divinely

THE THREE CLOTHS OF CHRIST by John C. Iannone

transformed that it was sufficient for those who could not see the Lord bodily in the flesh to see the transfiguration made on the cloth."

Historian Ian Wilson, who brought this quote to light from Ernst von Dobschutz' monumental work *Christusbilder*, goes on to say that:

"The Byzantines...devised a super-Mass for special private showings, in which the figure of Christ was made to rise in a series of stages from the casket, each stage being regarded as a symbolic part of Jesus' earthly life...at the first hour of the day as a child, at the third hour as a boy, at the sixth hour as an adolescent, and at the ninth hour in his full manhood, in which form the Son of God went to his Passion when he bore for our sins the suffering of the Cross."

Implied here is a *full-length cloth with a full length image* being raised (lifted out of a casing) to show the full image.

The Latin Abgar Legend:

In 800 A.D., the *Latin Abgar Legend* translated by Ernst von Dobschutz in *Christusbilder* quotes Jesus as saying:

"But if you wish to see my face in the flesh, behold I send to you a linen, on which you will discover not only the features of my face, but a divinely copied configuration of my entire body."

Also:

"He...spread out His entire body on a linen cloth that was white as snow. On this cloth...the majestic form of His whole body was divinely transferred."

Again, reference is made to a full-length image presumably on a full-length cloth made of linen. The facial image of the Image of Edessa (also known as the Mandylion, or Little Towel) was likely opened up to reveal the entire body image on a linen cloth.

The Second Council of Nicea (787 A.D.):

In 787 A.D. the Second Council of Nicea, ruling in favor of

THE THREE CLOTHS OF CHRIST by John C. Iannone

the veneration of icons, mentions the Image of Edessa,

> "the one 'not made by human hands' that was sent to Abgar."

The Council went on to say that:

> "one can and one must be free to use images of our Lord and God, in mosaics, paintings, etc."

and that:

> "the icon must be an image that bears a very close resemblance to its prototype,"

(presumably the Image of Edessa).

The Image Moves To Constantinople: *Narration on the Image of Edessa*

Constantinople was the seat of the Byzantine Empire and the Greek Church for over 1,000 years until the Ottoman Turks captured it and renamed it Istanbul in the middle of the fifteenth century. Constantinople had been built by the Emperor Constantine the Great around 325 and became the eastern seat of the Roman Empire, an impressive city envied by the Western world. The Emperor ruled from the Bucholeon Palace. Many of the relics of the Crucifixion were believed kept there, including such things as the cap of thorns and pieces of the Holy Cross. For centuries, the Emperors wanted to bring the Image of Edessa from the City of Edessa to Constantinople and capture it from the Moslems who now ruled in Edessa and had control of the Shroud.

Dr. Max Frei relates that he found pollen (in 1978) on the Shroud from the area around Constantinople/Istanbul and this confirmed information we learn from Byzantine texts about the movement to Constantinople of the Image of Edessa and its identification with the Shroud. On August 15, 944 the Byzantine army moved the Image of Edessa with great fanfare from Edessa to Constantinople, ransoming the Shroud from the Moslems for silver. A manuscript called *Narration on the Image of Edessa* (10th Century) describes in some detail how an "image not made by man (acheiropoietos) of Christ our God was transferred to Constantinople."

It has:

THE THREE CLOTHS OF CHRIST by John C. Iannone

"An impression of God's assumed human form by a moist secretion without coloring or painter's art. An impression of the face was made on the linen cloth."

(The colors of the Shroud have often been described in this fashion).

The Great Bucholeon Palace:

The Bucholeon Palace, also called the Great Palace, was a magnificent place, virtually a small city within Constantinople begun by the Emperor Constantine the Great when he moved the center of the Roman Empire from Rome to Constantinople in the period shortly after 325 A.D. The Byzantine Emperors ruled the Eastern Empire from the Great Palace, a sumptuous complex on the water overlooking the Straits called the Golden Horn.

The fourth century historian and biographer of Constantine, Eusebius, in his *Ecclesiastical History*, Book IV, 17 enumerated seven structures of the Bucholeon Palace which Constantine built. The Palace was later enlarged by Justinian I in 527-565 and was further built up by Justin II between 565-578. In 750 Constantine V Copronymos added the Pharos Chapel which was completed by Michael III around 865.

The Pharos Chapel:

The Pharos Chapel was a sumptuous chapel located within the Bucholeon Palace where the tenth century writers tell us the Image of Edessa was kept after being brought from Edessa to Constantinople. The term "Pharos" in ancient Greek referred to a "large piece of cloth...wide cloak or mantle without sleeves...used as a shroud or pall."

Henry George Liddell, in his classic *Greek English Lexicon* of 1887 points out that the word is used in this way in Homer's *Iliad*. The naming of the Chapel after the burial cloth of Jesus would seem to indicate knowledge by the Emperor's people of the full length of the Shroud. The Image of Edessa was a facial image on the cloth doubled-in-four. The Byzantine Greeks were steeped in the traditions of classical Greece and would have been familiar with Homer's use of this term.

THE THREE CLOTHS OF CHRIST   by   John C. Iannone

Sermon of Gregory the Archdeacon 944 A.D

Atlanta Sindonologist, the late Rev. Albert Dreisbach pointed out that Gregory the Archdeacon of the Hagia Sophia mentioned in a sermon of August 16, 944 the:

> "blood and water from the side wound of the cloth."
>
>> (Reference MS. Vatican Graec. 511 folio 149
>>
>> Verso trans. by Professor Gino Zanninotto).

Clearly, Gregory understood that this Image of Edessa was in fact a full-length Shroud containing the image of the Crucifixion. Some considered that the Mandylion - or little towel - was just that: only a facial image. However, as noted before, the Mandylion was the Shroud doubled-in-four or the tetradiplon, showing only the facial image.

Byzantine Emperor Romanus Lacapenus:

In the 10th Century we find a diptych showing the Byzantine Emperor Lacapenus holding the cloth showing the face. In the depiction it is called the *Mandylion*. However, the diptych also shows several Prelates next to him holding a long cloth unfolded with the facial image in the hands of the Emperor. During that same period the Emperor and his two sons along with Constantine (the new Emperor) had a private showing of the new relic by candlelight. Constantine stated:

> "As for the cause of the image, it is rather a moist secretion without colors or the art of a painting."

Those who have directly viewed the Holy Shroud, myself included, point out that this matches their impressions. The image seems to disappear as one gets closer to the cloth.

The Mandylion - The Little Towel:

As pointed out, the Mandylion is a term for the folded Shroud. The term Mandylion appears first in the biography of the ascetic Paul of Mt. Latros around 990 A.D.

"Paul, without ever leaving Mt. Latros was granted a miraculous vision of the 'Icon of Christ' not-made-by-hands

THE THREE CLOTHS OF CHRIST by John C. Iannone

> which is commonly called the 'Holy Mandylion.'"
>
> Robert Drews, *In Search of the Shroud of Turin*

Ian Wilson in *The Mysterious Shroud*, pp. 111-114 provides a list linking the Image of Edessa with the Holy Shroud and Mandylion:

1. The Mandylion is referred to as the acheiropoietos, or image not-made-by-hands.

2. The image appears on a linen cloth.

3. Those who view it think it was formed by a 'moist secretion.'

4. It is dim and difficult to perceive.

5. It contains bloodstains.

6. Its color is off-white or ivory.

7. It is mounted and framed on a board embellished with gold. (Note: the paintings show a trellis-like casing).

> "The shape of the Mandylion is a horizontal rectangle of the face versus the normal artist's upright vertical rectangle normal for a portrait. The encasement is like a slipcover of a jacket embroidered with a trellis or net pattern in gold thread...fringe racked to a board. We know that the Shroud image was folded and tightly packed against a board. It is referred to as a tetradiplon (doubled-in-four)."

In summary, the Holy Shroud is the Image of Edessa, and the Mandylion. It is referred to as the Mandylion - or "little towel" - the Shroud doubled-in four for manageability, framing and transport. It is an "acheiropoietos" and a "himation" or long cloth.

Such information provides historical evidence of the existence of the Holy Shroud which moved from Jerusalem (between 33-50 A.D.) to Edessa; then to Constantinople (944 A.D. to 1204 A.D.) clearly identifying the Shroud to have existed well before the Carbon-14 dating of 1260-1390 discussed in another place in this book.

THE THREE CLOTHS OF CHRIST   by   John C. Iannone

THE THREE CLOTHS OF CHRIST by John C. Iannone

Chapter Nine

THE JOURNEY CONTINUES:
THE SECOND THOUSAND YEARS

There exists "a cloth on which the image not only of my face but of my whole body has been divinely transformed."

Roman Codex 1130 A.D.

Where did the Shroud go from its presence in Constantinople in 944 A.D. to the current time?

Emergence of the Lamentation Scenes:

In the year 944 A.D. the Image of Edessa, now identified as the Shroud, was transported to Constantinople and located in the beautiful Chapel of the Pharos - a part of the Bucholeon Palace occupied by the Emperors. The long-sought prize for the Byzantine Emperor and Eastern Church was rescued from the Moslems in Edessa by the Byzantine army and brought to the Emperor.

Lamentation Scenes (Threnos):

Knowledge of the Shroud's existence and whereabouts began to spread to the West. In the eleventh century we note the appearance of the *Lamentation Scenes* (called *Threnos*). The late art historian Kurt Weitzmann tells us that in both the East and West scenes emerge in art in which the body of Christ is lying in front of the Cross as the central figure. Ian Wilson notes that, common to all these lamentation scenes is a long white cloth:

> "obviously intended to envelop the body over the head, a cloth we would unhesitatingly identify as a Shroud."

THE THREE CLOTHS OF CHRIST by John C. Iannone

Shroud Historian Professor Daniel Scavone (Indiana University) points out the new artistic theme of Jesus dead with hands folded as on the Shroud of Turin, lying upon a large white burial sheet.

Western References:

In 1080 Alexis I Comnenus Emperor of Constantinople sought the aid of the Western Emperor Henry IV and Robert of Flanders in defending the relics which were kept in Constantinople, especially "*the cloth found in the sepulcher after the resurrection*." This marks the beginning of the Crusades - the Western attempt to protect the Holy Land and the Christian relics.

In the *Roman Codex* No. 5696 of 1130 A.D. we read of

> "*a cloth on which the image not only of my face but of my whole body has been divinely transformed.*"

In 1142, Orderic Vitalis, an English monk, wrote in his Ecclesiastical History that:

> "Abgar, Toparch of Edessa, reigned there, to whom the Lord Jesus sent a sacred letter and the precious napkin with which He had wiped the sweat from His face and on which the image of our Savior Himself is miraculously preserved, which shows the lineaments and proportions of the divine body to the beholders."

This phrase suggests a full length cloth with image.

In 1147, King Louis VII of France venerated the Shroud in Constantinople and in 1157 Nicholas Soemundarson, an Icelandic Abbot, listing the relics of Constantinople, talks of both linen bands with the "sweat cloth" (*sveitakuk*) and a *maetull*, which scholars identified as the Mandylion (or little towel).

King Amalric I Visits Constantinople:

The noted medieval historian William of Tyre relates an incident in which King Amalric during the period of the Crusades paid a visit to the Emperor Manuel I Comnenus of Constantinople in 1171. At that time, the Eastern half of the Byzantine Empire was under threat from the Moslems who already occupied the Holy Land and Jerusalem since 638 A.D.

THE THREE CLOTHS OF CHRIST by John C. Iannone

The Western Church initiated the Crusades to drive the Moslems from the Holy Land.

Amalric, a French nobleman, was named King of Jerusalem during this early period. The Byzantine Emperor saw the political advantage of remaining close to the Crusaders for protection of the Empire's eastern borders from the Saracen invaders. He offered the hand of his daughter in marriage to King Amalric who then visited the Emperor in Constantinople. The writers of the period tell us that the King and his entourage were received with great pomp and circumstance.

Enter the Knights Templar:

King Amalric was accompanied by Philip de Milly (Grand Master of the Knights Templar) and others. More will be discussed shortly about this journey with Philip de Milly and the impact of this visit on future events relating to the Shroud's disappearance from Constantinople. The King and his entourage stayed at the sumptuous Bucholeon Palace and visited the Pharos Chapel. The Emperor, in a rare move, ordered all relics of saints to be exposed as well as the:

> "most precious evidence of the Passion of Our Lord, namely the Cross, Nails, Lance, Sponge, Reed, Crown of Thorns, *Sindon* (that is, the cloth in which He was wrapped) and the Sandals."
>
> William of Tyre Historia Belli Sacri, XX, 25 Migne's Latin Patrology Vol. 201.

This is the first time, to our knowledge, that dignitaries of the West were introduced directly to the Shroud and the many treasures of the Eastern Church. It is possible, and even probable, that this visit triggered the sequence of events among Western plotters that led eventually to the diversion of the Fourth Crusade in 1204 to Constantinople – a temporary occupation of Constantinople (the Crusaders wintered there in 1204) which permitted Western Crusaders to barbarously attack and plunder the treasure of the Eastern Church and remove the Shroud to the West. Philip de Milly as Grand Master of the Knights Templar may have been instrumental in the initiation of this plot. The Knights were involved in the Fourth Crusade. This is one of the tragedies of Christian history - the attack by a Christian army on the jewel of Constantinople with a thousand years

THE THREE CLOTHS OF CHRIST by John C. Iannone

of Christian history.

The Quest for the Holy Grail:

Genealogist and Shroud/Grail historian Noel Currer Briggs (*The Shroud and The Grail*, 1987) makes the intriguing case that the introduction of Western dignitaries to the relics of the East during the visit of King Amalric I marked the beginning of the Holy Grail legends. Currer-Briggs speculates that William of Tyre, the historian documenting the visit, told Walter Map at the Lateran Council in 1179 A.D., who in turn brought the story back to France. In 1180, Chretian de Troyes wrote his famous *Perceval: The Story of the Holy Grail (Conte del Graal)* at the request of Philip of Alsace, Count of Flanders and relative of King Amalric I.

This is the first mention of the Grail in Western literature. Currer-Briggs points out that the original Grail stories considered the Grail to be *a receptacle for the Shroud*. Somehow, the Grail contained the precious blood of Jesus as the story evolved and changed over the years, this receptacle became identified as a *chalice* containing the precious blood. However, the earliest legends show that it was not a chalice, but rather the *Shroud that contained the blood, the Grail being a receptacle for the Shroud*.

There appears to be a telltale link between the early Holy Grail legends and the appearance of the Shroud in Athens and in Europe after 1204 A.D. In 1204, Helinand, the Abbot of Froidmont, a Cistercian Abbey north of Paris wrote of:

> "the stories of the most holy vessel called the Grail into which the precious blood of the Savior was received on the day He was crucified to save mankind from hell."

Currer-Briggs relates that the Abbot used the word *gradalis* for Grail (a shallow dish) and *scutella lata* (dish, saucer, flat or broad bowl) referring to the receptacle in which the Shroud, containing the blood of Jesus, was placed for safe keeping and veneration.

The Sacristan of the Pharos Chapel:

In 1201, Nicholas Mesarites, the Sacristan and Keeper of the Relics from the Pharos Chapel wrote:

THE THREE CLOTHS OF CHRIST by John C. Iannone

> "Here He rises again, and the *sindon* with the burial linens is the clear proof...they are of linen...still smelling fragrant of perfumes, defying corruption because they wrapped the mysterious naked, dead body from head to feet."

Here again is a full-length cloth mentioned in 1201 and attention is drawn to the fact that the body was naked.

The Fourth Crusade and the Fall of Constantinople:

One of the most ignominious episodes in Christian history, East or West, involves the attack on Constantinople by the Fourth Crusade in 1204 A.D. Constantinople was the jewel of the Eastern world and home of the Eastern Byzantine Church. The Great Schism divided the Eastern Church from the Western Church and Rome. The Byzantine Emperors had collected over the centuries many relics, allegedly authentic, including the Holy Shroud and brought them to this great city.

Constantinople was replete with churches, including the famed Hagia Sophia and the Bucholeon Palace with the Pharos Chapel as well as the Palace of the Blachernae. The Western Church, after King Amalric's visit in 1171 with Philip de Milly, Grand Master of the Knights Templar, became acutely aware (and envious) of the many treasures contained in this great city. Perhaps jealous of its wealth and might, they looked for an opportunity to plunder Constantinople of its great resources, including the relics of the Passion. This opportunity came in 1204 A.D.

France and Venice - A Treacherous Alliance is Formed:

Several Chroniclers of the period, including Robert de Clary and Geoffrey de Villehardouin from the West and Nicetas Cholates of the East related the tragic events of this period. The Fourth Crusade was organized in Europe under the guidance of Pope Innocent III and Philip II, King of France to go to the Holy Land. Their mission was to defend Western pilgrims and drive back the Moslems from Jerusalem. The reward, as Villehardouin relates, was an indulgence:

> "All those who take the Cross and remain for one year in the service of God in the army shall obtain remission of any sins they have committed, provided

THE THREE CLOTHS OF CHRIST by John C. Iannone

> they have confessed them. The hearts of the people were greatly moved by the generous terms of this indulgence and many on that account were moved to take the Cross."
>
> Villehardouin and Joinville: *The Chronicles of the Crusades, 1963)*

The Crusade leaders worked closely with the Venetians and reached a treaty in 1202 with Enrico Dandolo, the Doge of Venice, to build a fleet of vessels - warships and troop transports - capable of carrying the army, including knights and their horses, to Palestine. It was a monumental task. The Doge told the French emissaries:

> "We will build transports to carry 4,500 horses and 9,000 Squires and other ships to accommodate 4,500 Knights and 20,000 Foot Sergeants."

Also included were nine months of rations and fodder for all the horses. Shortly thereafter, the army chose its leader, the Marquis Boniface de Montferrat. Throughout France people prepared for this "pilgrimage." The Venetians did their job and created a great fleet. Villardhouin tells us that:

> "the fleet they had got ready was so fine and well equipped that no man in the whole of Christendom has ever seen on to surpass it. It comprised so great a number of warships, galleys and transports that it could easily have accommodated three times as many men as were in the whole of the army."

The Fourth Crusade Diverts To Constantinople:

For political reasons, the Crusade temporarily diverted to Constantinople. Emperor Isaac in Constantinople had been treacherously overthrown by his brother Alexis. Isaac escaped and went to Venice to meet with Boniface de Montferrat - the Crusade's leader. Isaac made a deal that if he was restored to power in Constantinople he would make available to Boniface and his army the vast resources of the Byzantine army to help in the Crusade to free Jerusalem. Apart from the East's desire to gain assistance in protecting its easternmost border from the Moslems, and the West's desire to gain troops and resources to fight the

THE THREE CLOTHS OF CHRIST   by   John C. Iannone

"infidels" in the Holy Land, there was an underlying motive to help heal the rift created by the Great Schism between the Eastern and Western Churches.

The Crusaders left for Constantinople in what was to be a temporary diversion to restore Isaac to the throne. More sinister motives, however, may have been involved on the part of the leaders of the Crusade. The Crusaders laid siege to Constantinople and ultimately forced Alexis to flee, restoring Isaac to the throne. Constantinople was to pay a terrible price for this temporary occupation.

The Trojan Horse of the Western Crusade entered the gates of Constantinople. Most of these Crusaders were simple peasants and farmers from France and other parts of Europe. This crude army was overwhelmed by the riches and treasures of the cultured Constantinople, unmatched except perhaps by Rome. Villehardouin tells us that:

> "Many of our men... went to visit Constantinople to gaze at its many splendid palaces and tall churches and view all the marvelous wealth of a city richer than any other since the beginning of time. As for the relics, they were beyond all description for there were at that time as many in Constantinople as in all the rest of the world."

Perhaps overcome with greed and desirous of possessing the precious relics of this city to gain favor with their Western leaders, they turned to treachery. Here were relics of the True Cross and the Holy Shroud. The leaders of the Crusade (Boniface de Montferrat, Otto de la Roche - his right hand man - and Henri of Flanders) made the decision to attack and plunder Constantinople. The story of this vicious attack is outlined by the chroniclers. The Crusaders set fire to Constantinople and, beside the great loss of life, destroyed forever many of the priceless treasures of Christendom, including many of the Churches and their priceless works of art as well as valuable manuscripts.

Geoffrey de Villehardouin relates:

> "The rest of the army scattered throughout the City, also gaining much booty: so much, indeed, that no one could estimate its amount or its value. It included gold and silver, table services and precious stones,

THE THREE CLOTHS OF CHRIST by John C. Iannone

> satin and silk, mantles of squirrel fur, ermine and miniver and every choicest thing to be found on the earth...so much booty had never been gained in any city since the creation of the world."

The leaders of the Crusade carefully secured the two great Palaces. Marquis Boniface took the Bucholeon Palace with the Pharos Chapel and Henri of Flanders took the Palace of the Blachernae. The Shroud was in the Bucholeon Palace (Pharos Chapel).

The Shroud Disappears:

Robert de Clary, who was a part of the Fourth Crusade, wrote in his Chronicle: *The Conquest of Constantinople*:

> "...and among others there was another of the Churches which was called My Lady Saint Mary Blachernae where was kept the *syndoine* in which our Lord had been wrapped, which stood up straight every Friday so that the *figure* of our Lord could be plainly seen. No one, either Greek or French ever knew what became of the *syndoine* after the capture of the city."

The *sindoine* was the *sindon* or Shroud. Dr. Peter Dembowski advised that in Old French, the "figure" can be properly translated as "form or outline of the body of our Lord." The Shroud, normally housed in the Pharos Chapel, was taken by procession on Fridays to be displayed in the Church of Saint Mary Blachernae. Robert de Clary tells us that:

> "The Marquis took possession of the Palace of Bucholeon and the Church of Saint Sophia (Hagia Sophia) and the houses of the patriarch. And the other high men, like the Counts, took possession of the richest palaces and richest abbeys to be found there."

He goes on to say that in this great palace with over five hundred halls made of gold mosaics there were some thirty chapels, great and small, one of which was the Pharos Chapel. Within the chapel were two pieces of the True Cross, the iron lance that pierced Jesus' side, two nails, a phial with some of His blood, the tunic which He wore on His way to Calvary, the blessed Crown of Thorns and much more. Clary further related that there was still another relic hanging in a vessel - a cloth. Of the cloth he says that:

THE THREE CLOTHS OF CHRIST   by   John C. Iannone

> "Our Lord enveloped His face with it so that His features were imprinted on it."

Since the true Sudarium (face cloth in the tomb) had no image on it and was likely in Oviedo, Spain (as explained elsewhere in this book) and since the Veil of Veronica had been brought from Constantinople to Rome around 708 A.D. (as also explained elsewhere), this was likely a copy of the face of the Shroud or of the Veil. The *syndoine* disappeared during the Crusade and was likely confiscated by the Marquis Boniface de Montferrat. Where did the Shroud go?

Interim Movement of Shroud to Athens:

It appears that for a very short time, Boniface entrusted the Shroud to Otto de la Roche, his second-in-command. After the assault, Otto de la Roche was rewarded with the rule of Athens and Thessalonica. It is likely that he took the Shroud with him, based on information we read in a Letter to Pope Innocent III written by Theodore Ducas Angelos on August 1, 1205. Referring to the sack of Constantinople, Theodore states that:

> "The Venetians partitioned the treasure of gold, silver and ivory, while the French did the same with the relics of the saints and most sacred of all, the *linen in which our Lord Jesus Christ was wrapped* after His death and before the Resurrection. We know that the sacred objects are preserved by their predators in Venice and France and in other places, *the sacred linen in Athens*." (italics mine).

The Shroud was apparently kept in the Monastery at Daphni near the Parthenon. Three years later in 1207 Nicholas d'Orrante, Abbot of Casole and Papal Legate in Athens, listed the relics of the Passion that were:

> "in the treasury of the great palace before the City (Constantinople) was taken by the French Knight entering as robbers."

Speaking of the funerary cloths, he adds: "which we later saw with our own eyes" in Athens. Somewhere between 1207 and 1357 the whereabouts of the Shroud becomes a mystery. We will jump ahead and consider its reappearance in 1357 in France and then attempt to solve the riddle of the Shroud's

THE THREE CLOTHS OF CHRIST   by   John C. Iannone

whereabouts for the prior 150 years.

Knight Geoffrey II de Charny:

In the year 1357, France was being ravaged by the "Black Death," the Bubonic Plague, which hit Paris in 1350. Geoffrey de Charny displayed a cloth identified as the Shroud at an exposition in a small church in Lirey, France, twelve miles from Troyes and a short distance from Paris. This is the first documented public appearance of the Shroud in the West since the fall of Constantinople and its brief respite in Athens. The Church of Lirey had been founded there three years earlier by his father, Geoffrey I de Charny and his wife Jeanne de Vergy. Geoffrey I, who earned the title Porte Oriflamme, was a famous decorated knight who died in battle three years later fighting alongside King John the Good.

In the year of the exposition we find the famous *Pilgrim's Medallion* of Lirey, a medal minted specifically for the occasion of the exhibition, found in the mud of the Seine River, showing shields with the arms of Geoffrey de Charny and Jeanne de Vergy. His son, Geoffrey II with his daughter Marguerite de Charny - having obtained permission from Pierre de Thury, Cardinal of Sainte-Suzanne and Papal Delegate to King Charles VI of France, but without having obtained permission from the local bishop - displayed the cloth at Lirey to the crowds. He may have brought the Shroud "out of hiding" to give consolation to the people during the tragic Bubonic Plague where people received no answers from their leaders (Church and State) that would bring peace of mind. It was again a "palladium" - a consolation and protection for the people as they witnessed thousands dying during the Black Plague - to see the image of their Lord.

Alleged Memorandum of Bishop d'Arcis:

Thirty two years later in the year 1389 Bishop d'Arcis allegedly wrote a letter to Pope Clement VII claiming that the cloth displayed by Geoffrey II de Charney during the tenure of Bishop Henry of Poitiers, his predictors, was *cunningly painted* and the artist had "*confessed*." This purported Memorandum has been used by some to discredit the cloth of Geoffrey II de Charny as not having been the

THE THREE CLOTHS OF CHRIST   by   John C. Iannone

Shroud.

Scholars who have reviewed the Memorandum, however, point out that the "artist" was never named and that Bishop Henry of Poitiers did not object during the time of the exposition thirty-two years earlier. French sindonologist Brother Bruno Bonnet-Eymard has convincingly demonstrated that the Memorandum was in fact proved to be *an anonymous, unsigned, undated and unsealed paper copy not at all consistent with the official decrees by the Bishop.*

Eymard also point out that the artist was never named and that Pope Clement VII silenced the Bishop, even threatening him with excommunication. The Pope supported Geoffrey's exposition. Author Noel Currer-Briggs notes that the Shroud may have been confused with a painted copy known as the *Besacon shroud.* Geoffrey II de Charny really believed that the cloth he was exhibiting was more than just a painting. He presented the cloth with all the ritual and ceremony of a true relic and was certainly aware that the Shroud had been passed down through his family from 1204 A.D.

Marguerite de Charny:

Marguerite was the daughter of Geoffrey II and inherited the Shroud after his death. In 1443 the Canons of Lirey began to insist that the Shroud be returned to them. Marguerite ignored their demands and sought a more fitting home for the cloth. In the year 1453 she signed a contract with the Duke of Savoy and passed title of the Shroud to the House of Savoy. In return, she received some land estates that would ensure her decent survival in old age. Duke Louis of Savoy represented the House of Savoy which became the ruling family of Italy in the 19th century. Marguerite saw in the Duke and his wife a pious couple and a rising dynasty, wealthy and powerful enough to give security to the Shroud. The cloth remained with the Savoys until 1983 when King Umberto of Italy died and willed the Shroud to the Roman Catholic Church. Pope John Paul II left the Shroud in the care of the Cathedral of Saint John the Baptist in Turin, Italy where it remains today.

The Knights Templar and the Missing 150 years:

The Shroud, as was pointed out, disappeared from Constantinople in 1204 during the Fourth Crusade. Notwithstanding a brief reference to its presence in Athens

THE THREE CLOTHS OF CHRIST by John C. Iannone

between 1204-1207, the Linen basically remained in silence until its emergence in 1357 in Europe (Lirey, France) with Geoffrey II de Charny. What happened to the Shroud during this period? The most prominent theory is that the Shroud was in the possession of the Knights Templar. This conclusion is further supported by an Italian archivist who recently (2009) found further records in the Vatican Library of the Knight's involvement with the Shroud.

The most prominent theory is that the Shroud was in the possession of the Knights Templar. Who were these mysterious Knights and what role did they play in confiscating and protecting the Shroud from 1204 - 1357? The Templars were a military-religions order founded in the Holy Land in 1119 A.D. by Hughes de Payen during the Crusades. They were truly "warrior monks," religious Knights who believed in the medieval Christian ordeal of death in battle. Saint Bernard of Clairvaux, a famous Cistercian monk who founded many Cistercian monasteries throughout Europe during this period, had a strong affiliation with the Knights Templar and even drafted their "Rule" or "Constitution." St. Bernard summed up the Templar's ideal when he said:

> "Rejoice, brave warrior, if you live and conquer in the Lord, but rejoice still more and give thanks if you die or go to join the Lord. This life can be fruitful and victory is glorious yet a holy death for righteousness is worth more. Certainly, 'blessed are they who die *in* the Lord' but how much more so are those who die *for* Him.'"

The Order was formed initially to protect the pilgrims in the Holy Land from attacks by the Moslems. The Knights Templar were European noblemen who vowed poverty, chastity and obedience and who lived a monastic style life in Preceptories - fortresses with a monastic flavor that were at the same time barracks. They were Monks whose mission was to be Knights fighting in the Holy Land. Seward Desmond tells us that:

> "Just as mendicant friars lived a conventional life preaching the Gospel, the brother Knights lived a conventional life defending it...Monasticism had made a sacrament of battle. In the early 1100's there were three such Orders founded: The Hospitalers, The Teutonic Knights and the Knights Templar."

THE THREE CLOTHS OF CHRIST by John C. Iannone

At that time, the land of the Crusades was called Outremer, the West's first colony. The word derived from two French words: Outre Mer (over the sea). It encompassed the Holy Land with the Kingdom of Jerusalem as its center. Outremer was shaped somewhat like an hourglass, extending for nearly five hundred miles from the Gulf of Aqaba on the Red Sea to Edessa in modern Turkey.

The Crusaders and the Templars:

In 1095 A.D., Pope Urban II in Rome first called upon the faithful of Europe to recover Jerusalem from the Saracen armies who had occupied Jerusalem since 638. Shortly thereafter, the first attacks by the Crusaders occurred in 1099. Hugues de Payen was Lord of the Castle of Martigny in Burgundy, France, and may have been a relative of St. Bernard of Clairvaux. Hugues went to Outremer in 1115 and became a protector of pilgrims on the dangerous road from Jaffa to Jerusalem. He persuaded seven Knights from northern France to help him. They all took a solemn oath before him to protect pilgrims. King Baldwin of Jerusalem was impressed and gave them a wing in the royal palace thought to be in the Temple of Solomon in Jerusalem.

The Templars, as warrior Knights, were close to the Cistercian monks who were produced by the same wave of asceticism in Europe. In fact, Bernard of Clairvaux prepared a simple Rule for the Templars who thought of them as "military Cistercians." The Templars even wore a type of religious garb, a habit, white with a plain red crosses. Over the next two hundred years, the Templar Order became exceedingly wealthy and powerful throughout Europe. The Order set up a system of Preceptories - military fortresses throughout Europe - that were used for administering estates donated to the Templars, as well as for training and recruiting depots, arsenals for storing weapons and as homes for elderly brethren.

The Templars became professional bankers and financiers, collecting vast sums of money for the Holy Land efforts. The Knights acquired many European estates and in 1113 Pope Paschal II took them under his special protection. They were an independent army, answerable only to the Pope and the envy of local Church dignitaries and political leaders. Bishops and Kings did not always appreciate the fact that the Knights Templar had this special connection with the Papacy and police powers could not always control the

THE THREE CLOTHS OF CHRIST by John C. Iannone

Templar activities - a factor that many believe led to the plot to destroy the Order.

The Shroud and the Templars:

Against this background the theory emerges that during the period when the Shroud disappeared in 1204-1207 to its reappearance in Europe, *the Knights had possession of the Shroud in conjunction with several powerful French families*. While the evidence is circumstantial, it is quite strong and creates a credible link between Constantinople in 1204 and Lirey, France in 1357.

Philip de Milly, Grand Master of the Knights Templar - as noted earlier - accompanied King Amalric I of Jerusalem to Constantinople in 1171 A.D. The Knights were not privy to the whereabouts of the Shroud and were likely envious to possess the sacred cloth and please their European leaders including the Pope. Some thirty-three years later (in 1204) the Templars were "prominent, if not dominant, in the Fourth Crusade"

As Frank Tribbe noted:

> "in the weeks preceding the breaching of the city's walls they had been unwelcome guests roaming the city. They would have been very aware of the Shroud seen by Robert de Clary on display and would not have forgotten the stories told by their Grand Master Philip de Milly earlier about his visit to this precious Chapel of the Pharos."

Boniface and Mary Margaret:

During the assault, the leader of the Fourth Crusade, Marquis Boniface de Montferrat, took personal charge of the attack on the Bucholeon Palace and Pharos Chapel. Shortly thereafter it shows up in Athens under his right hand man Otto De Le Roche. During the attack, Boniface took charge of the Imperial Palace and here met the just widowed Mary Margaret, a Hungarian Empress who, as a child of ten, had been married to Emperor Isaac II Angelus of Constantinople. Boniface married Margaret and shortly thereafter moved to Thessalonica in Greece. Perhaps here Otto gave the Shroud back to Boniface.

Mary Margaret founded a Church of the Acheiropoietos (not-made-by-human-hands) known today as the *Eski Coma Cami*, or

THE THREE CLOTHS OF CHRIST by John C. Iannone

Ancient Friday Church. This seems to be more than coincidental, although several churches bore this name. Also, one of the finest of all known *epitaphoi* (embroidered cloths relating to the Passion and Death) originated in Thessalonica. In 1207 Boniface died and Mary Margaret married Nicholas de Saint-Omer. They had a son who became a Knight Templar. Wilson speculates that the Shroud was deposited with the Knights Templar for their making a loan to Baldwin.

Knights With Red Crosses:

Noel Currer-Briggs points out that in the famous Holy Grail legend Perlesvaus, written between 1206-1212 possibly by a Templar:

> "The Hermits who guard the Grail are also Knights who wear red crossed on their surcoats like the Knights of the Order of Templars."

The German legend of the Grail, *Parzival*, written between 1205-1208 by Wolfram Von Eschenbach mentions that the:

> "Formidable fighting men dwell at Munsalvaesche with the Grail."

While the identity of Munsalvaesche (which literally means "safe mountain') has been a matter of speculation, the "formidable fighting men" supports the theory that the Knights Templar, warrior monks who wore red crosses on their surcoats, were in possession of the Shroud and further strengthens the relationship between the Holy Grail and the Shroud.

The Trial of the Templars:

The Templars became a very powerful and secretive Order. King Philip IV of France was particularly resentful of the Knights and also envious of their great wealth which the King needed. On October 13, 1307 he ordered a well-executed raid on the Templar leaders in France, putting them on trial on various, often fabricated, charges. One charge in particular relates to our story namely idol worship. The King's men accused the Templars of "idol worship carried on in secret receptions and chapter meetings of the Order." Trials were held by the King supported by Pope Clement V. We can speculate that Philip IV was keenly aware of the fact that the Templars were in possession of the Shroud in

THE THREE CLOTHS OF CHRIST by John C. Iannone

their Preceptory in France, of which Geoffrey de Charny was in charge.

The king may have hoped to capture the Shroud in the secret raid while incarcerating the Templar leaders. His charge of "idol worship" seems to support that he was aware of some object in the possession of the Templars. The King demanded an inventory of all Templar wealth, but could not find the Shroud listed among their possessions. The Templars were careful to protect the Shroud, their most prized possession, from the greedy King.

Many members of the Order were tortured and forced to confess to a variety of alleged crimes. The lands of the Templars were seized. Among the leaders captured were Jacques de Molay, the twenty-second and last Grand Master, and Geoffrey de Charny, Preceptor of Normandy. In 1314 these two leaders were burned at the stake. Ian Wilson suggests that Geoffrey de Charny was the ancestor of Geoffrey I de Charny (Porte Oriflamme) and that this original Geoffrey, as Preceptor of Normandy, had possession of the Shroud which he stowed in the family castle for forty-one years until his successor, and possible grandson, Geoffrey II de Charny moved it to the Church of Lirey and publicly exhibited it in 1357. Interestingly Geoffrey de Charny told his inquisitors that he had been received into the Order forty-two years earlier (in 1265) by none other than Amaury de la Roche, Master in France. Amaury de la Roche may well have been a relative of Otto de la Roche who took the Shroud to Athens in trust for Boniface.

Templars Charged with Idol Worship:

The charge of "idol worship" involved the Templar's secret worship of:

> "a 'bearded head' which one of the leaders, Purred, admitted was made of wood. The brothers were accused of worshipping this head at secret Chapters. During the efforts to defend the Order, one of its members, Jean de Montreal, presented a document in which he spoke of the Order's foundation; its great efforts to fight the Saracens; its carrying of the Cross and the Thorns of the Crown of the Savior and the fact that they had been able to acquire a great collection of relics."

THE THREE CLOTHS OF CHRIST by John C. Iannone

Another Templar, Jean Taylafer de Gene, told his inquisitors that:

> "On the day of his reception 'a certain head' had been placed on the altar of the chapel and he was told to adore it...it appeared to be an effigy of a human face, red in color and as large as a human head."

The Templecombe Image:

What could this wooden, bearded effigy of a human head have been and how may it have been related to the Shroud? The answer to this may well have been found in modern times in the village of Templecombe in Somerset, England, and a site that was the former Preceptory of the Knights Templar in England. In 1945 a painting of the head of Christ on a wooden panel was discovered. It is strikingly similar to the face of the Shroud.

Australian sindonologist Rex Morgan indicates that the presence of a keyhole and hinge marks on the wooden panel suggest it was the lid to a chest that once likely held the actual Shroud - somewhat like the Grail. The Templars, then disbanded in France, likely took the Shroud to England in this chest where Geoffrey I de Charny acquired the shroud in 1350 when taken prisoner by the English.

The Templecombe image as a repository of the Shroud could well contain on its lid the picture of the wooden, "bearded image" worshipped by the Templars. There may have been an actual wooden image of the head or a series of wooden heads reproducing the face of the Shroud which circulated within the Templar communities to remind them that the Order possessed the Holy Shroud. After the trials of the Templars were completed, the Order was disbanded. However, the Shroud re-emerged almost forty-one years later in the possession of Geoffrey II de Charny in Lirey, France.

The Genealogical Link - the Shroud "Mafia"

All three Geoffrey's de Charney and other families associated with the Shroud appear to have been closely associated with, or members of, the Knights Templar. Rex Morgan contends that the Knights could have collaborated with powerful French families to conceal the Shroud. This is supported by Noel Currer-Briggs who presents intriguing information. Tracking the genealogical chart of Boniface de

THE THREE CLOTHS OF CHRIST by John C. Iannone

Montferrat (leader of the Fourth Crusade) and his wife Mary Margaret, he demonstrated that the family of Louis, Duke of Savoy and his wife Anne de Lisugnam-Chypre, were related to Boniface. It is hardly coincidental that there was a relationship between Boniface and the family that inherited the Shroud from Marguerite de Charny some 250 years later.

Somehow, the Shroud remained the closely guarded secret of these French families, primarily families from the regions of Burgundy and Champagne. These families, linked to the Knights Templar, utilized the Knights Templar with their wealth and power, to confiscate and protect the sacred cloth until the Templar dispersion after the trials in the early 1300's. The Shroud then moved under the protection of the powerful and rising House of Savoy.

These families, principally the Vergys, the Joinvilles, the Briennes and the family of Mont St. Jean included the deCharny family. Currer-Briggs relates the genealogy of Otto de la Roche, Boniface's right-hand man to Humbert de la Roche - Saint Hippolyte, and to Marguerite de Charney, his wife. These French families, whom Currer-Briggs calls the "Shroud Mafia" guarded a powerful secret over the years. But what is the link with the Knights Templar?

Linking the French Families to the Templars:

Authors Lynn Picknett and Clive Prince have provided additional evidence to show that these same families had links to the foundation of the Knights Templar in 1118. These authors point out that the members of Currer-Briggs "Shroud Mafia" were involved in secret dealings surrounding the formation of the Knights Templars. They state:

> "It also struck us as significant that the families involved in the origins of the Templars should have been involved in the equally mysterious events surrounding their end."

There was an intertwining of families and they go on to say that:

> "Guillaume de Champlitte, the part of the 'clique' surrounding Boniface of Montferrat during the Fourth Crusades - married into the Mont St. Jean - de Charny family."

Currer-Briggs pointed out that the "Shroud Mafia" was "all

THE THREE CLOTHS OF CHRIST by John C. Iannone

families descended from or linked with Fulk of Anjou" who died in 1143. Fulk became King of Jerusalem in 1131 and through intermarriage of his grandchildren eventually brought the title of Jerusalem to the House of Savoy. While I part company with Picknett and Prince in their efforts to prove that Leonardo Da Vinci created the Shroud, I agree that there were family links between the founding of the Templars in 1118, the visit of the Templar leader Philip de Milly with King Amalric I to Constantinople in 1171, the viewing of the Shroud and the plot involving the Templars to capture the Shroud in 1204 and transport it in secret to Europe.

The links were in the powerful French families orchestrating events, families involved in founding of the Knights Templar; the engineering of the Fourth Crusade and the confiscation/protection of the Shroud until it emerged in the public exposition at the Church of Lirey by Geoffrey II in 1357. The family was descended from Hugues, count of Champagne, the prime mover in the establishment of the Templars. The Templars and the French families had the motive (desire to possess the Shroud and enhance their power and stature in Europe); the method (military force of the Crusaders and Templars) and the opportunity (occupation of Constantinople during the Fourth Crusade at the invitation of the dethroned Emperor Isaac) to hatch and execute their plan to remove the Shroud from Constantinople.

Modern History of the Shroud:

The history of the Shroud after 1453 is well documented. In 1471 Pope Sixtus IV in his monograph *The Blood of Christ* states that:

> "The Shroud in which the body of Christ was wrapped....is now preserved with great devotion by the Dukes of Savoy and it is colored with the blood of Christ."

Shortly thereafter, in 1502, it was deposited in the Chapel of Chambery Castle in France and in 1506 Pope Julius II approved a special Mass and Office, allowing the public veneration of the Shroud.

The Great Fire of 1532:

THE THREE CLOTHS OF CHRIST by John C. Iannone

On the eve of December 4, 1532, a fire was accidentally set, most likely by a candle in the Sacristy of the Chapel of Chambery. The fire was quite intense, engulfing part of the castle and chapel. Philip Lambert, the counselor to the Duke of Savoy, along with two Franciscan priests rushed into the chapel, broke through the grille protecting the Shroud and carried the Shroud in its silver casket to safety. The intensity of the fire, some 900-960 degrees centigrade was so great that the fire melted part of the silver Reliquary in which the Shroud was kept. The melted silver helped scientist determine the intensity of the fire. The fire created burn holes and left a drop of silver embedded in the cloth. This was discovered by the STURP team in 1978.

The intense heat caused scorch marks along the longitudinal folds readily apparent on both sides of the body today. The Shroud was spared and during its rescue was stained by water. The water-marks of the fire are visible on the Shroud today. Very visible are the blood stains, the scorch marks, water stains, patches (removed recently in 2002) and burn holes. The Poor Clare Nuns patched and darned areas of the Shroud.

Many scholars today believe that the intensity of the heat of the fire in 1532 and the carbon produced by the fire chemically altered the linen and had an impact on distorting the accuracy of the Carbon-14 testing in 1988 by adding carbon atoms to the Shroud, thereby giving it a "younger" C-14 appearance. However, newer evidence better explains the error of the dating. C-14 scientists seem to agree that such "rejuvenation" by carbon of the fire of 1532 would have a minimal effect on throwing off the date and there are better explanations.

Fire of 1997: Accident or Arson?

Readers may recall another fire (April 11, 1997) involving the Holy Shroud. The New York Times (Sunday, April 13, 1997, p.4) reported that an electrical short circuit caused a fire in the Cathedral which was heavily damaged. Firefighters rescued the Shroud without damage to the fabric. Firefighter Mario Trematore used a hammer, and even resorted to his bare fists, to break through four layers of bullet proof glass protecting the reliquary while other Firefighters poured water on the vessel to keep it cool. It took almost 200 firefighters to extinguish the blaze to the

THE THREE CLOTHS OF CHRIST   by   John C. Iannone

cheers of thousands who gathered outside praying for their City's treasure.

Turin police indicated that the cause appeared to be a short circuit and did not believe at first that sabotage was involved, but were continuing investigation. Other reports suggested more sinister motives. The state-run Italian television network reported that the fire apparently started in the Cathedral's 314 year-old wooden dome which was scaffolded for restoration.

Archbishop Saldarini stated that the cloth was intact and that church authorities would go ahead with a rare public viewing in 1998. It should be noted that not all Italian writers agree that this was an accident but rather believe that it was arson based on some discrepancies in the stories of what happened. For a fuller explanation of the theories of conspiracy, readers may go to my new book *The Image and The Rose: Behind Vatican Walls*, 2002. See www.Amazon.com or www.Lulu.com or go to my website www.northstarproductions.org and visit the on-line store on the website.

Further History:

In 1535, to get it out of harm's way during a war, the Shroud was sent to Nice and, thereafter, to Vercelli where it remained until 1561 when it was returned to Chambery. In 1578, the Shroud was moved to the Cathedral of St. John the Baptist in Turin where it has remained ever since. It was venerated by notables of the day, including St. Charles Borromeo. In 1613 St. Francis de Sales held the cloth before the people at a rare exposition. In 1694 the Shroud was placed in the Royal Chapel in Turin designed by Guarini on an altar designed by Antonio Bertola.

It was given a new red silk back lining cloth. Over the following years there have been several limited expositions, the latest being in 1978, 1998, and 2000 (for the 2,000 anniversary of the Church). Pope Benedict XVI has chosen to put the Shroud on public exhibit from April 10 - May 22, 2010 likely due to the new findings supporting authenticity and challenging the Carbon-14 testing of 1988.

Public Exposition:

In the past, Church authorities were hesitant to expose the

THE THREE CLOTHS OF CHRIST   by   John C. Iannone

Shroud to the environment because of potential damage. Today, however, due to a new manner of exposing the Shroud since 2002, the cloth is kept behind bullet-proof glass; is air-conditioned to approx. 68 degrees Fahrenheit; is kept in an inert argon/nitrogen compound and it is laid flat to avoid wrinkling and the migration of blood-particles from folding and unfolding or rolling on a wooden roller as was done previously. Turin is an industrial city - home of Fiat Cars - and, as such, has an environment now recognized by the Church and scientists as damaging to the linen.

The patches have now been removed in 2002. There is always the concern for random or planned acts of terrorism. Turin Shroud authorities are constantly admonished to seek better protection of Christianity's greatest treasure. The current Papal Custodian, Cardinal Savarino Poletto, and the previous Custodian Cardinal Giovanni Saldarini, have taken steps for the protection of the cloth. Pope Benedict XVI is placing the Holy Shroud on rare public exhibit in 2010.

****

THE THREE CLOTHS OF CHRIST by John C. Iannone

Chapter Ten
ART AND THE SHROUD

"While the technology of our own age has mastered outer space exploration, we are still at a loss to explain the image on the Shroud or make another Turin Shroud. It is not the result of invention."

Artist Isabel Piczek

There is no information in the Gospels and Epistles that can serve as a guide to Jesus' physical or earthly appearance. We have no written description by His followers that tells us if the image we now see on the Shroud would explain John's sudden realization and acceptance of the Resurrection. Josh McDowell likewise concludes that something about the grave cloths themselves convinced John that Jesus had risen from the dead. It is possible that when Peter and John entered the tomb early that Easter morning, they witnessed the images on the sindon - an actual startling photo-on-linen imprinted by some mysterious process, obviously for some reason, that left them and all future generations a life-size image of their Lord at the moment of His Resurrection.

The Legend of Peter as an Artist:

In the early Church there developed the legend of Peter as an artist. St. Peter eventually left Jerusalem and journeyed to Rome. Rev. Albert Dreisbach of Atlanta established a continuous historical chain of evidence from the early Church affirming Peter's awareness of the images of the Shroud. Werner Bulst suggested that Peter took the Shroud out of the tomb and brought it to Rome where it inspired copies known as Veronicas. This does not appear to be the case. If one accepts the legend of Peter as an artist, it would appear that Peter drew the image precisely because he did NOT have the authentic Shroud with him in Rome. As noted earlier, the Apostle Thomas had authorized

THE THREE CLOTHS OF CHRIST by John C. Iannone

the Shroud's transfer to Edessa via the disciple Thaddaeus.

One legend, for example, tells us that when Peter arrived in Rome he visited the home of Prudens (a Roman Senator) and Claudia, his wife. Their daughters, Saints Prasside and Prudentia, asked Peter to show them what Jesus looked like. Peter, the legend relates, took a handkerchief and drew on it with ink and stylus. Peter's drawing became a pattern. Copies were made on cloth and later used to cover faces of martyrs of the Neronian persecution. Possibly, the handkerchief, its whereabouts having been lost in the annals of history, was also used as a model for paintings of the face of Jesus on the walls of the catacombs. The significance, according to Rev. Albert Dreisbach is that Peter is associated with an image of Jesus reproduced on a cloth.

The Image Disappears:

Earlier we referred to the disappearance of the image from men's minds after the reign of King Abgar. His son initiated a persecution of the Church and, it is believed, the Image was walled-up to hide and protect it from this persecution. As a tenth century document relates, the Bishop of the region is stated as having:

> "lit a lamp in front of the image and placed a tile on top. Then he blocked the approach from the outside with mortar and baked bricks and reduced the wall to a level appearance. Then a long interval of time elapsed and the erection of this sacred image and its concealment both disappeared from men's memories."

Image of Edessa Re-Emerges in the Sixth Century

Early in the sixth century, between 525-544 a very significant event occurred, namely the re-discovery or possibly re-emergence of the cloth hidden away in the walls of Edessa to protect it. The Icon was rediscovered either during the great flood of Edessa in 525 when the walls were being repaired, or later in 544 when the Persian King Chosroes was attacking the city and the Edessans built a tunnel under the wall to undermine the Persian defenses. Likely also because the Bubonic Plague was causing widespread death - the Black Death - the image may have been brought out as a consolation or Palladium for the people around 535 A.D.

THE THREE CLOTHS OF CHRIST   by   John C. Iannone

Impact of The Re-Emergence:

Ian Wilson is credited with making the enlightening association that links the Image of Edessa with the Shroud. We noted earlier that Wilson describes at length the impact of this rediscovery on the art of the period. It bears repeating at this point. Prior to the rediscovery, the common images of Jesus throughout the Roman period, with few exceptions which bare little or no resemblance to the image on the Shroud, were of a *young, beardless, Apollo-like man with short hair and no moustache, pictured usually in profile. Jesus was most often depicted as a Shepherd, Teacher or Healer in art in the Catacombs and elsewhere*. The themes were mostly of the risen, glorified Christ.

After the re-emergence of the Shroud in 1535, Christian art takes a radical turn. Jesus' images in art appear remarkably similar to that of the Shroud of Turin with Jesus now depicted as a *bearded man with long hair and moustache, pictured frontally with a full facial Image*.

An example of this is the fourth century face of Christ from the mosaic pavement found at Hinton St. Mary in Dorset, England and now in the British Museum. Shroud Historian Robert Drews points out that portraits from the third and fourth century show Jesus as *a teacher, miracle worker, shepherd or Christ in triumph*, but do not depict the passion and death of Jesus. He cites six examples, including the Tomb of the Aurelii.

Wilson relates that from this point on (535 A.D), with the re-emergence of the Shroud recovered from the wall of Edessa, a consistent *Shroud-like, long-haired, fork-bearded, front-facing likeness of Christ appears in Christian art*. The front view is striking as opposed to the profile images of most of the depictions of Jesus in earlier Christian art. He noted:

> "the universally recognized source of the true likeness of Jesus in art was an apparently miraculous imprinted image of Jesus on cloth, the so-called Image of Edessa or Mandylion."

The re-emerging Image, sealed for centuries in a niche above the city's gate of Edessa, had become the model for future artists. It was none other than the Image of the Shroud.

THE THREE CLOTHS OF CHRIST by John C. Iannone

Depictions of Jesus in Catacomb Art

Going back in time, Shroud historian Rex Morgan of Australia, through his study of the nineteenth century artist Thomas Heaphy's renditions of catacomb paintings, make the case that there are some paintings and frescoes in the catacombs with bearded images of Jesus. For example, Heaphy's painting of a fresco in the Catacomb of Saint Domitilla (dated to Apostolic times) which is now called the Catacomb of Saints Achilleus and Nereus (dating from the first century) and other catacomb renditions by Heaphy show Jesus *having dark hair to the shoulders, hair parted in the middle and a short beard.* Morgan makes the case that these earliest catacomb paintings may have been made by artists who directly witnessed Jesus or who had met people who knew Jesus. They do not, however, resemble the Shroud image and are profile, and not frontal, images.

Perhaps, as Rev. Dreisbach points out, they were copies of Peter's drawings with ink on cloth described earlier. Although these were most likely paintings made independent of the Shroud, they support the Shroud image as one of Jesus having long hair, a moustache and beard. However, they were not the image used to replicate Jesus after the re-emergence of the Shroud in 535. Morgan states, however, that the similarities give a true picture of Jesus.

> "I formed the theory early in 1984 that if these paintings could be judged to be similar in their characteristics to the image on the Shroud, then both sources were representations of the same man, which in turn suggested that the image we have on the Turin Shroud is, indeed, that of Christ as depicted in the earliest catacomb representations."

These images were early witnesses and when the catacombs were sealed by the Emperors and the Image sealed up in the walls of the Edessa, the actual image of Jesus was lost in the memory of the growing Church for a period of time (or carefully held secret by the Bishops). The more youthful, Apollo-like Roman god style image of Jesus as a young, beardless man with short hair and no moustache depicted usually as a teacher, shepherd or healer then came to dominate early Christian art.

THE THREE CLOTHS OF CHRIST by John C. Iannone

The Roman Catacombs

The Roman catacombs are ancient burial ground outside the original city some two or three miles. The volcanic soil, as Morgan points out, is soft enough for the excavation of tombs. However, the catacombs were not just burial grounds (as they originally were since Christians and Jews could not be legally buried in graves in Rome during the earliest years) but they became meeting places for worship for the earliest Christians. As Morgan points out:

> "These early Christians simply used their legal right to bury their dead rather than the Roman tradition of cremation, and use a form of burial similar to that of the Jews."

It appears that the very earliest artists in the catacombs painted the image of Jesus from having directly witnessed Him or having spoken with those who witnessed Him. Or, more likely depicted Jesus from the guidance of those who traveled to Rome and who knew Jesus (such as Sts. Peter and Paul). Frank Tribbe points out that perhaps, since the Shroud was not yet hidden between 33 A.D. and the time it moved to Edessa (approx. 40-50 A.D). copies may have been made in the catacombs and elsewhere directly from the burial cloth by those fortunate enough to view it in Jerusalem.

The Vignon-Markings

Wilson's theory linking the Image of Edessa with the Shroud receives strong support from the work done previously by the famous sindonologist Paul Vignon in the 1930's. Vignon points out that, among the family of the post-mid sixth century portraits of Christ, there was a recurrence of certain unusual markings seemingly derived from the Shroud. Tribbe notes that:

> "in each of these cases, the artist, wishing to be totally faithful to the original, incorporated these oddities even though they are irrelevant to or detracted from the naturalness of the face....all these artists must have copied from the same original and all of them misunderstood the nature of these imperfections."

However, because of the sacred status of the

THE THREE CLOTHS OF CHRIST by John C. Iannone

acheiropoietos, it was very important that every detail, even if odd or unusual, be faithfully duplicated by the Byzantine artists. Wilson, following Paul Vignon, cites fifteen such oddities or anomalies which have come to be known as the Vignon-Markings:

1. A starkly geometric topless square (3-sided) visible between the eyebrows (as found on the Shroud) which some believe was the prayer-box mentioned earlier.

2. V-shape visible at the bridge of the nose.

3. A transverse streak across the forehead.

4. A second V-shape inside the topless square.

5. A raised left eyebrow.

6. An accentuated left cheek.

7. An accentuated right cheek.

8. An enlarged left nostril.

9. An accentuated line between the nose and upper lip.

10. A heavy line under the lower lip.

11. A hairless area between the lip and beard.

12. The fork in the beard.

13. A transverse line across the throat

14. The heavily accentuated "owlish eyes."

15. Two loose strands of hair falling from the apex of the forehead.

The late Professor Kurt Weitzmann of Princeton University noted that:

> "… the eyebrow over Christ's left eye is arched higher than over His right. One side of the moustache droops at a slightly different angle from the other, while the beard is combed in the opposite direction."

THE THREE CLOTHS OF CHRIST   by   John C. Iannone

The Polarized Image Overlay Technique (PIOT)

Former Professor of Psychiatry and long-time sindonologist Dr. Alan Whanger of Duke University developed the technique called the Polarized Image Overlay Technique to point out these many oddities and anomalies relating the Shroud with post-sixth century Christian art. The technique basically utilizes two polarized filters at right angles to the other and enabled Whanger to superimpose two images over each other and shift back and forth to discover similarities or anomalies.

He discovered that *many images of later (post sixth century)* art must have been made directly from the Shroud or a copy of it based on the high number of congruencies between the images. He studied many portraits, mosaics, frescoes and coins and compared them, via the PIOT method to the Shroud images. He concludes that a consistent, shroud-like, long-haired, fork-bearded, front-facing likeness of Christ can be traced back through numerous works in the Byzantine tradition dating many centuries before the time of Geoffrey de Charny (1357).

Wilson had noted the same thing, citing as an example the **Christ Pantocrator** (meaning having power over all the universe) from Cefalu, Sicily. He also noted, a century earlier, the **Pantocrator of the Dome of the Church of Daphni**, near Athens, (a city that once served as the temporary home of the Shroud from 1204-1207); the **Christ Enthroned** in the Church of St. Angelo in Formis, near Capua Italy in the 10th century; and a similar Christ portrait from the 8th century found in the depths of the **Pontianus Catacomb** near Rome. In the 6th century the Christ Portrait appears on a **silver vase found at Homes** in present day Syria and on another beautiful Icon of **Christ Pantocrator** from the Monastery in the Sinai desert. As Wilson states:

> "Despite stylistic variations, each of these works seems inspired by the same tradition of Jesus' earthly appearance. And each has a strong resemblance to the face visible on the Shroud."

We can add to this list the 7th century coins, the **tremisses** and the **solidus** coins minted by Justinian II with shroud-like images; the **Spas Nereditsa** fresco (Savior of Neredica) in 1199 and the **icon in the Church of St. Bartholomew** of Armenia in Genoa, Italy. As mentioned

THE THREE CLOTHS OF CHRIST by John C. Iannone

earlier, I had the opportunity to hold the gold solidus ring minted by Justinian II in Dr. Alan Whanger's collection. I could easily see the points of congruence between the Shroud and the face on the coin.

The Epitaphoi - Embroidered Cloths:

In the tenth and eleventh centuries there developed the *Epitaphoi* in Byzantine art. These are large embroidered cloths used in the Good Friday liturgy explicitly symbolic of the Shroud. The body of Jesus is depicted frontally with hands crossed such as the epitaphoi of King Uros Milutin. All of these seem to point to the rediscovery of the full-length of the Shroud in Constantinople in the tenth and eleventh centuries. The Image of Edessa, when brought to Constantinople, was apparently removed from the board on which it was folded and mounted (*tetradiplon* - doubled-in-four) to show that the *Mandylion* (the little towel showing only the face), when stretched out, was the full length cloth of the Shroud. Hence, the full-body images (front and rear) and bloodstains were noted.

The Hungarian *Pray* Manuscript: Four Fingers and Four Circles:

On the Shroud today one notes that, in addition to the distinctive marks of the 1532 fire, there are *four sets of burn holes* that are the result of some incident previous to the famous fire that damaged the Shroud in 1532. This prior existence is known because a painting of 1516 from the Church of Saint Gommaire in Lierre, Belgium, clearly shows the four sets of holes.

In 1986 the French Dominican Father A.M. Dubarle, corresponding on the subject of the Shroud-like figure on the *Hungarian Pray Manuscript* (1192-1195) had his attention drawn to some curious holes noted on the Shroud in the illustration. Wilson points out that:

> "clearly visible on the sarcophagus in the scene of the Three Marys Visiting the Empty Tomb was a line of three holes with an extra hole offset to one side."

It is in the pattern of an L. It appears that the artist of 1192 who illustrated the Hungarian *Pray Manuscript* was aware of the "burn-holes" on the Shroud of his day. If correct, it sets the Shroud's date 68 years earlier than

THE THREE CLOTHS OF CHRIST by John C. Iannone

the very earliest date allowed by the Carbon-14 test which dated the Shroud from 1260-1390.

Significantly, Jesus is depicted as naked and laid on a Shroud. His arms are crossed with the right hand placed over the left (in actuality, the left was over the right but the image is reversed and only appears anatomically correct when photographed in the negative) and the hands showing only four fingers. There is a herringbone weave in the lower illustration, the weave identical to that of the Shroud which has a 3-over-1 herringbone twill. There is an imprint of a body on the inside and not on the outside of the Shroud. However, on the illustration there are four circles that appear to be burn holes on the Shroud. Kevin Moran pointed out to me recently that the othonia (other burial cloth or chinband) appears rolled by separately.

The appearance of only four fingers and four circles on the illustration matching the image on the Shroud is highly significant. Pathologists such as the late Robert Bucklin (former Medical Examiner of Los Angles) and Dr. Frederick Zugibe (Medical Examiner Rockland County, NY) note also that the four fingers appear to the viewer and the thumb is not seen. They agree that a nail driven through the upper palm damaging the Median nerve of the hand (where the crease in the palm closest the thumb meets the wrist) and exiting from the wrist has the effect, from their experience, of forcing the thumb into the palm.

Moreover, the four burn holes seen in the Hungarian *Pray Manuscript* correlate to four holes found in the corresponding area of the Shroud and predate the Carbon-14 dates and the fire of 1532. Much speculation has been devoted to how these holes were created. Wilson considered that it was some form of "trial by fire." Dreisbach notes that most likely the holes were made by fragments of hot coal or burning incense that fell on the Shroud perhaps by a careless or over-zealous member of the clergy.

No Paints, Pigments, Ink, Powders, Caulk or Dyes:

In 1978 the STURP Team was permitted a brief five day, 120 hour, nonstop round-the-clock period to examine the Shroud of Turin first-hand with the most sophisticated scientific equipment of the time. Their findings have been published in many scientific journals for peer review and their studies, combined with subsequent studies, have supported

THE THREE CLOTHS OF CHRIST by John C. Iannone

the antiquity and authenticity of the Shroud. Among the many findings of STURP were those related to art treated in this Chapter.

The scientists discovered, for example, that there are absolutely *no pigments, paints, inks, caulk or dyes* which in any way contributed to the formation of the image and *no capillary action* in the cellulose. Nor did they find any medium by which pigments would traditionally be applied - *no binders or cohesion of fibers to one another.* The ultraviolet and infrared evaluations as well as the X-Ray fluorescence and microchemistry of the fibrils preclude the possibility of paint, inks, dyes, powders or other substances being used as a medium for creating the images. This clearly refuted the "iron-oxide" theory of Dr. Walter McCrone. Iron oxide is found uniformly throughout the Shroud as a result of the retting process of linen in water as discussed earlier. It does not constitute the image.

Sanctification of Paintings:

As pointed out earlier, the STURP team noted the presence of some paint flecks on the Shroud but pointed out that these in no way were part of the image. Historians noted that during the Medieval period artists were allowed to come to Turin and paint copies of the Shroud. They would then be permitted to lay their paintings on the cloth for "sanctification" before returning to their home churches throughout Europe. This "sanctification of paintings" happened at least 40 times on record. As microscopists point out, such actions would allow the transfer of microscopic particles of paints but these particles do not constitute the image.

A Surface Phenomenon With No Brush Stokes:

Tests indicated *no brush strokes* and *no "directionality"* of any type which would be characteristic of an artist's painting. In addition, there are *no penetration or saturation* of the fibrils of the flax or linen fibers. The image is such that it tends to disappear when one looks at it closely and scholars point out that any artist would have had to work from a long distance away from the cloth to create such an image. The Shroud, as the team officially recognized, is certainly no painting.

THE THREE CLOTHS OF CHRIST   by   John C. Iannone

No Outline or Style Of Any Artist:

Internationally renowned artist Isabel Piczek of Los Angeles has said that the Shroud shows no affinity whatsoever with any of the styles which were practiced through the cultured world in the Middle Ages. Isabel notes that the Shroud image has no outlines and states that:

> "art always exhibits the mandatory use of the outline, the horizon event in art."

STURP scientists point out that the image, far from being a painting, appears to be a sort of scorch - or scorch-like - but not an actual scorch from heat. The coloring is sepia or straw-yellow.

They note that when ultra-violet and x-ray fluorescence are applied, *the image does NOT fluoresce* indicating that it is not made from heat. Their conclusion is that the image was produced through some unidentified process - most likely **LIGHT** and not heat which caused an accelerated dehydration, oxidation and degradation (rapid aging) of the cellulose fibers of the linen creating the image.

More recently, the late Dr. Ray Rogers, the STURP's chemist, after re-examining fibers, indicated that the medullas of the cellulose did not dehydrate but rather that whatever caused the image *affected the surface impurities of the linen - most likely starches*.

> "The image color resides only on the topmost fibers at the highest parts of the weave (A2); it resides on the thin impurity layer of outer surfaces of the fibers." Dr. Ray Rogers

What was the mysterious process that caused the imaging of the linen?

As Isabel Piczek states:

> "The practiced arts come to the conclusion: The Turin Shroud does not fit into the milieu of the Middle Ages. Whatever happened before, during or after the Carbon-14 testing of the Shroud, the test results are at great odds with the conclusive results drawn by the practiced arts - namely that the Shroud is definitely

THE THREE CLOTHS OF CHRIST by John C. Iannone

not a painting or the result of manipulations by a medieval artist."

****

THE THREE CLOTHS OF CHRIST by John C. Iannone

Chapter Eleven

RESOLVING THE CARBON-14 CONTROVERSY

"There seems to be an unhealthy consensus approaching the level of dogma...that C-14 dating will settle the issue...This attitude simply contradicts the general perspective of field archaeologists and geologists who view contamination as a very serious problem."

Archaeologist William Meacham

Background of the C-14 Testing and Controversy:

After the 1978 studies by the Shroud of Turin Research Project (STURP), several scientists, in spite of warnings from such renowned archaeologists as William Meacham not to rely too heavily on the Carbon-14 test, believed that only the C-14 test could definitively establish the age of the Shroud. The non-denominational STURP team, which included Catholics, Protestants, Jews and agnostics, supported authenticity and some warned of the pitfalls of Carbon-14 testing.

The Vatican was hesitant to utilize the procedure at the time because the Carbon-14 test, prior to the 1980's, required a relatively large piece of cloth (almost the size of a handkerchief) to be used. Such a test would result in the destruction of a large sample of the linen. Cardinal Anastasio Ballestrero of Turin, then Papal Guardian of the Shroud, refused to allow the test because he could not justify destroying a substantial piece of the sacred cloth to prove its authenticity.

However, in the 1980's, great strides were made with the improvement of the Accelerated Mass Spectrometer (AMS), the equipment used to measure Carbon-14 levels, which would

THE THREE CLOTHS OF CHRIST by John C. Iannone

allow the same test to be done on a *postage sized piece of cloth*. When this capability was demonstrated, the Vatican permitted samples to be taken from the Holy Shroud. A Commission was set-up in 1986 to outline the procedures and protocol to be followed in this testing to take place in 1988.

Carbon-14 - What is it?

Scientists tell us that in the food chain, all living things, whether human, animal or plant, ingest carbon, especially Carbon-12 and Carbon-13 (which are stable atoms, that is, atoms likely to hold on to their electrons) along with unstable, radioactive Carbon-14 in much, much smaller quantities. While something is alive, it contains C-12 and C-13 in high quantities and C-14 in very small quantities. Of significance is the fact that there is a constant measurable ratio of C-12 to C-14 in the organism as long as the creature is alive and participating in the food chain.

However, when the living object dies, it slowly begins to lose its unstable C-14 (a process called "atomic decay") and the unstable C-14 atoms decay at a certain rate, called its "half-life," or the period of time it takes for the creature or once-living object to lose half of the C-14. The "half-life" of Carbon-14 is 5,730 years. In other words, in 5730 years a human, animal, tree trunk, perhaps a fossil bone of a dinosaur, and so forth, will lose one half of its C-14, thereby altering the ratio what exists between the stable C-12/13 and the unstable C-14.

Since the initial ratio between C-12 and C-14 is known in living creatures, the object can be measured to determine the degree of decay or ratio left between the C-14 and C-12 and a date is then assigned to it. The stability of the decay or ratio assumes, however, that no other factors have interfered to alter the ratio over time, for example, by exposure to radioactivity from other sources or contaminants - like a forest fire - which can then possible seriously affect the accuracy of the dating by adding back Carbon-14.

With regard to the amount of C-14 in proportion to C-12, scientists advise that it is extremely small. Paul E. Damon, a University of Arizona geochemist and principal co-investigator with the University's Laboratory of Isotope Geochemistry, related that:

THE THREE CLOTHS OF CHRIST by John C. Iannone

"At death, the organism no long takes up carbon dioxide and the various types of carbon isotopes decay at different rates. The task will be especially difficult because only about one out of every trillion carbon isotopes is Carbon-14. It is like you had an acre of blue marbles, three feet deep, with one red marble mixed in with the blues. You job would be to find the red marble."

Credit for the discovery of the Carbon-14 test goes to Willard Frank Libby who won the Nobel Prize in Chemistry in 1960 for "his method of using Carbon-14 for age determination in archaeology, geology, geophysics and other branches of science." His first presentation or first formal public lecture describing the C-14 method was before a group of archaeologists and anthropologists in January 1948 in New York City. It was an historic moment. Scientists consider the use of C-14 method a landmark in the history of archaeology, particularly in prehistoric studies. Since the Shroud is made of linen, that is, cellulose fibers from the flax plant, scientists reasoned that the Shroud would be able to be dated using the C-14 test.

Shroud Submitted To The C-14 Test in 1988:

After reviewing the credentials of many laboratories that utilized the Accelerated Mass Spectrometer to perform the C-14 test, the Commission selected seven laboratories. However, at the last minute, for reasons unexplained, this number was reduced to three laboratories. The Carbon-14 test was performed on July 29, 1988 at Oxford as well as the Federal Polytechnic Institute of Technology of Zurich and the University of Arizona at Tucson.

A piece of cloth 3/8 of an inch by 2 1/4 inches was cut in the presence of Cardinal Ballestrero; Professor Luigi Gonella (Dept. of Physics, Turin Polytechnic and scientific advisor to the Archbishop); Professor F. Testore and G. Vial - two textile experts; Dr. Michael S. Tite of the British Museum; Giovanni Riggi (who removed the sample from the Shroud) and five representatives of the three radiocarbon dating laboratories (Professors P.E. Damon; D.J. Donahue, E.T. Hall, Dr. R.E.M. Hedges and W. Woelfli). Swiss Textile Expert Mechthild Flury Lemberg was scheduled to the cutting, but was removed inexplicably at the last minute and replaced by Dr. Giovanni Riggi who did the

THE THREE CLOTHS OF CHRIST   by   John C. Iannone

actual cutting.

They divided the sample into four parts: three were given to the laboratories and one was kept separately by the Vatican scientific advisor. The British Museum agreed to function as record keeper. The three laboratories were given two other dated fabrics as controls. (It should be noted that the Shroud fabric is easily identifiable by its three-over-one herringbone twill, so the Laboratories could easily identify it against the controls. Requests were made to separate the fibers so as to provide a "blind test." However this was not done.

The Actual Test Procedure:

It is worthwhile describing the method used to break down the Carbon-14 sample, as it will help the reader to understand concerns raised over the application of the C-14 as it pertains to the Shroud. An article in *National Geographic* described the process as follows:

> "Three laboratories received a snippet of linen from the Shroud. Each was thoroughly cleaned and burned to produce Carbon dioxide. A high-energy mass spectrometer separated the carbon isotopes and counted their atoms. From their ratio came the fabric's age."

...or did it?

The New York Times described the process as follows:

> "In the technique used by all three institutions, carbon and other atoms and molecules extracted from the sample are electrically charged and hurled through a series of magnetic fields by a special nuclear accelerator called a *tandem accelerator mass spectrometer (AMS)*. These fields deflect atoms of varying mass and electrical charge so they strike different regions of a detector target. Heavier atoms are deflected less by the magnetic fields than are lighter atoms and this difference separated the trajectories of atoms, according to their masses. By counting the atoms that strike any given part of the detector, the apparatus can estimate their abundance."

Postage stamp sized samples of the Shroud were utilized. The linen was first carefully cleaned, using both chemical and mechanical methods, according to Dr. Douglas J.

THE THREE CLOTHS OF CHRIST   by   John C. Iannone

Donahue. (However, we will describe some discrepancies that should have been noted). Next, the sample was burned in oxygen thereby converting the carbon in its molecules into carbon dioxide gas. The gas was then reduced to pure carbon in the form of graphite by heating the gas in the presence of iron powder. In the next stage, the graphite derived from the Shroud sample, consisting of a mixture of stable carbon isotopes with radioactive C-14, was bombarded by heavy celsium atoms. This process knocked the carbon atoms loose from the graphite, endowed some of them with electric charges and sent them toward the accelerator to be counted.

The C-14 Laboratory Test Results:

Unfortunately, the newspapers printed the results prematurely. The *London Times* stated on August 27, 1988 that Oxford scientists had leaked the results. Shortly thereafter, the Vatican made an announcement in Italy on October 13, 1988. The results of the test were first officially published in an article entitled "*Radiocarbon Dating of the Shroud of Turin*" in 1989 in *Nature Magazine*. The official report stated that the Shroud of Turin was dated between 1260-1390 and this would make the Shroud between 607 - 737 years old at the time of the testing.

The report stated the following:

> "The results of radiocarbon measurements at Arizona, Oxford and Zurich yield a calibrated calendar age range with at least 95% confidence for the linen of the Shroud of Turin of A.D. 1260-1390. The results, therefore, provide conclusive evidence that the linen of the Shroud of Turin is medieval."

Headlines all over the world jumped on this report and, ignoring the vast body of evidence to the contrary, and the warnings of the perils of the C-14 test, prematurely accepted the results of this one test to condemn the Holy Shroud as a "fake or fraud." Sensationalism was the operative work. The newspapers in New York, as an example, capitalized on the negative test results of the Holy Shroud. Some headlines read as follows:

> "Test Shows Shroud of Turin to be Fraud, Scientist Hints."   (*New York Times*, Sept. 22, 1988)

THE THREE CLOTHS OF CHRIST by John C. Iannone

"Turin Shroud Made After Crucifixion." (*Associated Press* headline in the Daily News, Sept. 28, 1988).

"Shroud of Turin Legend in Tatters: Carbon Tests Date It to the 14th Century."(*New York Post* September 28, 1988).

It was truly a bleak period for the Holy Shroud - no stranger to difficult periods - and for scientists who had carefully studied the "preponderance of evidence." They knew that the mass of evidence supported the authenticity and antiquity of the Shroud while one test contracted this evidence. Unfortunately, the Press, in a highly unbalanced approach, simply ignored the body of evidence and never questioned the reliability of the Carbon-14 test. The Vatican, to the dismay of sindonologists, exercised poor "spin-control" on the one-sided view of the Press and provided credibility to the C-14 tests by failing to question the reliability of the tests. As one Shroud scholar, Barrie Schwortz (photographer of the STURP team) puts it: "This is science by press release."

If the Church erred in this matter, its error, as later found out, was in accepting unquestioningly the results of the Carbon-14 test, especially with regard to the linen, as will be demonstrated. In this respect, the Church was in good company since the world press and many members of the world scientific community also accepted the initial results without putting the information in the broader context of many other pieces of evidence supporting authenticity and antiquity.

A Litany of Contaminants Affecting the Shroud:

The scientists who conducted the Carbon-14 test were very concerned with the potential of foreign elements that might affect the test on the Shroud, as was noted in the report in *Nature Magazine*. Throughout history, the Shroud was exposed to many and varied contaminants. The exposure of the Shroud linen to washing and soap prior to its being used as a burial cloth and many other contaminants combined with the questionable cleaning of the test patch, likely affected the test results. Such contaminants as ointments (aloe and myrrh), sweat, blood, saliva, candle wax, and finger oils from continued handling by the faithful in earlier years; atmospheric dusts; limestone dust from the tomb (calcium carbonate); dirt (travertine aragonite)

THE THREE CLOTHS OF CHRIST   by   John C. Iannone

pollen, mites, mold/mildew and the smoke, soot and steam of water used to douse the fire in 1532 fire which added some carbon isotopes to the Shroud, and silk fibers from the Holland backing cloth - all contributed to the litany of contaminants that left their marks on the Shroud over two thousand years.

The Conspiracy Theory:

There were numerous violations of protocol involved in the testing of the cloth by a relatively small group of scientists which raised questions around the world about the accuracy of the C-14 in the light of findings which contradicted many other tests. However, it also raised questions about whether or not there was a conspiracy to discredit the Holy Shroud in 1988 for some reasons unknown and even to destroy the Holy Shroud in the fire of 1997 just before the 1998 public exhibition set-up by Pope John Paul II with Cardinal Giovanni Saldarini - Papal Custodian of the Shroud in Turin.

There were several questions brought to light after the testing which raised serious doubts about the handling of the testing.

1. In the protocol committee sessions held in 1986 to prepare for the July 29, 1988, it was agreed that members of the scientific team that handled the 1978 investigation were to help be an oversight committee. Yet they were mysteriously eliminated at the last minute.

2. In addition, the Pontifical Academy of Science, a world-respected group, was likewise eliminated from oversight without explanation.

3. In a strange move, Cardinal Agostino Casaroli, then Vatican Secretary of State in Rome, sent a letter in 1987 to Cardinal Ballestrero (then Papal Custodian of the Shroud in Turin) indicating that only the British Museum in the person of Dr. Michael Tite was to be the supervising institute along with Professor Luigi Gonella, the Cardinal's scientific advisor from the Polytechnic Institute. Italian newspapers reported that Cardinal Casaroli was alleged to be a Freemason, a member of the rogue P2 Lodge in Italy which was not part of Freemasonry

THE THREE CLOTHS OF CHRIST   by   John C. Iannone

but imitated it for its own political ends in Italy. If the allegation is true, this would be troubling.

4. The 1986 Commission selected *seven labs, including the notorious Harwell Labs in England (part of the United Kingdom Atomic Energy Commission),* to conduct the test. At the last minute it was narrowed to three eliminating Harwell without explanation. Only Zurich, Arizona and Oxford were to be involved.

5. As analytical chemists have noted, the test area must be representative of the whole cloth. In fact, the protocol requested that *threads from several areas* of the Shroud be utilized. However, Professor Riggi who did the cuttings took samples from the lower left front (ventral) section, *agreed by all to be the most contaminated area of the Shroud.* Scientists who had seen discrepancies in Carbon-14 testing of other objects recommended multiple test sites but this was ignored. The late Dr. Harry Gove, inventor of the Accelerator Mass Spectrometer and acknowledged expert in the C-14 method, had *proposed this multiple sampling method to assure a representative sample by taking threads from different parts of the Shroud.*

6. The test was to be *a "blind-test,"* that is, the fibers of the Shroud sample were to be separated so that the testing Labs could not tell it was the Shroud. Two other test cloths from the Medieval period were tested also. The Labs, however, *admitted that they knew immediately which sample was the Shroud because of the unique 3-over-1 herringbone weave of the Shroud linen.*

7. Swiss textile expert Mechthild Flury-Lemberg (currently one of the custodians of the cloth) was going to do the actual cuttings. Flury Lemberg was replaced at the last minute by Dr. Giovanni Riggi with no explanation.

8. The entire session was to be video-taped. However, the scientists got into a heated discussion, turned off the cameras and went into another room raising questions about the proper taping of the test and failing to account for what was discussed during the "missing time."

THE THREE CLOTHS OF CHRIST by John C. Iannone

9. Dr. Riggi noted "rogue fibers" on the test sample taken adjacent to a Medieval repair but proceeded with the test. It is interesting that Professor Edward Hall, head of the Oxford Laboratory involved in the C-14 test noted odd fibers in the C-14 sample. He enlisted the opinion of Peter South of Derbyshire Labs who concluded that:

> "the rogue fibers were fine dark yellow strand cotton...and may have been used for repairs in the past."

His statement was prophetic, as we shall see.

It is also interesting that Professor Riggi had given assurances that the excised C-14 samples provided to the labs were free of foreign threads. In this regard, the University of Arizona C-14 Labs indicated that they documented both *red silk and blue satin* in its sample. (The threads were likely from the backings of the cloth). In fact, Archaeologist William Meacham cited a letter he had just obtained that was written by one of the labs' directors to the British Museum in January 1988 in which the current C-14 project was described as:

> "A rather shoddy enterprise...which the British Museum may live to regret."

10. It was further noted that the *samples weighed twice as much as expected*. This would occur if a blend of original linen with rogue cotton fibers existed in the test area.

These were not ignorant men but rather trained scientists. When taken as a whole, these multiple violations of protocol do not appear to be the work of ignorance or accident. The debate went on for over 14 years regarding not only a possible conspiracy to discredit the Shroud in the eyes of the world, but about the validity of the Carbon-14 test on the Shroud.

Astonishingly, according to the German paper *Die Welt*, dated September 5, 1997, Cardinal Ballestrero made some remarks which appear surprising in the light of the declarations he made in 1988 backing the results of the dubious C-14 dating test. In particular, *Die Welt* says the following regarding the Cardinal's comments:

THE THREE CLOTHS OF CHRIST by John C. Iannone

> "The Turin Shroud is, in Cardinal Anastasio Ballestrero's opinion, authentic. The laboratory tests conducted in the 80s, which dated the cloth back to the Middle Ages, would appear to have been performed 'without due care.'"

At the time, the Cardinal had himself published the results of this research. After the publication of these results, criticism was swift to follow.

A Major Breakthrough In Shroud Studies - A Medieval Reweave:

In 1978 STURP scientists (Photographer Vernon Miller) used a special type of photography called Quad Mosaic Photography utilized by NASA in space studies. Thanks to Shroud photographer Barrie Schwortz who made Miller's photographs available, scientists were able to view these photographs. This type of photography was able to distinguish *color as a function of chemistry on the cloth*. For example, the lower front section of the ventral (front) area of the Shroud is *orange-yellow*. Yet *the lower left corner of the cloth is a bluish-green*, indicating to chemists that this area is *anomalous* to the rest of the Shroud. Yet, this was the area chosen for the test.

Shroud Chemist Dr. Alan Adler had noted in a different chemical test that there was the presence of *aluminum oxide* in the lower left corner. He did not know the ramifications of this at the time.

Shroud scholars Joseph Marino and retired NASA scientist Edwin Prior pointed out in a recent article (2008) that the Shroud's current scientific advisor, Professor Piero Savarino, co-authored a booklet on the Shroud before being appointed advisor to Cardinal Poletto in 1998 in which he stated that the 1988 C-14 testing:

> "might have been erroneous due to 'extraneous thread' left over from invisible mending routinely carried out in the past on parts of the cloth in poor repair."

Savarino went on to say:

> "...if the sample taken had been the subject of 'invisible mending', the carbon-dating results would

THE THREE CLOTHS OF CHRIST by John C. Iannone

not be reliable. What is more, the site from which the samples actually were taken does not preclude this hypothesis."

What did he mean by "invisible mending"?

In 2000, a highly credible theory emerged from new findings. The late Sue Benford (who unfortunately died of cancer at a young age as this book was going to publication) and her husband Joseph Marino claimed that a *virtually invisible darn* dating back to the 16th century was used to repair a damaged piece of the Cloth in the lower left corner of the Shroud. A piece of the lower left corner of the linen was removed due to possible damage or more likely was removed from the Shroud from a corner area perhaps as a souvenir taken by Margaret of Austria of the Savoy family - owners of the Shroud at that time. *An adjacent area was expertly repaired to mend the unraveling edges.*

The Benford-Marino Theory:

Sue Benford and Joseph Marino suspected that when the repair was originally made on the Shroud, it was done through a process of "invisible weaving" - a specialty of French Medieval tapestry weavers. They pointed out that between about 1520 and 1560 some of the 30 to 40 master weavers were experts. Thomas Campbell in his work *Tapestry in the Renaissance: Art and Magnificence* calls the Sixteenth century weavers 'magicians."

Sue Benford noted that:

> "All of the major European courts had teams of skilled weavers and embroiderers who were employed in the repair of high-quality textiles. The Savoy family would certainly have had the wealth to afford these experts."

The repair was carefully rewoven using Medieval cotton fibers to repair the original ancient cloth. The cotton fibers were *dyed with a Madder Root dye (yellow)* and attached using an *aluminum mordant and Gum Arabic binder*. This was confirmed by STURP chemist Dr. Ray Rogers who utilized samples remaining from the test. This explained the findings of Dr. Alan Adler as to why he found aluminum

THE THREE CLOTHS OF CHRIST by John C. Iannone

oxide in his earlier chemical tests. At the request of Sue Benford and Joseph Marino, Dr. Ray Rogers, who himself had originally accepted the 1988 C-14 results, re-examined the fibers expecting to easily refute the Benford-Marino theory. However, he quickly noted to his surprise that when patches were cut for examination by the Carbon-14 labs, there was an *intrusion of Medieval cotton fibers from the repair into the old linen of the cloth.*

In essence, Medieval cotton fibers, dyed with a yellow Madder root dye and bound to the cloth by aluminum mordant and Gum Arabic binders, were expertly rewoven into the old Shroud. The testing was done on this area that contained both Medieval cotton and ancient linen. Beta-Analytic Labs of Miami, Florida determined that a mix of about 60% new fibers with 40% old would give a Medieval date.

A "Spurious Sample":

Dr. Rogers made a very important statement in his writings "*A Chemist's Perspective On The Shroud of Turin*" just before his recent death.

> "The Church officials appear to be content to have society view the Shroud as a Medieval hoax, and the radiocarbon laboratories have refused to consider the possibility that they were given a spurious sample. In a manner uncharacteristic of rigorous scientists they refuse to allow observation of retained samples. They also refuse to do their own simple chemical observations. They refuse to discuss or show any photomicrography of samples they might have."

Dr. Rogers went on to say:

> "Control samples should always be retained to enable confirmation of results at a later date. Retained samples, if any, have not been made available for study. This leads one to question the ethics or rigor of any 'scientists' involved in the process. Is something being hidden?"

We ask the same question: "Is something being hidden?"

The results of the new findings on the Medieval reweave which affected the old linen, and thereby threw off the

THE THREE CLOTHS OF CHRIST by John C. Iannone

Carbon-14 testing, when combined with all the other evidence, outlined proves beyond a reasonable doubt the authenticity of the Holy Shroud as the actual burial cloth of the historical Jesus of Nazareth - one that contains His images, His bloodstains and evidence of His Resurrection. Science, faith and history come together to tell the compelling story of the passion, death and resurrection of Jesus.

****

THE THREE CLOTHS OF CHRIST   by   John C. Iannone

THE THREE CLOTHS OF CHRIST by John C. Iannone

Chapter Twelve

THE SUDARIUM CHRISTI:
THE FACE CLOTH OF JESUS IN THE TOMB

"Then Simon Peter, who was behind him (John) arrived and went into the tomb. He saw the strips of linen lying there as well as the burial cloth (sudarium) that had been around His head. The cloth was folded up by itself separate from the linen (sindon)."

John 20:6-7

In the Cathedral of San Salvador in Oviedo, a city in northern Spain at the foothills of the Pyrenees Mountains, is a linen cloth called the "Sudarium Christi" or the Face Cloth of Christ. It is often referred to as the Cloth of Oviedo and is believed to be the cloth mentioned in the Gospel of St. John that was "folded up by itself..." Modern studies by the Spanish Centre for Sindonology (Dr. Jose Villalain, Jaime Laquierdo and Guillermo Heras of the University of Valencia, as noted by Sudarium scholar Mark Guscin) using infrared and ultraviolet photography and electron microscopy, have demonstrated that the Cloth in Oviedo, along with the Shroud of Turin, both touched the same face (that of the historical Jesus of Nazareth) at different points in the Crucifixion.

Tradition and historical information, now supported by contemporary scientific research, support the belief of millions of people that the face that touched both cloths was that of the historical Jesus of Nazareth. This cloth is NOT the cloth called the Veil of Veronica as discussed in the next chapter, which is the alleged Veil which early Christian legend claims was used by Veronica to wipe the face of Jesus while still alive on the Via Dolorosa. This Veil is an imaged cloth with eyes open.

The Oviedo Cloth - the Sudarium Christi - was placed around the head from the time death occurred on the Cross until

THE THREE CLOTHS OF CHRIST by John C. Iannone

the body was laid in the tomb when it was covered (enveloped) by the Shroud in the Garden Tomb. At that time the Face Cloth was removed and placed to one side (John 20:7).

British born classicist Mark Guscin living in Spain notes that the practice of covering the face is referenced in the Babylonian Talmud (Moed Katan 27a):

> "Formerly, they would uncover the face of the rich (corpse) and cover the face of the poor because their faces became blackened by famine. And the poor people were ashamed. The sages therefore instituted that all faces should be covered out of deference for the poor."

He further notes that Rabbi Alfred Kolatch in New York talks of the Kevod Ha-Met or "respect for the dead" as the reason for covering the head. Rabbi Michael Tuktzinsky of Jerusalem in his *Sefer Gesher Cha'yim* (Volume 1, Chapter 3, 1911) offers as a reason that it is a hardship for onlookers to gaze on the face of a dead person. We note the modern practice of covering bodies or faces of people who have died in the street.

Describing The Sudarium:

Scientifically, there are at least six points of congruence between the Holy Shroud and the Sudarium:

1. The blood type of the Shroud matches the Type AB of the Sudarium - a "bio-type of the Middle East."

2. The pollen on the Shroud matches pollen on the Sudarium - Gundelia tournefortii - the thorn-thistle bush.

3. The blood-serum ratio 1:6 matches the ratio of pulmonary fluids found on the Shroud.

4. Puncture marks on back of head of Shroud - presumably piercing of thorns - match exactly the marks noted on Sudarium

5. The length of nose matches both cloths.

6. Wounds on the back of the neck of the Shroud match

THE THREE CLOTHS OF CHRIST by John C. Iannone

markings on the Sudarium.

The Blood Type:

The blood type of the Shroud - namely, AB blood - matches the blood type of the Sudarium. Dr. Garza Valdez of the University of Texas Health Science Center notes that only 3.2% of the world population has AB blood and the majority of these cases are in the Middle East. In fact, AB blood has been called a bio-type of the Middle East.

Pollen Match:

Pollen grains found on the Cloth of Oviedo by Dr. Max Frei in 1973 and 1978 and studied also by Monsignor Giulio Ricci match pollen grains found on the Shroud of Turin. Dr. Frei found at least four different pollen matching both the Shroud and the Sudarium. Dr. Uri Baruch (expert Palynologist from the Israel Antiquities Authority) has indicated that one of these pollen is *Gundelia tournefortii* - a thorn thistle bush that is indigenous to the Holy Land.

Dr. Avinoam Danin (botanist and expert on the flora of the Holy Land who teaches at the Hebrew University in Jerusalem) reports that *Gundelia tournefortii* serves as a "geographic and calendar indicator" of the provenance of the cloths in the Holy Land. In addition, on the Oviedo cloth "were found pollen representative of Israel, North Africa and Spain, exactly in accord with the cloth's known history."

Sudarium scholar Mark Guscin notes:

> "The Pollen: We have seen that historical testimony fits in with what we know about the sudarium, and there is no reason to doubt the historicity of the few references that exist. Its (the Sudarium's) stay in Jerusalem and its route through the north of Africa can be further confirmed by studying pollen found on the cloth. As is well known, this method of study has also been used on the Turin Shroud, and the pollen found coincides with the historical route of this cloth through Edessa, Constantinople, France and Italy. ... From the pollen found, it is undeniable that the Shroud was in Palestine, Edessa and

THE THREE CLOTHS OF CHRIST by John C. Iannone

> Constantinople. Most people who have read any book about the Shroud will be familiar with the name Dr Max Frei, the Swiss criminologist responsible for the pollen studies related to the Shroud."

Before Dr Frei died, he also analyzed pollen samples from the sudarium in Oviedo. Guscin notes:

> "The results perfectly match the route already described. He found pollen from Oviedo, Toledo, north Africa and Jerusalem. There was nothing relating the sudarium to Constantinople, France, Italy or any other country in Europe."
>
> (Guscin, *The Oviedo Cloth*, 1998, p.22)

Blood-Serum Ratio:

The Sudarium does have bloodstains and serum stains from pulmonary edema fluid which match the blood and serum patterns of the Shroud. As Shroud historian Ian Wilson noted:

> "The Sudarium's "blood and body fluid stains" are "very compatible with Gospel writer John's observation that at the conclusion of Jesus' crucifixion", when pierced with a lance, "immediately there came out blood and water." John 19:34.
>
> Wilson and Schwortz, *"The Turin Shroud: The Illustrated Evidence"* (Michael O'Mara Books: London, 2000, pp. 77-78, 92).

Wilson and Schwortz go on to say:

> "Although it bears no photograph-like 'body' image in the manner of the Shroud, Mark Guscin and his Spanish colleagues have very convincingly demonstrated that its `blood and body fluid' stains exhibit shapes so strikingly similar to those on the Shroud that there has to be the strongest likelihood that both were in contact with the same corpse. Two groups of stains particularly indicate this. The first are what I would call the nasal stains, which appear to derive from a nose and mouth soaked in bloody fluids. These are repeated mirror-image-style, apparently because of the cloth having been partly doubled on itself. Forensic

THE THREE CLOTHS OF CHRIST by John C. Iannone

analysis indicates that they consist of one part blood and six parts pulmonary edema fluid."

"This finding is therefore strikingly consistent with the strong body of medical opinion that the man of the Shroud's lungs would have filled with fluid caused by the scourging. They are also very compatible with gospel writer John's observation that at the conclusion of Jesus' crucifixion `immediately there came out blood and water' John 19:34, as from the same edematous fluid, when a lance was plunged into Jesus' side. In the case of the Oviedo cloth's back-of-the-head group of bloodstains, if these are photographed to the same scale as their equivalent on the Shroud, and then matched up to each other, there are again enough similarities to indicate … that these two cloths were in contact with the same wounded body."

Puncture Marks:

A series of puncture marks noted on the Sudarium match those on the back of the head (occipital area) of the Holy Shroud consistent with the puncture marks from the capping of thorns. As Shroud Historian Ian Wilson noted:

"If the Oviedo cloth's back-of-the-head group of bloodstains are photographed to the same scale as their equivalent on the Shroud, and then matched up to each other, there are again enough similarities to indicate...that these two cloths were in contact with the same wounded body."

The Length of Nose:

The length of the nose on both cloths is 8 centimeters (3 inches). Mark Guscin notes:

"The length of the nose which produced this stain has been calculated at eight centimeters, just over three inches, which is exactly the same as the length of the nose on the Shroud."

The Sudarium Christi is an ancient linen venerated in Oviedo, Spain for more than 1,200 years. Mark Guscin notes that:

THE THREE CLOTHS OF CHRIST by John C. Iannone

"It was originally a white linen cloth with a taffeta texture, now stained, dirty and wrinkled. It is rectangular, somewhat irregular and measures approximately 34 by 21 inches (855 mm x 526 mm) or 84 x 53 cm. Unlike the Holy Shroud (Shroud of Turin), it does NOT have an image, having been removed from the face before the image was created on the Holy Shroud."

Wounds on Back of Neck:

Guscin notes:

"The image of the back of the man on the Shroud is covered with wounds from the scourging he received before being crucified. The wounds on the man's back are obviously not reproduced on the sudarium, as this had no contact with it. However, there are thick bloodstains on the nape of the man's neck, showing the depth and extent of the wounds produced by the crown of thorns. This crown was probably not a circle, as traditional Christian art represents, but a kind of cap covering the whole head. ... The stains on the back of the man's neck on the Shroud correspond exactly to those on the sudarium."

(Guscin, M., "The Oviedo Cloth," Lutterworth Press: Cambridge UK, 1998, pp.30,32).

Match of Beard and Blood Stains on The Side of The Mouth:

"Perhaps the most obvious fit when the stains on the sudarium are placed over the image of the face on the Shroud, is that of the beard; the match is perfect. This shows that the sudarium, possibly by being gently pressed onto the face, was also used to clean the blood and other fluids that had collected in the beard." Guscin, *The Oviedo Cloth*.

If the stains of the Sudarium are placed over the nose of the image on the Shroud, one stain is seen to proceed from the right hand side of the man's mouth. This stain is hardly visible on the Shroud, but its existence has been confirmed by Dr John Jackson, who is well known for his studies on the Shroud using the VP-8 image analyzer. Using the VP-8 and photo-enhancements, Dr. Jackson has shown that

THE THREE CLOTHS OF CHRIST by John C. Iannone

the same stain is present on the Shroud, and the shape of the stain coincides perfectly with the one on the Sudarium. The gap between the blood coming out of the right side of the mouth and the stain on the beard is visible.

> "The principal bloodstains clearly form a mirror image along the axis formed by a fold that is still present. They are fundamentally light brown in color, in varying degrees of intensity. Although the linen has been traditionally called the 'Holy Sudarium' or 'Holy Face,' there is no visible image of a face on the relic, only blood that is believed to be that of Jesus of Nazareth."
>
> J. Bennett, *"Sacred Blood, Sacred Image: The Sudarium of Oviedo"* (Ignatius Press: San Francisco CA, 2001, p. 13).

Dr. Alan Whanger of Duke University, N.C. found at least seventy matches between a polarized image overlay of the blood stains of the Shroud and those found on the Cloth of Oviedo.

> "Further computerized comparative studies by Nello Balossino of the University of Turin indicated that the traces of blood present on the two pieces of cloth matched perfectly."
>
> John C. Iannone, "The Mystery of the Shroud of Turin: New Scientific Evidence," St Paul's: Staten Island NY, 1998, p.91).

> "The PIOT methodology (Polarized Image Overlay Technique) (Whanger & Whanger, 1985, 1998) allows comparison of various objects and images with the Shroud images or stains. This affords confirmation, image by image, stain by stain, painstakingly, of the historical authenticity of the Shroud. Representative observations include: … Sudarium (face cloth) of Oviedo, dated to the 1st century in Jerusalem, kept in El Salvador Cathedral of Oviedo, Spain, since the mid-8th century (Guscin, 1998), 120 points of congruent bloodstains between the Sudarium and the Shroud." (Whanger & Whanger, 1998).

THE THREE CLOTHS OF CHRIST by John C. Iannone

See also: Danin, A., Whanger, A.D., Baruch, U. & Whanger, M., *"Flora of the Shroud of Turin,"* Missouri Botanical Garden Press: St. Louis MO, 1999, pp.6-7).

Brief History of the Sudarium:

A very early reference is noted in speaking of the history of the Shroud. It is a reference to the Sudarium Christi. *"The Mysteries of the Acts of the Savior"* of the second century, reports that the Lord Himself, appearing to Joseph of Arimathea, showed him the Shroud (*Sindon*) and the Face Cloth (*Sudario*).

The Sudarium Christi also known as the *Sagrado Rostro* or Holy Face has a well-documented history. One source traces the cloth back as far as 570 A.D. Pelayo, Bishop of Oviedo in the 1100's noted in his *Chronicles* that the Oviedo Cloth left Jerusalem in 614 A.D. in the face of the Persian invasion of the Holy Land and made its way across North Africa to Spain.

In advance of Moslem assaults into Spain, the Sudarium was transported to Oviedo, Spain in a silver Ark (large box) along with any other sacred relics. This wooden reliquary housed the Sudarium in Carthage, North Africa and in Monsagro and Toledo, Spain. In Oviedo, the Sudarium was placed in the Cathedral of St. Stephen in the *camera santa* (holy room) specially built for it.

In 1075 it was reliably recorded as being taken out of its still extant *arca* or chest in the presence of the Spanish King Alfonso VI. The fact that both cloths touched the same face at different points in the Crucifixion and that the Oviedo Cloth can be traced historically to a date as early as 570 A.D. are further proof that the Carbon-14 dating in 1988 which dated the Shroud to between 1260 - 1390 cannot be correct. New evidence discussed elsewhere has confirmed a flawed testing in 1988. Those wishing a highly detailed study of the Oviedo Cloth by Mark Guscin may look up *The Oviedo Cloth* (The Luttenworth Press) 1998, Cambridge, CT. ISBN 07188-2985-9.

The key date in the history of the Sudarium, according to Guscin, is 14 March 1075. On this date the ark or chest where the Sudarium was kept was officially opened in the presence of King Alfonso VI, his sister Dona Urraca,

THE THREE CLOTHS OF CHRIST by John C. Iannone

Rodrigo Diaz de Vivar (el Cid Campeador) and a number of bishops. This official act was recorded in a document now kept in the Capitular Archives of the cathedral in Oviedo, Series B.2.9. This is not the original document from the year 1075, but rather it is a copy, which was made in the thirteenth century.

The copy is so exact that even the signatures are imitated - the vertical signature of Urraca is clearly legible. ... The document states that even in the year 1075, the chest had been in the church for a long time ... The sudarium has been in Oviedo ever since, kept in a wooden ark. Alfonso VI had this ark covered with silver plating, on which the twelve apostles, the four evangelists and Christ are portrayed.

There are inscriptions in Arabic and Latin, both of Christian origin. After the conquest of the kingdom of Toledo, Christian- inscriptions were often written in Arabic. The Latin inscription invites all Catholics to venerate this relic that contains the holy blood. The silver plating dates from the year 1113, and gives a list of the contents of the ark. One of these items is clearly registered as `el Santo Sudario de N.S.J.C.' These letters stand for `Nuestro Senior Jesucristo', and the inscription means, `The Sacred Sudarium of Our Lord Jesus Christ'." (Guscin, 1998, pp.17-18).

****

THE THREE CLOTHS OF CHRIST   by   John C. Iannone

THE THREE CLOTHS OF CHRIST by John C. Iannone

Chapter Thirteen
THE VEIL OF VERONICA:
FACT OR FICTION?

"Your Face, O Lord, will I still seek; hide not your Face from me."

Psalm 27: 8-9

Introduction:

In Churches around the world we find an early practice formalized much later in the Medieval period called the Stations of the Cross (14 of them) which depict visually various incidents during the passion and death of Jesus until His entombment. The Church dedicates the Sixth Station to *Veronica Wiping The Face of Jesus*. The legend says that Jesus, as a reward to Veronica for wiping the sweat and blood from His face with her veil, left His imprint miraculously on the linen.

Is this an actual event or just a pious story? And what do we know of this Veil on which Jesus is believed to have left His image?

We will divide this question into two parts.

In the first part we will discuss whether there is any historical or traditional basis for the Legend of Veronica.

In the second part we will examine two claims. One claim is that the Veronica is, today, in Rome. The second claim is that the Veronica is in the town of Manoppello, Italy in a Capuchin Monastery approximately 150 miles East of Rome since the early 17th century.

THE THREE CLOTHS OF CHRIST by John C. Iannone

PART I:

Is There An Historical or Traditional Basis for The Core Legend?

The Veronica Veil is often confused with the Sudarium Christi. However, the Veronica Veil is an imaged cloth that allegedly touched Jesus during His walk to Golgotha while He was still alive. The Sudarium, on the other hand, is the Face Cloth wrapped around His head from His death on the Cross to His entombment when it was folded and put to one side. The Sudarium does NOT have an image - only bloodstains and serum as well as pollen.

Veronica: Vera Icona (True Image - Latin) or Eikon (Greek)

The Story of Veronica's Veil is *not found in the New Testament*. It appears in early Christian history. This was not the real name of the woman alleged to have wiped Jesus' face, but rather a name ascribed to her. The name given was Veronica from the Latin *Vera* (true) and *Icona* (image) or Greek *Eikon*. Her name was Bernice in the Greek literature. Later legend, which we will examine shortly, says that Veronica brought the Veil to Rome where the Veil cured the Emperor Tiberius from an unknown malady. In addition, she is said to have given the veil to Pope Clement - the 4th Pope.

However, other historical texts take the Veronica in a different direction, as we shall see. Veronica was also identified with the woman with the hemorrhage who touched the hem of Jesus' garment and was healed (Mark 5:29) of a 12 year problem of bleeding. Jesus stopped and asked who touched Him. He stated that power (*dunamin* in Greek) went out from Him and healed her. The New Testament story is worth repeating here:

> "And a great crowd followed Him and pressed around Him. And a woman who had had a hemorrhage for twelve years, and had had a great deal of treatment from various doctors and had spent all that she had and had not been benefited at all but had actually grown worse, had heard about Jesus. And she came up in the crowd behind Him and touched His robe, for she said, 'if I can only touch His clothes, I shall get well.' The hemorrhage stopped at once and she felt in her body that she was cured. Jesus instantly perceived

THE THREE CLOTHS OF CHRIST by John C. Iannone

that healing power had passed from Him and He turned around in the crowd and said, 'Who touched my clothes?' His disciples said to Him, 'you see the crowd pressing around you and yet you ask, Who touched me?' But He still looked around to see the person who had done it. The woman, knowing what had happened to her, came forward frightened and trembling and threw herself down at His feet and told Him the whole truth. And He said to her, 'my daughter, it is your faith that has cured you. Go in peace and be free from your disease.'"

Mark 5: 24-34. See also Matthew 9:18-26; Luke 8:40-56

This woman healed by Jesus came to be identified in early Christian history as Veronica.

Early Sources of the Evolving Legend:

The Veronica Veil, as indicated above, does NOT appear in the New Testament, although the story of the woman with the hemorrhage DOES appear when she touches the hem of Jesus' garment and is cured. She is later identified as Veronica.

Eusebius (Church Historian circa 325 A.D.)

Eusebius of Caesarea, who wrote the *History of the Church* during the reign of the Emperor Constantine, does NOT mention Veronica or the Veil, but does talk of the woman with the hemorrhage. (Eusebius: Ecclesiastical History: V11-18, 325 A.D.) mentioned in Matthew, Mark and Luke. At this time, the woman is not named by Eusebius.

ACTS OF PILATE (ACTA PILATI).

It was not long before a name was given to this woman in a work called the *Acts of Pilate* - an apocryphal writing also called the *Gospel of Nicodemus* - around 380 A.D. In this work, mention is made for the first time (that we know of) of the name of Veronica. She is named and associated with the woman healed of the hemorrhage by Jesus. No mention is made of the Veil or Legend yet. However, it should be noted that, since the term Veronica means Vera Icona or True Image, it is possible that the Legend was known earlier but not reiterated in this work.

Further, the *Acts of Pilate* dating from approximately 380 A.D. are considered by historians to be a work which grew

THE THREE CLOTHS OF CHRIST by John C. Iannone

over the centuries allegedly from the records Pilate kept at the Praetorium at the Fortress Antonia when he was Governor. He, however, was not the author. The text, according to scholars, contains multiple parts which are "uneven in style and would seem to be by different hands." The oldest section called the *Report of Pilate To The Emperor Claudius,* added as an Appendix, may have been composed in the late 2nd century (or earlier).

The *Acts of Pilate*, Chapter VII states:

> "And a certain woman named **Bernice** (**Veronica** in the Latin) crying out from afar off said: 'I had an issue of blood and touched the hem of His garment and the flowing of my blood was stayed which I had twelve years.'"

Now, for the first time in our known literature we see the woman with the issue of blood in the New Testament, and mentioned in Eusebius, given the name Veronica.

Justin Martyr - 160 A.D.

Justin, an early Church Father, who wrote *The First and Second Apology* (Apology here means defense of the faith) in Chapter 35 mentions the *Acts of Pilate* around 160 A.D. in two letters which he wrote to the Roman Emperor Pius and the Roman Governor Urbicus. All three of these men lived between 138 and 161 A.D. In his letter he indicates that:

> "And that these things did happen, you can ascertain from the *Acts of Pontius Pilate*."

While no mention is made of Veronica or her veil in Justin's letters, it is possible that this early version to which Justin refers might have been circulating and included some information about the Veronica Legend since the *Acts of Pilate* was known to Justin as well as to Roman authorities.

Tertullian:

Tertullian, an early Church Father, also mentions the *Acts of Pilate* toward the end of the Second Century but does not mention Veronica. Likewise, Epiphanius refers to an *Acta Pilati* in 376 A.D. but the extant Greek texts show evidence of later editing. Noted scholar Joannes Quasten in his *Patrology* believes that it is likely this legend was known

THE THREE CLOTHS OF CHRIST by John C. Iannone

at an earlier date.

St. Irenaeus of Lyon:

St. Irenaeus of Lyon, a Bishop living in what is now France, was one of the great theologians of the second century. Fr. Heinrich Pfeiffer, a world renowned scholar of early Christian art, makes an interesting statement:

> "St. Irenaeus of Lyon (130-200) recounts in his work *'Against Heresies'* that the followers of the Egyptian Gnostic heretic Carpocrates (2nd century), possessed and venerated *images of Christ* '...some are painted images, others made of other materials and are made according to *the model executed by Pontius Pilate* 'during the time in which Jesus was among men.'"
>
> Francesco Barbesino, Cristianita n. 311 (2002) *The Holy Face of Manoppello*

Another translation of *Against Heresies* from the Christian Classics Ethereal Library states:

> "They (Carpocratians) also possess images, some of them painted, and others formed from different kinds of material; while they maintain that *a likeness of Christ was made by Pilate* at that time when Jesus live among them."

In addition, the Carpocratian Marcellina "possessed a picture of Christ which she honored...with prayer and incense."
   (cf: www.thenazareneway.com/likeness_of_our_saviour.htm)

It is possible that even in the time of Pilate (when Veronica would have lived) the image referred to as "the model" or "the likeness of Christ" could have been the Veronica which Pilate or his soldiers possibly saw. They could refer to the Veronica Veil since soldiers were present when Veronica wiped Jesus' face and would have reported this to Pilate. The Carpocratians were likely aware of this and created images from this original.

While modern historians say that the *Acts of Pilate* around 380 A.D. was a later, complete edition, it is very possible that the Veronica Legend was contained in the earlier, less developed work around 163 A.D. which continued to evolve to

THE THREE CLOTHS OF CHRIST by John C. Iannone

the fourth century - making the legend much earlier in Church history.

The Avenging of the Saviour:

In the late 7th Century (680 A.D.) mention is made of the name of Veronica and, for the first time, the Legend of the imprinted cloth which healed the Emperor Tiberius is outlined. The work is also referred to in the *Cura Sanitatis Tiberii - The Cure of the Emperor Tiberius* and identifies Veronica as the woman with the issue of blood as well as mentioning the imprinted cloth. (Matthew, Mark and Luke).

In the *Avenging of the Saviour* we read:

> "...and another woman named Veronica, who suffered twelve years from an issue of blood, and came up to Him behind and touched the fringe of His garment, was healed."

Later in the text we read:

> "Then they made a search about the face or portrait of Jesus, how they might find it. And they found a woman named Veronica who had it."

> "Then they made a search with great diligence to seek the portrait of the Lord; and the found a woman named Veronica who had the portrait of the Lord. Then the Emperor Tiberius said to Velosianus: How hast thou it?"

The story goes on to say that:

> "Velosianus spread out the cloth of gold on which the portrait of the Lord had been imprinted. The Emperor Tiberius saw it...and his flesh was cleansed ...and all the blind, the lepers, the lame, the dumb, the deaf and those possessed by various diseases, who were there present, were healed and cured and cleansed."

From all this we see that the Gospels talk of the woman with the issue of blood. Eusebius mentions her again in 325. The *Acts of Pilate* around 380 gives her the name Veronica (true image) and the *Avenging of the Saviour* (680 A.D.) identifies her as Veronica who had the imprinted cloth with Jesus' face.

THE THREE CLOTHS OF CHRIST by John C. Iannone

Egeria - a 4th Century Christian Pilgrim:

Egeria, a woman from Gaul who traveled to the Holy Land in the 4th century (approximately 381-384 A.D.), recalls in her legendary *Diary* how she joined Christians from all parts of the Roman world walking westward on Holy Thursday from the Garden of Gethsemane to the Church of the Holy Sepulcher where they celebrated Jesus' death and resurrection. We don't know if they were aware of or honored this aspect of the passion (Veil of Veronica), but they may have been aware. As one writer noted:

> "It is...impossible to say with confidence what Egeria did NOT describe, since we now have only a fraction of what she wrote."

Over the years the route of pilgrim processions - beginning at the ruins of the Fortress Antonia (the Praetorium where Jesus was scourged) and ending at the church of the Holy Sepulcher was accepted as the way that Jesus went to his death. Today the procession winds through the crowded areas of Jerusalem's Old City.

Pilgrims contributed to European development of the Stations. Returning from the Holy Land, they brought oil from lamps that burned around Jesus' tomb as well as soil and relics from the holy places. They also brought memories of the liturgies, devotions and shrines they experienced. Model shrines were built in imitation around Europe. Since the Veronica was added to the Stations at this time, it is possible that they brought this custom and information back from the Holy Land. In the 1500's villages all over Europe started creating "replicas" of the way of the cross with small shrines commemorating the places along the route in Jerusalem.

Sometimes European artists created works depicting scenes of Jesus' journey to Calvary. The faithful installed these sculptures or paintings at intervals along a procession route, inside the parish church or outdoors. Performing the devotion meant walking the entire route, stopping to pray at each Station

The Moslem conquest of Palestine in the 7th century contributed to the building of replicas of the holy places in Europe, as Christians, finding access to the holy places

THE THREE CLOTHS OF CHRIST by John C. Iannone

more difficult, sought places of pilgrimage nearer home.
cf: www.communitiyofhopeinc.org

The Importance of Legends:

While the Veronica Veil is considered a legend transmitted down through time, it does not imply that it is not true. We simply do not know all of the information on which these earlier legends were based. They are like pieces of the puzzle that are missing to us but likely *known in the ancient world*. We must remember that legends – often embellished with time - likely have a kernel of truth from written or oral tradition.

Historian Steven Runciman, author of *"Some Remarks on the Image of Edessa"* (Cambridge Historical Journal 111, No. 3, 1931), a highly respected scholar, once said that:

> "Historians should not be so much victims to their skepticism as to dismiss a legend as false unless they can suggest how it was that the false legend arose."

There is often a kernel of truth which may be embellished with time but this does not invalidate the tradition on which the story was based. When dealing with early sources we need to keep in mind that earlier writers (of the first few centuries) *likely had access to information from both literature and oral tradition* which may easily have disappeared later. Great works and smaller ones (manuscripts, legal documents, letters, etc.) go through many dangers including:

1. Being hidden, lost and never found in the desert sands. Consider that the Nag Hammadi Library of Gnostic Literature and the Dead Sea Scrolls were found in modern times and give great insight into the early Jewish and Christian faith.

2. Being suppressed by authorities in disagreement with various groups or hidden by those fearing persecution.

3. Being destroyed - by accident or on purpose. The tragic burning of the famous Library of Alexandria in Egypt was a great loss of early source material. This Library, built by the successor of Alexander the Great in 283 B.C. was destroyed in 48 B.C. by fire, blamed by some as started deliberately by Caesar. Often in history, authorities (civil or church) sometimes had book-burnings to destroy

THE THREE CLOTHS OF CHRIST by John C. Iannone

unwanted literature that did not agree with their thinking. They say that history is often written by the victorious who efface the unwanted material of the past.

4. Suffering disintegration and deterioration due to age and climate if not properly stored.

5. Being stolen. Many manuscripts are kept in private archives by Collectors, etc.

It is safe to assume that this legend which appears later in time was based on a valid tradition alluded to by Eusebius, *The Acts of Pilate, The Avenging of the Saviour* and carried into Medieval tradition as a Station of the Cross. We know that many religions treasure oral traditions passed down by their leaders and shamans.

The Journey of the Veronica Veil:

Historically, Professor Heinrich Pfeiffer, Professor of Early Christian Art at the Pontifical Gregorian University in Rome, traces the movement of the Veil from Jerusalem to Ephesus with the Apostle John and then to Camulia (Kamulia) in Cappadocia in eastern Turkey, (near Edessa). While Pfeiffer does not explain how the Veil was in the hands of the Apostle John, this is still possible. Peter and John were the first to see the Shroud in the tomb. Peter went to Rome and we know that the Shroud went to Edessa in Turkey and not with him to Rome. The Sudarium, or Face Cloth, remained in Jerusalem until 614 A.D. John went to Turkey – Ephesus – and the Veil may have been with him, working its way to Camulia near Edessa. However, we do not have clear proof of the involvement of the Apostle John.

The Veil In Camulia (Kamulia) in Cappadocia, Ancient Turkey:

We do know that it was in Camulia, a city near Edessa (home of the Shroud) in eastern Turkey. A later Byzantine Historian, Cedronos, writing during the reign of Emperor Alexios Comnenos (1081-1118), noted that the Veronica moved from Camulia to Constantinople - the seat of the Byzantine Empire - by order of the then Emperor Justin II around 574 A.D. It was referred to as an "*acheiropoietos*" or image not made from human hands, a title also ascribed to the Holy Shroud.

THE THREE CLOTHS OF CHRIST by John C. Iannone

The Veil In Constantinople:

In Constantinople, the Image of Camulia became a "palladium," that is, the protective image of the capital guaranteeing protection to the city and victory to the imperial army.

> "It is said that the relic was received with enthusiasm in Constantinople and was raised up during the battle of Constantina in Africa in 581 and also at the battle of the Arzaman River in 586 and that it was present in many other battles. The Emperor Eraclio (575-641) on his departure for a military campaign in Persia, held in his hand a standard on which was carved the Image of Camulia. Later, in 626 during the attack on Constantinople by the Avars, the holy image was displayed on the walls of the city in order to defend it."
>
> Francesco Barbesino, Christianita n.311 (2002) *The Holy Face of Manoppello*

J. Gretsei (opera, XV, 196-7, Regensburg, 1741) relates that in Constantinople:

> "It was regarded as so sacred that a special festival was instituted in its honor and it was frequently carried in war as a potent icon."

Zacharias, MPG, Ixxxv, 1159) indicates that:

> "It (the cloth) was frequently carried in war as a portent icon. In the war against the Persians the General Philippicus had a picture of Christ which the Romans believed to be supernatural in origin, and the same portrait served to quell a mutiny in the army of Priscus, the successor of Philippicus. This icon was apparently on cloth and was a copy of an original."

While the battle standard may not have been the original Veil, it was likely made as a copy of the Veil in Constantinople.

Professor Pfeiffer points out in an article *"The Holy Face: From Jerusalem to Rome,"* three other references referring to the Veronica related to Constantinople:

THE THREE CLOTHS OF CHRIST by John C. Iannone

"Theofilatto Simocatta in a praise-poetry written to celebrate the victory of the Byzantine troops in the battle near the river Arzamon (586) obtained thanks to the presence of the Image, described it: 'not painted, not woven, but made with divine art.'"

"Giorgio Piside defined it as: "a prototype written by God.""

"Theofane (758-818), even after the disappearance from Constantinople declared that: 'no human hand could have drawn this Image, but only the creative and everything-forming Word produced the shape of this divine-human figure.'"

(See also: H. Pfeiffer, *"But the 'Veronica' is in Manoppello"* 30 Days Magazine, No. 5, May 2000, pp 78-79.)

The Patriarch Germanus I Sends The Veronica To Rome:

Barbesino relates that:

"One day the image disappeared never to be seen again in Constantinople...In the *Vita* of Germano I, Patriarch of Constantinople (715-730) it is narrated that he saved the Acheropite by throwing it into the sea. Miraculously the image reached the shore of Ostia where it was pulled from the water and brought to Rome. Despite the legendary aspect of the narration, there are other documents which seem to confirm the substance of what happened, namely the sending of the relic to Rome."

Pfeiffer places the date of this transfer between the first and second reign of Justinian II (679-711) between 695-705.

Barbesino notes that:

"The same information, stripped of its legendary characteristics, is furnished by the Byzantine chronicler Giorgio Monaco in his *Chronikon* published in 842. In this document it states that Saint Germano I, patriarch of Constantinople...exiled by the Emperor Leo III Isaurico (717-741) for his firm opposition to the Iconoclasts, carried the relic with him into exile and later sent it to Rome to Pope St. Gregory II (715-731). These facts are related also in some Greek

THE THREE CLOTHS OF CHRIST by John C. Iannone

codices of the Vatican dating from the 11th century, copies of a document which is judged to be not more than 130 years removed from the events narrated."

It appears, however, that the Veronica was received a few years earlier by Pope John VII in 708 A.D.

The Second Council of Nicea (787 A.D.):

It wasn't until 787 A.D. that the Second Council of Nicea, as mentioned earlier, ruled in favor of the veneration of icons. Until that time, the Veil was considered to be in danger in Constantinople from the Iconoclasts who wanted to destroy images.

The Council declared:

> "One can and one must be free to use images of our Lord and God, in mosaics, paintings, etc."

Pope John VII Receives The Veronica in Rome:

Later history confirms that, during the Iconoclastic debates in the 8th century when Icons were threatened with destruction, the Veronica was sent to Rome in 708 A.D. by the Byzantine Patriarch Germanus for temporary safe-keeping but remained there with the fall of the Byzantine Empire. The assumption is made by later writers that the Veronica Veil was present in the Old St. Peter's (built by Constantine the Great circa 325) in the papacy of John VII (705-708). Pope John VII had a Chapel (or Oratory) called the *Oratory of St. Mary of the Veronica* built and the Pope had placed the precious relic received from Constantinople in this Chapel during his reign.

Pope Stephen II:

In 753, the Lombard King Aistulfo besieged the city of Rome. When this happened, a procession was recorded with Pope Stephen II carrying an "Achieropsita" - that is, an icon on which a veil was placed. It was known at the time as the Holy Face of the Sancta Sanctorum Chapel in the Pope's Lateran Palace - likely, according to Pfeiffer, the Holy Face now in Manoppello. It is thought that the Veil was hidden after its arrival in Rome, perhaps attached, as noted by Bianchi, on top of the icon called the "Acheropsita" in the Sancta Sanctorum of the Lateran and then, under Innocent III (1198-1216), taken off and removed

THE THREE CLOTHS OF CHRIST by John C. Iannone

to Saint Peter's with the name Veronica.

Pilgrims in Rome in 1199 A.D. Mention Veronica:

Recording of Veronica's presence in Rome is attested to in 1199 A.D. when two pilgrims, Gerald de Barri (Giraldus Cambrensis) and Gervase of Tilbury made two accounts at different times of a visit to Rome which made direct reference to the existence of the Veronica Veil. In 1211, Gervase of Tilbury called it:

> "Est ergo Veronica pictura Domini vera."
>
> "The Veronica is, therefore, a true picture of the Lord."
> Gervase of Tilbry: *Otia Imperialia* (iii 25)

From the 12th Century until 1608 the Veronica was kept in the Vatican Basilica as it was a popular destination of pilgrims. In 1297 by order of Pope Boniface VIII, the image was brought to St. Peters. In 1456 its veneration was established by Pope Innocenzo III who called it "Veronica."

Veronica Veil as a "Mirabilia Urbis":

In the Holy Year 1300 the Veil was publicly displayed and became one of "Mirabilia Urbis" (wonders of City) for pilgrims. Dante Alighieri mentions the Veronica in *The Divine Comedy - Paradiso*, Canto XXXI (verses 103-111) - "the people coming to Rome to see the Veil." During the fourteenth century it became a central icon in the Western Church - in the words of Art Curator Neil Macgregor:

> "From the 14th century on, wherever the Roman Church went, the Veronica would go with it."

The Veil Is Believed Taken from The Vatican:

Then, during a rebuilding of St. Peter's Basilica between 1506-1626, at one point involving Michelangelo who designed the Dome, Professor Pfeiffer says *the Veil was stolen from the Vatican* and brought, eventually, to Manoppello. The claim is made that in 1506 during construction of the new St. Peter's Basilica, as recorded in the *Capucine Provincial Archive* - a mysterious stranger brought the Veil to Manoppello and gave it to a gentleman of the place, Dr. Giacomo Antonio Leonelli.

THE THREE CLOTHS OF CHRIST by John C. Iannone

The precious veil was kept in the Leonelli family for over a century. Then, in 1608, it was included in the nuptial gifts for Maria Leonelli for 400 scudi (an old Italian unit of currency), but the gift was never delivered. In 1608 Maria's husband, Pancrazio Petrucci stole it from his father-in-law's home. Later, in order to have her husband released from prison in Chieti, she sold the veil to Dr. Donato Antonio De Fabritis who placed it in a Walnut Frame adorned with Silver and gold between two pieces of glass and presented it to the Capuchins in 1638 as recorded between 1640 and 1646 by Padre Donato da Bomba who wrote a "Relatione Historica" (Historical Report).

The Veil Stolen From Rome In 1606 or 1608:

We note that historical research found that in 1608 during St. Peter's restoration under Paul V's papacy (1605-1621) the Chapel where Veronica's veil had been kept was demolished. Pfeiffer thinks it likely that on this occasion (the demolishing of the old chapel) the veil was stolen and brought to the Capuchin Monks at Manoppello. However, it may have been in 1606 as we will see shortly.

In the *Relatione Historica* of Padre Donato it states:

> "Taking the scissors Father Clemente himself cut away all the hanging threads and cleaning the most sacred image well of dust, moths and other filth, made it in the end just as it is now. The above-mentioned Donat'Antonio, eager to enjoy the sacred image with greater devotion, had it stretched in a wooden frame with glass on both sides, embellished with little frames and walnut work by one of our Capuchin monks named Brother Remigio da Rapino (not trusting other lay masters)".

It is noteworthy that in 1618, the Vatican archivist Giacomo Grimaldi made a precise list of the objects held in the Old Saint Peter's. On his list was the reliquary containing Veronicas' veil. He writes that the reliquary's crystal glass was "broken". Pfeifer notes that the veil in Manoppello has, on its bottom edge, a small piece of broken glass.

(See Antonil Gaspari: *Has Veronica's Veil Been Found?* www.catholic-forum.com).

THE THREE CLOTHS OF CHRIST by John C. Iannone

PART 2:

Is the True Veronica In Rome or Manoppello?

Pfeiffer announced recently, after years of research, that he believes that the true Veronica is not in Rome but rather in the Capuchin Monastery of the Sacred Face in Manoppello, Italy which lies approximately 150 miles to the east of Rome on a mountain top near the Adriatic Sea. The Sanctuary of the Holy face was built between 1617 and 1638. He made this announcement after years of study. But why does he believe the Veil is not in Rome, but rather at the Santuario del Volto Santo (Sanctuary of the Holy Face) in Manoppello?

The Case Against Its Presence in Rome:

The case against the Veil's presence in Rome after 1608 stems from some information that Pfeiffer and others have noted:

1. The Veronica that was kept in St. Peter's Basilica in Rome no longer shows any image. Lorenzo Bianchi notes that:

> "The few scholars of the past who were able to see it close up, such as DeWaal and Wilpert …saw only a few brown stains. The people who have been able to observe it recently (including Pope John Paul II) found no trace of the image."

2. Pope Paul V (1617) ordered that no reproductions of the Veronica in the 1600's (after the cloth was allegedly stolen in 1608) were to be made unless by a "Canon of St. Peter's." Pfeiffer believes the Pope made this statement because the Veil was stolen. They had no reason to give this order if they were in possession of the Veil in Rome.

3. The eyes on the reproductions of the cloth BEFORE the theft were OPEN. AFTER the theft, the eyes on reproductions of the Veronica are CLOSED. The original Veil showed the eyes open since Jesus was alive at the time Veronica wiped His face.

4. Pope Urban VIII (1623-1644) not only prohibited reproductions of Veronica's veil but also ordered all existing copies to be destroyed. Pfeiffer believes that these orders by Pontiffs of no duplication and destruction of reproductions indicates that the Vatican no longer

THE THREE CLOTHS OF CHRIST by John C. Iannone

possessed the original.

5. As noted by Lorenzo Bianchi in his article "The Veil of Manoppello":

> "The cloth currently in Rome is not transparent, while the 1350 reliquary that contained the Veronica in Rome, kept in the treasury of the Vatican Basilica, consisting of two panes of rock crystal, was evidently intended for an object that could be viewed from both sides. This reliquary, square in shape and of a size compatible with the veil of Manoppello than which it is slightly larger (but we have seen that the veil was trimmed) was replaced by another in the mid 16th century (now lost), itself replaced by the current one. A document testifies to the solemn installation of the new relic, that is, as one assumes, by a forgery – on 21 March 1606, in a niche cut into the pillar of the dome called 'of the Veronica.'"

The Vatican cloth in Rome is only on view one time per year – the Sunday before Palm Sunday – for a very brief time from a balcony high up in St. Peter's. People do not see an image. Renowned artist Isabel Piczek once relayed to me that she had the honor of viewing the (purported) veil in Rome as a young girl and claimed she saw no image, only some stains. Other scholars noted above confirmed this same thing.

Further, the Vatican will allow no study of its possession. Vatican custodians have steadfastly refused all requests for any photographs to be taken.

It is interesting to note that Pope Benedict XVI visited Manoppello Sept. 1, 2006 recently after taking his office and prayed before the Image. Some interpret this as a possible concern by the Holy Father that the true image may not in Rome but rather in Manoppello. This is, however, conjecture.

Describing the Veil:

The description of the Veil at Manoppello is that it is 6.7 x 9.5 inches (17.5 x 24 cm) after having been trimmed in the early 1600's by the Capuchins. There are 26 warp by 26 weft threads in a square centimeter not always at a regular distance from each other. The Veil is white, almost

THE THREE CLOTHS OF CHRIST by John C. Iannone

transparent, and is kept on a high altar in a silver monstrance. The fabric is made of a rare silk called Byssus - a precious thread woven from a fine, yellowish flax referred to as "sea silk" and used by ancient Egyptians and Hebrews. It is a kind of fabric found in the graves of the Egyptian Pharaohs. The Face is displayed in a walnut frame adorned with silver and gold between two pieces of glass. This Manoppello image has two panes of glass with broken chips on bottom which the Vatican archivist Giacomo Grimaldi in 1618 indicated was true of the image that was believed to be in Rome.

Sister Blandina Paschalis Schlomer, a German Trappistine nun and iconographer living now in Manoppello, claimed that the image of the Shroud of Turin and that of the Veil are super-imposable. There are tufts of hair on the forehead as found on the Shroud. The face on the Veronica reflects a high forehead, long, shoulder length hair, a beard and moustache with a long nose that appears to have broken cartilage like the Holy Shroud image. There are dark red features and open eyes and the face is asymmetrical like someone beaten and swollen. The mouth appears slightly open and the eyes are looking upwards.

Pfeiffer notes that the cloth is so thin one can read a newspaper through it. The image appears on both sides of the cloth like a photo slide. There are similarities to the Image on the Holy Shroud as noted by both Pfeiffer (an expert on the Veil) and Fr. Werner Bulst (an expert on the Holy Shroud). Pfeiffer carried out systematic studies of the main works of art which represent Veronica's Veil before the image imposed by Pope Paul V in 1617 when Pope Paul prohibited copies of Vernonica's veil being made unless made by a canon of St. Peter's Basilica.

In Pfeiffer's study of the main works of art representing the Veil, several details of these works of art all reflect a single model: they were copies of The Image in Manoppello. Similarities include:

...The cut and flow of the hair (shoulder length).

...The blood traces.

> (Note: there is a claim of clotted blood on His nose and one pupil of the eye is slightly dilated. We note that the blood has not yet been directly tested as has

THE THREE CLOTHS OF CHRIST by John C. Iannone

that of the Shroud of Turin and the Sudarium Christi, so we must reserve judgment as to whether this is, in fact, an ancient human blood.

...The shape of the face.

The cheeks are dissimilar: one rounder than the other and appear considerably swollen((John 18:22: 19:1-3). It is consistent with the reality of an asymmetrical face of a beaten man. The lack of symmetry could support a claim of authenticity.

...The beard's characteristics and size match those of the Shroud.

...The cloth's folds all reflect a single model - the Image in Manoppello.

...The tufts of hair on the forehead.

Pfeiffer notes a point recognized in Medieval times:

"The fact that the face appears and disappears according to where the light comes from was considered a miracle in itself in medieval times."

In the judgment of Pfeiffer:

"When all different details are assembled in one image, it means the image must have been the model for all the others. So, we can say that the veil of Manoppello is nothing other than the original Veronica Veil."

However, judgment must be reserved until further testing is done to include microscopic examination; infrared and ultraviolet fluorescence; blood studies and pollen studies, chemical analysis - to name a few.

Is There Paint or Water Color on the Veil?

As noted by Roberto Falcinelli in his excellent article *"The Veil of Manoppello: Work of Art or Authentic Relic?"* in 1999 the Friar responsible for the Monastery of Manoppello contacted Professor Donato Vittore, a traumatologist at the Medical Center of the University of Bari (Italy). Vittore utilized a digital scanner and a photographic optical machine to obtain high-resolution images of the Veil. As Falcinelli notes:

THE THREE CLOTHS OF CHRIST by John C. Iannone

> "The first impression he (Vittore) got when he stood in front of the Holy Face was as if looking at a painting. After having photographed it, he studied the images rendered at the computer and said that no traces of residual paint were visible in the spaces between the threads in the fabric. He also ruled out the possibility that it could have been watercolor, as the image's outlines are extremely precise around the eyes and the mouth, while watercolor paint would have unevenly soaked the fabric causing fuzziness in the details."

Falcinelli notes that "this affirmation of the Professor Vittore remains to be verified."

Lorenzo Bianchi notes in his article "*The Veil of Manoppello*,"

> "In 1998-1999 some initial investigation of a scientific nature was conducted on the Holy Countenance of Manoppello by Donato Vittore, a professor in the Faculty of Medicine at the University of Bari. The Veil was digitally scanned at high resolution. Vittore found that the interstices between the weft and the warp of the thread show no paint residues. This allowed him to rule out the possibility that the Holy Countenance was produced by oil painting, given the lack of paint deposit, nor by watercolor painting, since the outlines of the image are very sharp in the eye and mouth and there are no smears in the lines as would have occurred had the fabric been soaked by painting."

However, Bianchi also mentioned the work of Professor Guilio Fanti of the University of Padua. Fanti did further scientific studies and noted:

> "Further microscopic and spectroscopic examination was carried out by Giulio Fanti, professor of Mechanical and Thermal engineering at the University of Padua. Ultraviolet analysis using a Wood's lamp confirmed the results of a test done in 1971: neither the tissue nor the image of the Countenance show appreciable fluorescence, to be expected in the presence of an amalgam of colors, whereas there is considerable fluorescence where there are signs of restoration, at the top right and left corners. Yet traces of

THE THREE CLOTHS OF CHRIST by John C. Iannone

> substances (pigments?) seem present on other parts of the Veil. Infrared analysis, however, has also shown the absence of preparatory drawing below the image, and the absence of corrections. A 3-D construct shows more points of correspondence between the image of the Veil and the Shroud. It was noted in conclusion that, contrary to appearances, the two images (front and back) on the veil do not perfectly mirror each other: there are unusual differences in some details between front and back, difficult to explain, and so subtle that the idea that we can speak of painting is technically very problematic."

The absence of a "preparatory drawing" is noteworthy. Artist Isabel Piczek, talking about the Holy Shroud, once noted the same thing and mentioned that the lack of outline, which she called the "horizon event in art" would not be how an artist would have worked.

Professor Fanti does note that:

> "The image of the Holy Face on the other hand seems to carry different actual shades of color. No chemical tests have yet been carried out on the image of the Holy Face, which makes it impossible to draw certain conclusions; however, in some areas, like around the pupils and the hair, the presence of pigment has been ascertained: the paint is possibly due to some Middle Ages retouch. For the moment we cannot rule out that the whole cloth was painted in watercolor technique... In some spots, due to possible retouches in Medieval times, some of the fibrillae of the Holy Face image clearly appear clinging together as if cemented."

In summary, the coloring on the Veil could be representative that the Veil was a painting or that the Veil is authentic and affected by a Medieval touch-up.

A Painting or Authentic Veil with Medieval Touch-ups?

Along these lines, Roberto Falcinelli believes that this is likely a watercolor painting by Albrecht Durer which Durer gave to the Renaissance master Rafael. However, Fr. Pfeiffer maintains that the Roman Veronica was taken in 1608. Durer was born in 1471 and died in 1528 while Raphael was born in 1483 and died in 1520. While Falcinelli makes an interesting case, we would have to consider:

THE THREE CLOTHS OF CHRIST by John C. Iannone

1. Why such a great object as the Veronica was not credited by historians of the period to Durer or Rafael.

2. How the work of this German master arrived in the small village of Manoppello (or) how it got to Rome before 1608? An image was already in place in Rome for centuries up to this point. If Rome believed it had the authentic Veronica since 708, why would authorities replace it with Durer's work?

3. Does Durer have other works in watercolor on Byssus and are these two-sided? Note: Prof. Fanti writes of an image of the head and possibly of the hands on the Holy Shroud after analyzing the back side of the Shroud on pictures taken after its restoration in 2002. He refers to this find as a *"double superficiality of the frontal image of the Turin Shroud."*

   The image may appear on both sides - similar to the Veronica.

We would need to explain the appearance of an Imaged Cloth representing the Veronica for several centuries in Rome before Durer or Rafael lived.

Scientific Notes:

...The image clearly appears on both sides of the transparent cloth like a photo slide.

...The Veil is believed to be made of Byssus, a sea silk, and extremely fine, rare and valuable fabric produced from the long silky filaments or Byssus secreted by a gland in the foot of several bivalve mollusks by which they attach themselves to the sea bed. The shell of the mollusk is almost a meter long, adheres itself to rocks with a tuft of very strong thin fibers, pointed end down in the interdidal zone.

The hypothesis about the fabric being marine Byssus was supported in 2004 by Chiara Vigo, one of the last weavers of this material. Final confirmation will come from direct tactile examination or other studies. It should be noted that marine Byssus is a smooth and impermeable fiber and is considered technically not paintable because the paint, as Bianchi notes, "would tend to slip forming crusts which do

THE THREE CLOTHS OF CHRIST by John C. Iannone

not appear on the cloth."

...Image is claimed to be super-imposable with the face on the Holy Shroud. Fr. Enrico Sammarco and Sister Blandina Paschalis Schlomer have demonstrated that the dimensions on the face of the Holy Shroud are the same as on the veil of Manoppello.

Need for Further Study:

Pollen studies have not been done on the Veronica Veil and this would help greatly. It would be revealing if there is evidence of "Gundelia tournefortii" pollen (the thorn thistle pollen prevalent on both the Holy Shroud and the Sudarium Christi) or other pollen of the Jerusalem area. It would also help greatly if there was the spread of pollen from Turkey (Camulia and Constantinople) and Italy.

Blood studies would help to determine if the blood is Type AB found on both the Shroud and Sudarium. Also, the presence of the bile pigment "bilirubin" (found in Shroud blood studies) indicating high trauma and stress would greatly support authenticity. Finally, the DNA testing, if this is real human blood, could reveal, as it does on the Holy Shroud, whether or not this is a male blood and contains "a degraded DNA consistent with the supposition of ancient blood" as Dr. Victor Tryon of the University of Texas DNA labs noted of the occipital blood sample (at the back of head) of the Holy Shroud.

The Veil Lacks Three-Dimensionality:

It should be noted here that Professor Fanti indicated that the Manoppello Veil does not show as three dimensional under the VP-8 Image Analyzer, as does the Shroud photographic images. This is interesting but does not of itself indicate that the Veil may not be authentic. We must be careful not to mix apples and oranges. If the Shroud was created, as we suspect, from a form of radiant energy emanating from within the body and creating vertical relief reflecting a cloth-to-body distance and three dimensionality, this does not mean that the Veil was created in the same manner.

The body in the tomb was deceased and, Christians believe, came to life in the Resurrection. The face in the Veil, on the other hand, is believed to be of the living Jesus whose

THE THREE CLOTHS OF CHRIST by John C. Iannone

face is being wiped as He carried His cross on the Via Dolorosa. A cloth is pressed onto His face by the alleged Veronica and leaves an imprint. The process of the creation of the Veronica, which admittedly we do not yet understand, was one that differed from the radiant energy believed by many involved with the creation of the Shroud images. It may be likened to the image of Mary on the Tilma of Guadeloupe – a mysterious imprint not yet understood.

The Value of Christian Tradition:

Today, the Church honors the Veronica Legend in the Sixth Station of the Cross: "Veronica Wipes the Face of Jesus." There is some credibility added to the Veronica Veil Legend by the fact that Church tradition from earliest times honored the story of the woman who met Jesus on the path taken in His crucifixion and wiped His face of sweat and blood, imprinting His image on the cloth.

Promotion of the devotion to the Stations began in earnest with the Franciscans who were given custody of the Holy Places in the Holy Land in the 1300s. During the time of the Crusades (1095-1270) it became popular for pilgrims in the Holy Land to walk in the footsteps of Jesus to Calvary. However, after the Moslems recaptured the Holy Land, pilgrimages were too dangerous. As a result, the Stations became a popular substitute for the Holy Land pilgrimage by bringing these practices to Europe. The Stations were originally done outdoors but the Stations were allowed inside churches in the mid-18th century.

However, the origins of the Stations (and possibly the Veronica) go back even earlier to 4th century (and likely 1st century) Jerusalem when pilgrims flocked to the Holy Land from all parts of the world to seek the path of Jesus during His passion. The path was not clear and became complicated because the Jerusalem of Jesus' day was almost completely destroyed by the Roman armies in 70 A.D. with the fall of the Second Temple and Jerusalem. The pilgrims often had to guess where some incidents took place. The most popular site was the Church of the Holy Sepulcher which had been built by the Emperor Constantine in 335 AD atop Calvary and the tomb of Jesus. Processions of pilgrims to the church were common.

THE THREE CLOTHS OF CHRIST by John C. Iannone

Conclusion:

We do have a line of references to this early legend of Veronica and a credible historical path leading from Jerusalem to Camulia, then to Constantinople and Rome and possibly to Manoppello. There are likely other references lost or not yet found that can fill the gaps.

We have also the tradition of the Church which has revered the Veronica from earliest times to the contemporary presence of the Veronica in the Stations of the Cross. While many do not yet place the Veronica on the same level of credibility as the Holy Shroud or the Sudarium, we continue to fill the gaps and hope that the authorities who possess the Veronica will allow careful scientific study of the Veronica to determine if the blood stains are comparable to those of the Shroud and Sudarium or whether the pollen tells a tale of the Veil's journey.

I draw four conclusions from these studies:

1. There is credible early historical and traditional support for the existence of the Veil of Veronica.

2. The Veil is NOT to be confused with the Sudarium Christi (Face Cloth) which has its own proven independent historical and scientific validity.

3. The original Veil is NOT currently in the Vatican in Rome.

4. The Veronica Veil MAY be in Manoppello. This will require further historical and scientific analysis especially with regard to blood and pollen studies.

We encourage the Capuchins to allow further non-destructive studies by a team of experts as was permitted by the Vatican on the Holy Shroud and by Spanish authorities on the Sudarium in Oviedo.

These are truly emerging treasures of our Christian heritage. As with the Holy Shroud, Jesus may have chosen to leave His mysterious images on the Veil of Veronica for all generations to ponder. If so, as with the Holy Shroud, there is a reason that He did this and we need to continue to study these treasure of our Christian heritage to seek to understand why the Images-on-Cloth visually support the words of the Gospel as to who Jesus really is and what He accomplished for us. *****

THE THREE CLOTHS OF CHRIST by John C. Iannone

Chapter 14

The Image Of Our Lady On The Tilma of Guadalupe

"Let not your heart be disturbed. Do not fear that sickness (of his uncle) nor any other sickness of anguish. Am I not here, who am your Mother? Are you not under my protection? Am I not your health? Are you not happily within my fold? What else do you wish? Do not grieve nor be disturbed by anything."

Words of Our Lady to Juan Diego

Background:

In 1521, the Aztecs in Mesoamerica, who ruled much of Central and South America, fell under Spanish forces. For many centuries earlier the Aztec culture professed a polytheistic religion that utilized human sacrifice. Aztec priests, believing that the end of the world was near, sacrificed thousands of men, women and children to their gods to appease the gods and stall the end. They would cut out the human hears of their unwilling victims.

It is recorded that in 1487, in a single four day ceremony for the dedication of a new temple in Tenochtitlan, over 80,000 captives were killed in human sacrifice. When the Spanish conquered the Aztecs in 1521, the Spanish missionaries stopped the sacrifices and attempted to convert the Aztecs to Christianity. They were having little success.

The Basic Story of Our Lady of Guadalupe:

An event occurred in 1531 that changed the course of Aztec

THE THREE CLOTHS OF CHRIST by John C. Iannone

history and religion. A humble peasant, Juan Diego, a native American at Tepayac, was walking many miles to Church as he did each week. Juan was on a hill about 20 kilometers (14 miles) northwest of what is now Mexico City. Suddenly, Our Lady appeared to him wanting to help the people. Our Lady told Juan that she wished a Church to be built on the site and directed him to go to the Bishop and make this request. Juan went to see Bishop Juan de Zumarraga who was naturally skeptical and asked for a sign.

When Juan returned to the hills, Our Lady appeared to him again "speaking to him as a beautiful Aztec princess talking to him in his own Aztec language." (www.catholic.or/saints). The Virgin Mary asked that he climb a hill and bring back flowers as a sign to the Bishop. It was December 12, 1521 and it was cold. The hill was bare and Juan knew that no flowers grew at this time. However, he trusted the Lady and climbed the hill, hearing many beautiful song birds and finding many sweet smelling Castilian Roses not common to the area. Juan placed them in his TILMA (his mantle consisting of a poor quality cloth made from the Cactus plant also called Ayate) and brought them to the Bishop who was understandably shocked. Everyone present suddenly noticed the Image of Our Lady on the Tilma.

Meanwhile, nearby, Juan's uncle, Juan Bernardino, had an apparition from Our Lady and it was claimed that he was miraculously cured of an ailment from which he had been dying. This cure is relayed to the Bishop. Our Lady tells Juan Bernadino to call this as being "of Guadalupe" and he relayed this to the Bishop who then had a Church built on the site.

The Name of Guadalupe:

The question of why this name was used has been discussed by scholars. Many believe that the Lady called herself "of Guadalupe" because of the miraculous statue of Our Lady of Guadalupe in Estremadura, Spain given by Pope Gregory the Great to the Bishop of Seville, Spain. The statue was lost for 600 years and found in 1326. The village of Guadalupe was located near the place of discovery.

THE THREE CLOTHS OF CHRIST   by   John C. Iannone

Conversion of the Aztecs:

Within a short period of time, astonishingly, over 9,000,000 Aztecs were converted to Christianity - a feat that the local Spanish missionaries were unable to accomplish. This fact alone is considered by many to be a miraculous result of the vision. The story of the apparitions is described in the "Nican Mopohua" a 16th century document written in the native Nahuatl language. The first formal investigation by the Church about the events, the "Informaciones Guadalupanas", was written in 1666.

The Basilica of Guadalupe:

The new Basilica of Guadalupe (built between 1974- 1977) is a circular structure 330 ft. in diameter and accommodates up to 50,000 people. It was built on the site of the earlier 16th century church finished in 1709 which in turn replaced the first Church in 1567. Each year between 18-20 million pilgrims visit the Basilica, making it Christianity's most visited sanctuary. Pope John Paul II visited the Basilica in 1999 and in 2002 Juan Diego was canonized and named as a Saint.

Brief Description of the Image:

The Image of Our Lady of Guadalupe represents an Aztec Pictograph and it is believed the Virgin Mary did this so that it would be quickly and easily understood by the Aztec Indians. In the Image, Mary stood in front of the Sun (showing her to be greater than their dreaded sun-god Huiltzilopochtli). Her foot rested on the Crescent Moon (symbolizing the vanquishing the Aztec's foremost deity, the feather serpent Quetzalcoatl). There were stars strewn across the mantle (which some scholars indicate were the stars of Dec. 12, 1531 showing the constellation of stars that appeared in the sky that day). Cf: www.catholiceducation.org .

The Science of the Tilma:

There are some remarkable facts that lend support to the authenticity of this event, elevating the event to a truly miraculous phenomenon.

THE THREE CLOTHS OF CHRIST by John C. Iannone

In the Image, Mary is standing on a serpent, crushing its head. The Serpent was an almost universal symbol of the Aztec religion. "Temples were richly decorated with snakes. Human sacrifices were heralded by the prolonged beating of huge drums made of the skins of huge snakes. Nowhere else in human history had Satan, the ancient serpent, so formalized his worship with so many of his own actual symbols." Courtesy of: www.sancta.org/nameguad.html.

1. **The "Radiant" Image of Mary:**

The Tilma measures approximately 6 1/2 by 3 1/2 feet. Many believe, based on Juan Diego's description, that the Virgin Mary appeared in her glorified body, ("a young girl of fifteen to sixteen surrounded by light" radiating the image onto the cloth). Juan Diego noted that when he reached the summit, he saw a Lady. Approaching her, he marveled at her superhuman grandeur.

> "Her garments were shining like the Sun; the cliff where she rested her feet pierced with glitter, resembling an anklet of precious stones, and the earth sparkled like the rainbow." Courtesy: www.sancta.org.

A 1772 report described the "rays of light" around the Guadalupe image. There are great similarities to the Image on the Holy Shroud (described earlier in this book) which many modern physicists believe was a result of the radiant energy emanating from within the body of Jesus at the moment of Resurrection. This same phenomenon of radiant light (auto radiation) was described by the Gospel writers in their recounting the Transfiguration of Jesus. They described His appearance as brighter than the Sun or a flash of lightning while not hurting the eyes of the three Apostles Peter, James and John who witnessed this manifestation of the glorified body of Jesus before His Crucifixion.

It should be noted that there is no under-sketch or outline used by an artist nor any sizing and no protective over-varnish. There are no brush strokes. This also bears similarity to the Image of the Holy Shroud.

2. **Song Birds and Flowers:**

It was mid-winter and there were normally no birds in the

THE THREE CLOTHS OF CHRIST by John C. Iannone

area, and certainly no flowers. More surprisingly, the many fragrant flowers were Castilian Roses native to the Bishop's home not indigenous to the area. This greatly surprised the Bishop. Juan Diego was surprised by the singing of many birds.

3. **The Image is Almost 500 Years Old:**

The Image on the cactus Tilma has not disintegrated in almost 500 years, defying the normal disintegration of the cactus fibers. The area normally has high salt and humidity in the air and local fabrics of the cactus plant disintegrate within 20 years.

...In 1979 Dr. Phillip Callahan took 40 frames of infra-red photographs of the image and later concluded that the original image is unexplainable as a human work. He concluded that portions of the face, hands, robe and mantle appeared to have been painted in one step, with no sketches or corrections and no apparent brush strokes.

... Biochemist Richard Kuhn analyzed a sample of the fabric in 1936 and found "he could not identify the pigment used as being from mineral, vegetable or animal sources." The image did not have natural animal or mineral colorings. "Given that there were no synthetic colorings in 1531, the image is inexplicable."
                    Courtesy: www.catholiceducation.org

4. **The Remarkable Eyes of the Virgin:**

One of the most fascinating discoveries involved the eyes of the Virgin which appear to reflect images.

...in 1929, Alfonso Marcue, the official photographer of the old Basilica, found in his black and white photos what appeared to be *a clear image of a bearded man reflected in the right eye of the Virgin*. This reflection appeared to fit the description of Juan Diego before the Bishop. This was kept secret at the request of authorities.

...in 1951, however, Jose Carlos Salinas Chavez examined a good photograph of the face and rediscovered the image of what seemed to be the bearded man in the right eye of the image and located it on the left eye also. Since then, (according to www.sancta.org) more than 20 physicians and

THE THREE CLOTHS OF CHRIST by John C. Iannone

Ophthalmologists have examined the eyes of the Virgin on the Tilma to verify these results.

...In 1956, Dr. Javier Torroella Bueno, MDS, a prestigious Ophthalmologist, certified the presence of the triple reflection (identified as the Samson-Purkinje Effect) characteristic of all live human eyes and states that:

> "the resulting images are located exactly where they are supposed to be according to such effect, and also that the distortion of the images agree with the curvature of the cornea." Courtesy: www.sancta.org.

...Also in 1956, Ophthalmologist Dr. Rafael Torrijo Lavoignet with an ophthalmoscope observed the apparent human figure in the corneas of both eyes, with the location and distortion of a normal human eye. He found that the eyes looked strangely "alive" when examined.

...In 1979, Dr. Jose Aste Tonsmann, Ph.D., a graduate of Cornell University, worked with an IBM scanner at high resolution off a good photograph from the original face on the Tilma. He filtered and processed the digital images to eliminate "noise" and enhance them and noted not only the human bust clearly present in both eyes, but other human figures. He wrote this in his book "El Secreto du sus Ojos" that he noted the image of various human figures that seem to constitute a family, including various children. He insisted that the basic image "has not been painted by human hands" As early as the 18th century, scientists demonstrated that it was impossible to paint such an image in a fabric of that texture. The "ayate" fibers deteriorate after 20 years.

...In 2009, Dr. Aldofo Orozco told participants at the international Marion Congress of Our Lady of Guadalupe that:

> "one of the most bizarre characteristics of the cloth is that the back side is rough and coarse, but the front side is as soft as the most pure silk, as noted by painters and scientists in 1666, and confirmed one century later in 1751 by the Mexican painter Miguel Cabrera." Courtesy: www.catholicnewsagency.com.

THE THREE CLOTHS OF CHRIST by John C. Iannone

5. An Acid Spill:

Another feature noted was that in 1791 a worker accidentally spilled a 50 percent nitric acid solvent on the right side of the cloth.

> "Besides any natural explanation, the acid has not destroyed the fabric of the cloth, indeed it has not even destroyed the colored parts of the image." according to Dr. Aldofo Orozco.
> Courtesy: www.catholicnewsagency.com.

6. A Mysterious Bomb Explosion:

> In 1921 a bomb was set off near the image. According to Dr. Aldofo Orozco, the explosion broke the marble floor and windows 150 meters away from the explosion but "unexpectedly, neither the Tilma nor the normal glass that protected the Tilma was damaged or broken." The only damage near it was a brass crucifix that was twisted by the blast."
> Courtesy: www.catholicnewsagency.com.

7. Miracles Ascribed to the Image of Guadalupe:

Finally, numerous miracles including healings have been attributed to the image.

The official Sanctuary Web Site: http://www.virgendeguadalupe.org.mx

This fascinating information on the Image of Guadalupe has remarkable similarities to the images on the Holy Shroud. We hope that the authorities who control the Tilma at the Basilica in Guadalupe, Mexico will continue to allow non-destructive testing of the Image. God's use of such images-on-cloth, not-made-by-human hands (acheiropoietos) will continue to intrigue the world and open up new dimensions in the physics of the universe and our understanding of the mysteries of our faith.

****

THE THREE CLOTHS OF CHRIST by John C. Iannone

THE THREE CLOTHS OF CHRIST by John C. Iannone

After Forward

There have been more recent findings related to the Holy Shroud which merit our attention. We will outline the key ones here:

Aramaic Letters on an Oval Placard:

Recent studies of the Shroud have determined that there is holographic information on the cloth (discussed below). One of the finds determined by Dr. Petrus Soons from these holograms indicated that there are three letters identified on an oval object just under the beard. These letters are in Hebrew or Aramaic and read **AYIN-ALEPH-NUM**.

Dr. Soons, a retired M.D. from the Netherlands, in his article *"The Shroud of Turin, The Holographic Experience"* noted, via holograms or 3D images of the Shroud, some lettering just under the beard of the image on the Shroud. He indicated that calligraphy was his hobby and that the letters **AYIN-ALEPH-NUM** are written in calligraphic form. Since he did not read Hebrew or Aramaic, he consulted experts in old Hebrew and Aramaic. These scholars consulted Hebrew and Aramaic dictionaries including: "A *Comprehensive Etymological Dictionary of the Hebrew Language for Readers of English*, by Ernest Klein, and "A *Dictionary of the Targum, The Talmud Babli and Yerushalmi and the Midrashic Literature"* by Marcus Jastrow. The Hebrew word is translated as: "small cattle, sheep, goats." They concluded that the meaning of a flock of little animals in the translation from Hebrew to Aramaic of Psalm 119:176 as translated by ibn Ezra is that the word AN meaning the LAMB. The Aramaic word **Ayin-Aleph-Num** means "**THE LAMB**."

Psalm 119:176 in English is:

> "I have gone astray like a lost sheep; seek your servant, for I do not forget your commandments."

As Dr. Soons points out:

> "Now, here we have the Shroud of Turin with the image of a crucified man, who according to tradition was

THE THREE CLOTHS OF CHRIST by John C. Iannone

Jesus Christ, and under the beard an object (oval) upon whose surface is written in Aramaic the word **"THE LAMB."**

This is an extraordinary finding seen on the holograms of the Holy Shroud. As Dr. Soons points out, the designation of Jesus as **THE LAMB** makes great biblical sense because:

> ...The Gospels mention that Jesus approached the river Jordan where John the Baptist was teaching and baptizing. When John sees Jesus he tells the people: "Behold, here comes THE LAMB OF GOD that takes away the sins of this world."
>
> ...During the Catholic Eucharist, when the priest shows the bread, he says: "This is the Body of Jesus Christ, THE LAMB OF GOD that takes away the sins of this world."
>
> ...In the book if the Apocalypse of John, the word LAMB is mentioned 28 times and always means Jesus Christ.
>
> ...During the last Supper, where according to the Jewish tradition of the Pesach-meal, wine, bread and lamb should have been present. The Gospels only mention the bread and wine. The reason is that Jesus himself is THE Lamb and will be sacrificed the next day."

The Holographic Information On The Shroud:

Dr. Soons, in the same article and in a joint presentation at the Missouri Botanical Gardens along with Prof. Avinoam Danin of Hebrew University in Jerusalem, presented his work on the holography of the Shroud while Danin discussed the plant images.

As noted earlier, Dr. Avinoam Danin, Emeritus Professor of Botany at the Hebrew University of Jerusalem, has spent decades examining images of plant remains he discovered on the Shroud; collectively, these indicate a geographic origin of the burial in the vicinity of Jerusalem during the months of March or April. Dr. Petrus Soons has used digitized photos of the linen cloth to create another device for study: three-dimensional holograms.

THE THREE CLOTHS OF CHRIST by John C. Iannone

Dr. Soons utilized the digitization of excellent Shroud photographs taken in 1931 by Giuseppe Enri. Soons enhanced the original photos to improve details, and then translated the enhanced grayscale images into depth data. The result was a sequence of nearly 625 images for each photo, which computer expert Bernardo Galmarini combined using a Holoprinter to produce three-dimensional (3-D) holographic images of the Shroud. This unprecedented new view of the artifact yielded the discovery of previously unseen details, confirmation of many previous findings, and a few surprises.

Since the Shroud contained three-dimensional images as noted by Physicists Dr. John Jackson and Eric Jumper in 1978 and confirmed by Professor Tamburelli of the University of Turin, Dr. Soons believed that this information could be translated into a 3-D hologram. He recalled that after the fire of 1997, Aldo Guerreschi, a professional photographer familiar with the image, was asked to photo-document the examination of the Shroud. Guerreschi observed the following:

> "Moving around the table (with the Shroud laid out horizontally) I saw this image so faded as if to practically disappear, while from other angles, it seemed as if the figure was almost outside the sheet."

With this information, Dr. Soons formed a team of experts to produce holograms based on the scientifically proven 3D information in the grayscale of the image. Readers are referred to his article "The Shroud of Turin, The Holographic Experience" for a detailed explanation of how a hologram is formed. For our purposes, we will examine the results.

Essentially, he utilized excellent second and third generation copies of the Giuseppe Enrie photos of 1931. He then digitalized the Enrie negatives to facilitate translation of image density information into gray scale numbers. Bernardo Galmarini, an Argentinean 3D expert, translated the gray-scale levels into depth-data on the Z-axis and repaired and softened existing image areas that were void of 3D information. Bernardo generated a sequence of 625 images which were integrated into a 3D shroud image using a Holoprinter.

THE THREE CLOTHS OF CHRIST   by   John C. Iannone

Some Observations:

Dr. Soons made some interesting observations. Among them:

He noted that some image areas were void of 3D information and showed up as "holes." There were multiple, little "holes" or gaps on the forehead, the right and left sides of the face, the anatomical right side of the moustache and beard and the middle of the lower part of the beard. He recalled photographs of the face in the book by Dr. Alan and Mary Whanger where Professor Danin had drawn in images of flowers and plants. *It appeared that these flowers blocked the formation of the body-image information of these areas ("holes") of the face and the body around the arms and hands.* We recall that there is no image under the bloodspots. As Dr. Soons notes:

> "Whatever the image formation process was, it seemingly did not penetrate solid objects such as bloodspots or flowers. Two flowers also appear in the middle of the tip of the beard."

He also observed that both legs are bent (flexed at the knees) with the anatomical left leg bent a little more than the right leg and partly covering it. We noted earlier that this was the result of rigor mortis on the Cross fixing the position of the legs as slightly flexed at the knees.

In addition, the anatomical left foot crosses over the right foot in the form of an X and the tips of the toes of the left foot are visible.

There are many more observations indicating that the head is bent forward (again reflecting the position of the head at the time of crucifixion) and the observation that the hair falls down along the neck and the back and "looks wet." It appears to Dr. Soons as "rope-like" in the middle, similar to a ponytail or braid mentioned in the literature.

We have much more to observe and learn from these holographic images.

Other Claims of Letters on the Shroud:

In the past years there have been claims made that other words were found on the Shroud. While we do not categorically deny them, they do not appear to have the same evidence as those claimed by Dr. Petrus Soons above.

THE THREE CLOTHS OF CHRIST by John C. Iannone

Among them, a recent book published by Vatican archivist Barbara Frale in her new book *The Shroud of Jesus The Nazarene* claims that she has "discovered" inscriptions on the Shroud that prove its authenticity. She based her conclusions on the 1997 work of French researchers Andre Marion and Anne Laure Courage from the Institut d'Optique Theorique et Appliqué d'Orsay. Earlier claims were made by the Italian Piero Ugolotti in 1979 and Fr. Dubois, a French priest in 1982. (in the late 1990's).

As Shroud scholar Barrie Schwortz points out, however, their evidence is not at all clear, being based only on the Enrie photos, which he states are deceiving. In addition, language scholar Mark Guscin studied their findings and concluded that the inscriptions noted in the 1990's:

> "None of the inscriptions which some claim to be able to see make enough grammatical or historical sense." He carefully reviews them and demonstrated that these phrases were not historically or grammatically accurate for their time.

The Fabric of Time:

In a recent DVD entitled: *The Fabric of Time: Are The Secrets of the Universe Hidden in an Ancient Cloth?,* we see evidence of the 3-D hologram of the Shroud as developed by Dr. Soons. Particle physicists talk of the Shroud as "taking a quantum leap" in physics. As Particle physicist (and artist) Isabel Piczek indicates, the Shroud takes us to a threshold gate which leads to extraordinary world with extraordinary laws and redefines a physics we do not yet understand. She calls it an "event horizon in physics. Fred Alan Wolf, Ph.D., author of *Taking The Quantum Leap*, talks of an exponential growth of our knowledge of the laws of physics to which the Shroud introduces us.

The Executive Producers, Vance Syphers, Paul Shubert and Joseph Call, and writer Joseph Meier, show us the holograms of Dr. Soons (you wear 3-D lenses to watch portions of this unique DVD. The DVD is produced by Grizley Adams Productions. Optical Engineer Kevin Moran talks of the image being created by a type of atomic laser as yet unknown. The hologram is developed off the 1931 Enrie Photos which required more time to develop and more light, leading to more information contained therein. Reader are encouraged to view this fascinating movie which talks of

THE THREE CLOTHS OF CHRIST   by   John C. Iannone

different information at different levels seen on the Shroud.

Double Sided Image:

A recent find on the Shroud, still under review, was made by Professors Giulio Fanti and Roberto Maggiolo in 2002. Fanti writes of an image of the head and possibly of the hands after analyzing the back side of the Shroud on pictures taken after its restoration in 2002. They refer to this find as a *"double superficiality of the frontal image of the Turin Shroud."* The reverse side of the Shroud remained hidden for centuries beneath a piece of Holland cloth sewn on by the nuns in 1534 after the fire of 1532.

Recently, in 2002, when the backing of the cloth was removed along with the patches from the fire, Monsignor Giuseppe Ghiberti, one of the custodians of the cloth, photographed the back of the Shroud in detail. He published his photographs. He did not notice any images.

Professor Giulio Fanti, Professor of Mechanical and Thermic Measurements at Padua University, however, after study and enhancement of the photographs, stated:

> "As I saw the pictures in the book, I was caught by the perception of a faint image on the back surface of the Shroud. I thought that perhaps there was much more that wasn't visible to the naked eye."

Fanti utilized several techniques to enhance what he believed he saw. Using Fourier transform, digital enhancement, template matching and Gaussian filters, he noted the image of the face and possible image of the hands.

Fanti noted that the image on both sides was "superficial" – that is – a surface phenomenon, a known characteristic of the images on the front side of the Shroud which affect only the topmost fibrils of the fibers. This was, Fanti noted, also true of the back image. There was nothing between the front and back images. The image is above and below on front and back surfaces, but not in the middle which would have occurred if the image bled through the cloth from any substance.

THE THREE CLOTHS OF CHRIST by John C. Iannone

As Fanti noted:

> "It is extremely difficult to make a fake with these features."

More research is being done on the superficiality of the front and back images.

> Cf: Rossella Lorenzi, Discovery News: *Turin Shroud Back Side Shows Face*. April 11, 2004
>
> Cf: Belle Dume, *Physics Web: Reversal of Fortune for Turin Shroud*.
>
> Cf: Prof. Giulio Fanti: *Journal of Optics: Pure and Applied Optics*, 2004, 491-503

Public Exposition of the Holy Shroud:

Pope Benedict XVI has announced the public exposition of the Holy Shroud in Turin at the Cathedral of St. John the Baptist from April 5 – May 22. Those interested in going on a pilgrimage to both Manoppello to see the Veronica and Turin to see the Holy Shroud are welcome to visit my website: www.shroudinfo.com

or contact me via e-mail at: jciannone@gmail.com

to ask questions or provide helpful comments. Thank you.

For in-depth scientific articles on the Holy Shroud, please visit the website of Barrie Schwortz, Shroud photographer of the STURP team at www.shroud.com .

****

THE THREE CLOTHS OF CHRIST   by   John C. Iannone

THE THREE CLOTHS OF CHRIST by John C. Iannone

INDEX OF AUTHORS

Abbot Helinand 124
Abgar, king 105, 107-9, 110,112, 114-117, 122, 144
Accetta, Dr. August 102 - 103
Achilles 26, 104
Adler, Dr. Alan, 68-9, 72, 97, 164-65
Aistulfo, king 188
Alexander large the 47, 52, 184
Amalric the 122-125, 134, 139
Ananias 108-110
Andrew of Crete 115
Avi-Yonan, Michael 43
Balossino, Dr. Nello 43
Ballone, Dr. Baima 43, 68, 85
Barbescino, Francisco 181, 186
Barbet, Dr. Pierre 54.61
Baruch, Dr. Uri 34, 35, 170.175
Basil of Jerusalem, 115
Benford, Susan 6, 23, 165-66
Bernard of Clairvaux 132-33
Bianchi, Lorenzo 191, 194-5, 197
Bishop D' Arcis 130
Blanco, Dr. Jose Delfin 69
Boniface de Montferrat 126
Bonnet-Eymard, Brother 131
Braulio 114
Bucklin, Dr. Robert 17, 44, 51, 54-59,61-62, 66, 69, 151
Bulst, S.J., Werner 32, 82-83, 193
Caiaphas 54
Cameron, Dr. James 43-44, 59
Cardinal Anastasio Ballestrero 155, 157, 161, 163-4
Cardinal Augustino Casaroli 161
Cardinal Giovanni Saldarini 8, 71, 141-142
Cardinal Louis de Gorrevod 13
Cardinal Michelle Pellegrino, 15, 20
Cardinal Savarino Poletto, 142, 164
Carter, Dr. Giles 102-103
Cases, Giuseppe 69
Chosroes, king the 112, 144
Clement, Father 190

THE THREE CLOTHS OF CHRIST by John C. Iannone

INDEX OF AUTHORS - CONT.

Clotilde, Prince 13
Comnenus, Alexis, 122
Comnenus, Manuel I, 122
Coon, Dr. Carleton 16
Currer-Briggs, Noel 16, 122, 124, 131, 135, 137-8
Curto, Silvio 20
Damascene, St John 115
Damon, Paul 156-7
Daniel-Rops, Henri 16
Danin, Prof. Avinoam 29-30, 33-36, 57, 170, 175, 202, 204
Dante Alighieri 189
DeLage, Prof. Yves 14, 25, 54, 75, 104
De Milly, Philip 123, 125, 134, 139
D' Muhala, Dr. Thomas
Dreisbach, Rev. Albert 26, 32, 119, 143-4, 146, 151
Drews, Robert 120, 145
Egeria - 108, 183
Enrie, Giuseppe 15, 33-34, 40-42, 44-45, 47, 203, 205
Erbach, Rabbi Eleaxor 18
Essenes 17, 76, 85
Eulalius, Bishop 113
Eusebius of Caesaria 108-9, 118, 179-180, 182, 185
Evagrius 114
Fabric of Time (DVD) 205
Fabritis, Antonio 189
Fanti, Prof. Giulio 195, 197, 206-7
Feinbrun, Naomi 34
Filas, Fr. Francis 15, 41-47
Flury-Lemberg, Mechthild 113, 17, 87, 157, 162
Frale, Barbara 204
Frei, Dr. Max 21, 28-31, 33-35, 107, 109, 117, 170-171
Gambeschia, Dr. Joseph 54
Valdes Garza, Dr. 26, 67, 170
Gaspari, Antonio 190, 199
Geoffrey de Charny 130-131, 135-137, 139, 149
Geoffrey Villehardouin 125, 127
Germanus I, 187-188
Gervase of Tilbry 188
Giordano, Dr. 88
Goldoni, Dr. Carl 67
Gonella, Professor Luigi 157, 161

THE THREE CLOTHS OF CHRIST by John C. Iannone

INDEX OF AUTHORS - CONT.

Graeber, Ralph 95-97
Greeman, H. 17
Greenhut, Zvi 44
Gregory Archdeacon 119
Gruber, Elmar 71
Guscin, Mark 168-176, 205
Habermas, Gary 49
Haralick, Dr. Robert 42, 44-45
Heller, Dr. John 19, 68-69, 72-73, 90
Henri of the Flanders 127-128
Horowitz, Aharon, 29
Hughes de Payen, 132
Iannone, John C., 9, 174, 207
Irenaeus of Lyons, 181
Isaiah, Prophet, 50, 60
Jackson, Dr. John 15, 39-50, 99, 103, 112, 173, 203
James of Antioch, 115
Jerome, St, 105
Jeanne de Vergy, 130
Jehohanan 60, 63-64
John of Jerusalem, 115
Johnson, Kendall, 96
Josephus 52, 57, 72, 81, 107
Judica Cordiglia, Giovanni, 15
Jumper, Dr. Eric 15, 39, 40, 62, 94, 99, 203
Justin, Martyr, 180-181
Justin II 118, 185
Justinian 37, 113, 118
Justinian II 37, 149-150, 187
King Alfonso VI, 175
King Louis VII, 122
King Philip IV, 135
Kirlian, Semyon, 47, 95 - 97
Kersten, Holger, 71
Kohlbeck, Dr. Joseph 62
Kubler-Ross, Dr. Elizabeth 101
Lacapenus, Emperor Romanus 119
Lavoie, Dr. Gilbert 72
Leonelli, Maria 189

THE THREE CLOTHS OF CHRIST by John C. Iannone

INDEX OF THE AUTHORS - CONTINUED

Libby, Frank Willard 157
Lynn, Donald 51
Maggiolo, Prof. Roberto 206
McCrone, Dr. Walter 91, 152
Maloney, Paul 22, 29
Marine, Joseph 23, 164-166
Marx, Michael 42
McDowell, Josh 143
McNair, Philip 522.61
Meacham, William 35, 65, 155, 163
Meissner, Peter 46
Miller, Vernon 15, 45, 164
Moedder, Dr. Herman 54
Moody, Dr. Raymond 101
Moran, Kevin 40, 48, 151, 205
Morgan, Rex 137, 146-7
Moroni, Mario 41
Morse, Dr. Melvin 101
Moss, Thelma 96
Mottern, William 39
Nicephorus 115
Nicholas Mesarites 124
Nitowski, Eugenia 79-80, 93
Orderic Vitalis 122
Otto de la Roche 127, 129, 136, 138
Pellicori, Dr. Sam 62
Pia, Secondo 14, 40
Pfeiffer, Prof. Heinrich 181, 185-191, 193-4, 196
Phillips, Dr. Thomas 101
Phillip de Milly 1123, 125, 134, 139
Philo of Alexandria 57, 75
Piczek, Isabel 73, 90, 143, 153, 192, 195, 205
Pilate, Pontius 12, 18, 39, 41-7, 52-3, 55-56, 64, 81, 102, 180-182, 185
Piside, George, 186
Pliny 20, 57
Pope Benedict XVI 9, 25, 141-42, 192, 207
Pope Clement IV 178
Pope Clement V 135
Pope Clement VII 130-131

THE THREE CLOTHS OF CHRIST by John C. Iannone

INDEX OF THE AUTHORS - CONTINUED

Pope John VII, 187-188
Pope Gregory II 115
Pope Innocent III 125, 129
Pope Stephen II 188
Pope Stephen III 115
Pope Urban II 133
Pope Urban VIII 191
Prior, Edwin 164
Raes, Dr. Gilbert 21-23
Rahmani, L.Y. 78-9, 83
Ricci, Monsignor Giulio 88, 170
Richmond, Prof. I.A. 60
Ricket, Charles 26
Riggi, Dr. Giovanni 26, 30, 32, 71, 157, 162-3
Ring, Dr. Kenneth 101
Robert de Clary 125, 128, 134
Robinson, Rev. John 77, 84
Rogers, Dr. Ray 6, 23, 37, 87, 89, 92, 97, 153, 165, 166
Runciman, Prof. Steven 112, 184
Sabom, Dr. Michael 101
Sargon 26
Sammarco, Father Enrico 197
Schlomer, Sr. Blandina Paschalis 192, 197
Schwortz, Barrie 9, 15, 102, 160, 164, 171, 201, 205, 207
Schoenfeld, Rabbi Hugh 71
Scavone, Dr. Daniel 70, 121
Schuermann, Oswald 34
Segal, J.B. 106
Septa, Dr. Levi 62
Soemundarson, Nicholas 122
Soons, Dr. Petrus 201-205
Suetonius 57
Stevenson, Dr. Kenneth 16, 18-19, 28, 30-33, 39-40, 48-49, 51, 86
Tacitus 52, 57
Tamburelli, Giovanni 40, 203
Testore, Frank 157
Thaddaeus 108-110, 144
Theodore Ducas 129
Theofilatto Simocatta 186

THE THREE CLOTHS OF CHRIST by John C. Iannone

INDEX OF THE AUTHORS - CONTINUED

Tiberius Caesar 48, 178, 182
Trematore, Mario 140
Tribbe, Frank 20, 63, 97, 134, 147
Tryon, Dr. Victor 70-71, 197
Tryer, John 23
Valdez, Dr. Garza 26, 69
Veronica (Veil) 9-10, 102, 115, 129, 143, 168, 177ff
Vignon, Paul 83, 86, 93, 147-8, 213
Vittore, Prof. Donato 194
Volkringer, Dr. Jean 94-95
Von Dobschutz, Ernst 116
Walsh, John 14
Weitzmann, Prof. Kurt 121, 148
Whanger, Dr. Alan 11, 18, 28, 33-37, 43, 46-48, 97, 102, 149-150, 174-5, 204
William of the Tyre 122-124
Willis, Dr. David 54
Wilcox, Robert 19, 93, 95, 97
Wilson, Ian 11, 15-16, 22, 26, 31, 39-41, 51, 63, 66, 85, 109, 111-114, 116, 120-1, 135-6, 145, 147-9, 150-51, 171-2
Wuenschel, Fr. Edward C.Ss.R., 75, 83
Yarbrough, William 42, 46
Zanninotto, Dr. Gino 12, 119
Zohary, Michael 34
Zugibe, Dr. Frederick 26, 54, 58, 62, 69, 151

*****

THE THREE CLOTHS OF CHRIST   by   John C. Iannone

INDEX OF THE SUBJECTS

AB - Blood Type 68-69, 169-170
Acheiropoietos 109-110, 117, 120, 134, 148, 185
Athens, 124, 129-131, 134, 136, 149
Auto Radiation, 97
Bacteria 26-27
Bean Caper (see Zygophyllum dumosum)
Benford-Marine theory 165-166
Bilirubin 69, 71, 73, 197
Blood, human, (see Blood Type AB)
Blood and water (to see serum) 64, 66, 73, 119, 171-2, 18, 194-196
Bones of Jehohanan 60
Bones - Isaiah 60
Bones of wrist 61
Bone Box (Ossuary) 63, 77
Bones and teeth 102
Braid - 16, 204
Bucholeon Palace 117-118, 121, 125, 128, 134
Burial Attitude 17, 66, 85
Burn Holes 13, 140, 150-151
Calcium carbonate 18, 80 160
Calendar Indicators, 35
Camulia 185-186, 199
Cap of Thorns   see Crown
Carbon & C-14 test 6,9,13,21 - 24,28, 38, 87, 120, 140-1, 151-3, 155ff, 166, 175
Catacombs 36, 144ff.
Cave Tomb 18, 76-79, 82
Chafing Marks (see shoulders) 59
Chin Band 83-84
Chier (Gk: wrist) 61
Chrysanthemum coronarium 34-5
Cistus Creticus 35
Clotting (coagulation blood) 72-74
Coins over eyes 15, 18, 37, 39-49, 56, 82, 94-5, 99, 149
Conspiracy Theory 71, 141, 161ff
Constantinople 16, 31-33, 37, 106-7, 114, 117-119, 121-123, 125-130, 150, 170, 185, 187-188
Contaminants (on Shroud) 156, 160-1
Coronal Discharge 47-48
Cotton on Shroud 9, 21-24, 38, 163, 165-66

THE THREE CLOTHS OF CHRIST by John C. Iannone

INDEX of Subject- Continued

Crown of thorns 12, 36, 57-58, 67, 117, 136, 173
Crucifixion by Romans 12, 16, 18-19, 35, 50-60, 117, 119,
    160, 168, 171-2, 175, 178, 198, 204
Crucifragium 63-64-65, 67
Degradation (aging of linen) 24, 92, 94, 153
Dehydration (linen) 24, 92, 94, 153
Description of Jesus 16
D'Arcis Memorandum 126
Dirt on Shroud 18, 28, 55, 59, 62, 160
DNA 70-73, 197
Double Superficiality of image 204
Dunamin - energy/power 102, 179
Edema (to see the pleural edema)
Edessa 20, 29, 31, 33, 37, 106-117, 144-147, 150, 170, 184-5
Embroidered cloth 120, 135, 150
Enrie Photo 11, 12, 30-31, 38, 40-42
Epitaphoi 135, 150
Epsilon mark 57
Exactor Mortis 56
Fifth Gospel 9
Fingerprints on heel 88
Fire of 1532 12-13, 40, 139-40, 150, 161, 206
Fire of 1997 140-141, 161, 203
Flash photolysis 97
Flagrum 12, 55-56, 67
Floral images, flowers, images 18, 28, 33-38, 82, 85, 94, 99, 204
Fluorescence 90, 152-3, 194-5
Four Fingers (se Missing Thumbs) 61, 150-1
Geographic indicators 35
Grail, 124 Holy, 135-137
Guadalupe, Our Lady of, 207
Gundelia tournefortii 36, 57, 169-170, 197
Halos - Kerlian 96
Halos - serum albumin 72-73, 178
Haralick Report 42, 44-45
Healers 96
Height of Jesus 17
Haematidrosis 54, 58
Himation 115, 120
Hiroshima 97-98
Holograms, 201-205
Holy Grail 124, 135

THE THREE CLOTHS OF CHRIST by John C. Iannone

INDEX OF THE SUBJECTS

Hungarian pray manuscript 13, 150-151
Image of Edessa 31, 109, 111-120, 206
Infrared light 15, 21, 90, 152, 168, 194, 195
Iron oxide 91-92, 152
Juan Diego, 207
Julia Lepton 18, 39, 41-48
Kamulia 185-186, 199
Keriai 82, 8
Knights Templar 16, 123, 125, 131-139
Lamentation Scenes 121
Lance wound 12, 63-67, 72-73, 123, 127, 145, 149, 171-172
Lepton 16, 35-38, 41-44
Light - radiant 21, 83, 91-6, 149
Loculus 80
Mafia - the Shroud, 137-8
Mandylion 11, 36, 109, 111-112, 114, 116, 119-120, 122, 145, 150
Manoppello 177-8, 181, 186, 188-197, 199, 207
Measurement of Shroud 87
Metatarsals 102-103
Mineral Coated pollen 32
Missing thumbs 61-62
Mites 18, 28-30, 32-33, 161
Nails 12, 52, 60-63, 81, 88, 123, 128
Natron 26-27
Natronococcus 26
Negativity of photos 40
Ossuary 63, 78, 80
Othonia (burial strips) 82-83, 151
Oxidation 24, 89, 92, 94, 153
Paint on the Shroud: 12, 14-5, 40, 53, 68, 73, 78, 89-90, 91-92, 105, 110, 111, 115, 117-120, 130, 137, 144, 146, 150-4, 186
Paint on Veil: 194ff
Palladium (Shroud as) 113, 130, 144, 186
Pantocrator 37, 141
Passover Plot
Patibulum (cross beam) 53, 58, 59
Peridedeto 84
Peter as an artist 143
Phalanges - 102-103
Pharos Chapel 118, 124, 128, 134
Phylactery 15, 99
Pigment 90-2, 110, 151-2, 195-6

THE THREE CLOTHS OF CHRIST by John C. Iannone

INDEX OF THE SUBJECTS

Pigment (bile, bilirubin) 69, 71, 197
Medallion 130 of the pilgrim
PIOT - to see the image polarized
Pleural Edema 60
Pollen 15, 18, 25-33, 51, 73, 100, 102, 110, 157, 165-7, 174, 182, 192
Polarized Image Overlay Technique, 15, 19, 31, 42-43, 145, 170
Ponytail 16, 204
Post mortem blood flow, 72-4, 93
Prayer Box (see Phylactery)
Puncture marks 168
Raking Light Test 112
Red crosses 133-135
Reweave 9, 24, 164-6
Retting of 20, 24, 92, 152
Rigor mortis, 17, 62, 66-67, 72, 83, 166, 204
Rock Rose (see Cistus creticus) 35
Sainte-Chapelle 13
Saponaria 20
Sanctification of paintings 92, 152
Sedile (seat) 52
Selvedge 11
Sepia color 11, 24, 41, 89, 94, 153
Serum 60, 58-59,60, 66-67, 165, 167, 174
Serum albumin 72-73-74, 178
Shroud defined 10 ff
Signature of Roman Crucifixion, 50ff
Sindon (Shroud) 10, 77, 80, 82, 106, 115, 123-4, 128, 143, 168, 175
Sindoine 128
Soap Weed 20
Solidus 149-150
Spurious sample 9, 166
Stations of cross 59, 177, 183, 198, 200
Stipes (upright of cross), 53,59, 63
Sudarium/Sudario 9-10, 80-82, 85, 129, 168ff, 178, 197, 200
Surface phenomenon of fibers 24, 68, 89, 94, 98, 152, 206
Teeth 102
Trial of Templars, 135, 137-8
Templecombe 137
Tephillin (to see Phylactery) 18, 99
Tetradiplon 110-112, 119-120, 150
Textile, ancient, 19, 20-23, 28, 37, 70, 75ff, 157

THE THREE CLOTHS OF CHRIST by John C. Iannone

INDEX OF THE SUBJECTS

Thermonuclear Flash 98
Thorn-Thistle Bush (to see the tournefortii of Gundelia) 170, 197
Thumbs (see: Missing / Hidden Thumbs
Title over the crosspiece - to see Titulus
Titulus (title) 64
Transfiguration 100, 116
Tremisses 149
Travertine Aragonite (to see soil) 18, 55, 59, 62, 160
Tufts of hair 192, 193
Vanillin, 37, 87
Venetians 126, 129
Veil - see veil of the Veronica
Veronica Veil 9-10, 102, 115, 129, 143, 168, 177ff
Vignon Markings 83, 86, 93, 147-8
Vaporgraph 93-94
Volkringer Effect 94-95
VP-8 Image Analyzer, 15, 39, 40-42, 90, 173, 197
Warrior Monks 132, 135
Water and Blood (to see serum) 60, 58-59,60, 66-67, 165, 167, 174
Water stains, 13, 140
Weave anomalies 43
Weight of Jesus 17
Whip (Roman) - to see Flagrum
X-Rays 102-103
Zygophyllum dumosum 35-36

******

THE THREE CLOTHS OF CHRIST by John C. Iannone

 Dr. Frei (right) with Chemist Dr. Ray Rogers takes "sticky tape samples" of the pollen on the Shroud. Photo: Courtesy of Barrie Schwortz, Official Shroud Photographer.

 The sole of right foot (left) showing blood soaked sole with exit wound in lower center. Dirt (travertine aragonite) was found on heel of right foot.

THE THREE CLOTHS OF CHRIST by John C. Iannone

 Micrograph of the Thorn-Thistle Pollen (Gundelia tournefortii). Courtesy: Dr. Max Frei.

 The Hungarian Pray Manuscript of 1197. Note burn holes and Shroud weave demonstrating presence of Shroud before the earliest Carbon-14 dating of 1260.

THE THREE CLOTHS OF CHRIST by John C. Iannone

IMAGE OF CHRIST PANTOCRATOR
ST. CATHERINE'S MONASTERY - MT. SINAI
CIRCA 550 A.D.

Jesus in early art taken off images on the Holy Shroud which resurfaced circa 535 AD. Photo Courtesy of Archbishop Damianos, St. Catherine's Monastery, Mt. Sinai, Egypt. Recent findings indicate floral images in the halo.

THE THREE CLOTHS OF CHRIST by John C. Iannone

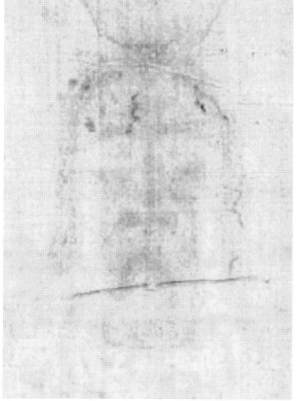

Shroud Face as actually seen with the naked eye. Courtesy: Barrie Schwortz.

THE THREE CLOTHS OF CHRIST by John C. Iannone

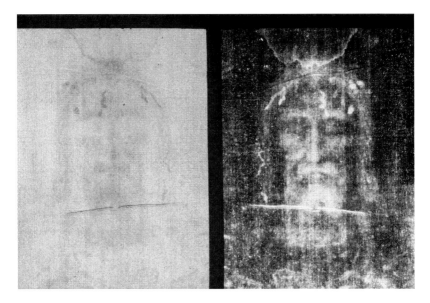

Shroud as seen with naked eye (left). Shroud as seen on a photographic negative which becomes a positive image on the negative plate. First noted by Secondo Pia in 1898. Courtesy: Barrie Schwortz.

THE THREE CLOTHS OF CHRIST   by   John C. Iannone

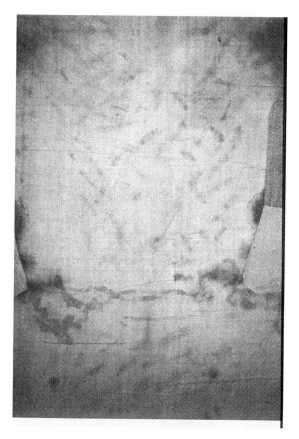

Scourge Marks on the back. Blood and Serum flow across lower back. The Romans used a Flagrum (whip with three leather thongs and two pieces of bone or lead on ends, leaving six contusions with each strike). Courtesy of Barrie Schwortz.

THE THREE CLOTHS OF CHRIST by John C. Iannone

(Puncture Marks and blood flow on back of head from cap of thorns). Courtesy Barrie Schwortz.

Jesus is scourged by two men with hand in front or over head. The instrument used is a Roman Flagrum – a whip with three leather thongs with two pieces of bone or lead on the ends, leaving six contusions for each strike. Courtesy: Holy Shroud Guild – NY.

THE THREE CLOTHS OF CHRIST by John C. Iannone

The Rock Rose (Cistus creticus) noted as a bouquet on the Holy Shroud. This plant is indigenous to the Jerusalem area and is a "calendar indicator of the provenance of the Shroud as being from this area." Prof. Avinoam Danin, Professor of Botany, Hebrew University, Jerusalem. Photo Courtesy of Prof. Danin.

The thorn-thistle bush (Gundelia tournefortii). Pollen of this plant are found on the Shroud, likely from the cap of thorns placed on the head of Jesus. Photo: courtesy Prof. Avinoam Danin – Hebrew University, Jerusalem.

THE THREE CLOTHS OF CHRIST by John C. Iannone

Three-Dimensional image of the face from the NASA VP-8 Image Analyzer first noted by Physicists Dr. John Jackson and Eric Jumper in 1978. Note the button-like objects over the eyes found to be images of coins. Courtesy: Barrie Schwortz.

Another view of the three dimensionality of the image, demonstrating that a real human body lay under the linen.

THE THREE CLOTHS OF CHRIST by John C. Iannone

The Roman lepton (Widow's Mite). Images of this coin are found over the eyes. This small coin has unique characteristics including the words Tiberiou Caisaros imprinted around the edges; a Augur's staff and a clipped area from the 1:00-3:00 position, helping to identify it. These coins were minted by Pilate from 28-31 A.D.

Below: The coin digitalized by Dr. Robert Haralick. Note the UCAI in upper left quadrant from Tiberio**u Cai**saros.

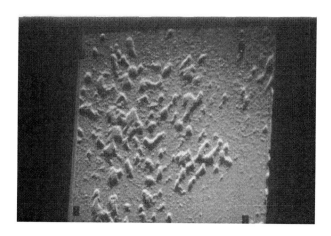

THE THREE CLOTHS OF CHRIST by John C. Iannone

(Above: imaged area showing fibrils as a "surface phenomenon" limited to very top of fibers. Below: blood area of the Shroud showing "red" color from high levels of bile pigment bilirubin. Courtesy: Barrie Schwortz.

THE THREE CLOTHS OF CHRIST by John C. Iannone

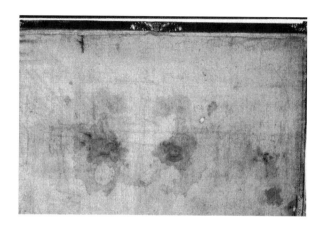

Top: Photo of the Sudarium showing double stains from cloth folded back over itself. Center: Face of Shroud overlaid on Sudarium (Courtesy: J. Bennett). Bottom: Cathedral of St. Stephen – Oviedo, Spain where Sudarium Christi is located. (Courtesy: Mark Guscin).

THE THREE CLOTHS OF CHRIST   by   John C. Iannone

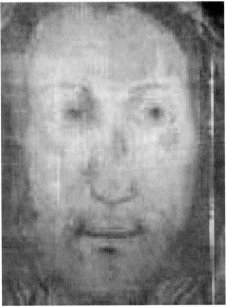 The Veil of Veronica image found in the Capuchin Monastery at Manoppello, Italy – 150 miles east of Rome in the Apennine Mountains.

THE THREE CLOTHS OF CHRIST by John C. Iannone

The Tilma (Cloak of Juan Diego) bearing image of Our Lady from Guadalupe near Mexico City.